NETWORK SYSTEM ARCHITECTURE

NETWORK SYSTEM ARCHITECTURE

Robert B. Walford

ADDISON-WESLEY PUBLISHING COMPANY INC.
Reading, Massachusetts   Menlo Park, California   New York
Don Mills, Ontario   Wokingham, England   Amsterdam   Bonn
Sydney   Singapore   Tokyo   Madrid   San Juan

Library of Congress Cataloging-in-Publication Data

Walford, Robert B.
  Network system architecture / Robert B. Walford.
    p. cm.
  Includes bibliographical references.
  ISBN-0-201-52409-0
  1. Business — Communication systems. 2. System design.
3. Information networks. I. Title.
HF5548.2.W2923 1990   90-31455
650'.028'546—dc20   CIP

Sponsoring Editor: Ted Buswick
Jacket design by Mike Fender
Text design by Patricia Dunbar
Set in 11 point Trump Mediaeval by DEKR Corporation, Woburn, MA

ABCDEFGHIJ–MA–9543210
First printing, April 1990

This book and its companion volumes are dedicated to my wife

Carolyn Mary

and our children

Ann, Roberta, Jim, Dennis, Christopher, Randall, and Mary

who endured this project with humor, patience, and understanding. They helped me balance the needs of this book, university duties, office responsibilities, and most of all, the family. Without their help, this book never would have been written.

CONTENTS

FOUR   DATA ARCHITECTURE

FIVE   SERVER ARCHITECTURE

SIX   COMMUNICATIONS ARCHITECTURE

SEVEN   NETWORK MANAGEMENT ARCHITECTURE

EIGHT   APPLICATION DEVELOPMENT ARCHITECTURE

TABLES

INTRODUCTION

FIGURES

INTRODUCTION

ONE

PREFACE

Most of the current intense interest in information networks has occurred because of the recognition that they are — or could be — an important component of an enterprise's structure and strategy. The recent emphasis on the use of information as a strategic asset (or weapon if you prefer) in the conduct of business is a case in point. Utilizing information networks in this way requires a multidimensional and well-ordered approach.

To provide the required framework, the major focus of the discussion in this book and its two companion volumes is on the topics of environment, architecture, and methodology. The environment encompasses technical and nontechnical constraints and requirements that are central to the proper development and use of the information network technologies.

It is widely recognized that the implementation of an information network and its associated systems requires the use of an architecture. Unfortunately, there is no agreement among practitioners in the field as to what an architecture is, what it is supposed to accomplish, and how one is to be constructed. Much of the confusion occurs because of the lack of definition concerning the overall development environment and the inherent processes it contains. Once this environment has been defined, the answers to the questions about an architecture become easy to answer.

The architecture is defined as a knowledge base that contains the knowledge necessary to develop network-based systems using a custom shop development model. It must be designed such that it is flexible and yet provides enough structure so that design and implementation decisions can be made effectively. Principles, which are derived from the architecture definition and structure, form the means by which these decisions are determined and evaluated.

The development methodology provides the means of implementing products and services that are consistent with the architecture, cost-effective for the organization, and yet meet the needs of the marketplace effectively. As the last phase of the development process, the methodology must also bridge the gap between the consistent and orderly architecture and the rough-and-tumble characteristics of the real world.

As mentioned earlier, the overall discussion of these topics is presented in three books: the first covers the environment, the second (this volume) covers the architecture, and the third covers the development methodology. This partitioning helps organize the considerable amount of material and keeps the discussion from becoming unmanageably complex. In addition, the location of the information of immediate interest can be identified quickly.

Because each book is designed to be a "stand-alone" discussion of the major topic addressed, enough background information is included in each book to put the main subject of the book in proper relationship to the other major topics. Thus, it is not necessary to read the books in serial fashion. The book that contains the discussion of immediate interest can be consulted directly. Of course, information presented in one of the companion books may be necessary for a full understanding of the subject in its complete context. The companion volumes to this book are *Information Systems and Business Dynamics*, and *Information Networks: A Design and Implementation Methodology*.

The first companion book, *Information Systems and Business Dynamics*, contains an in-depth discussion of the technology and business aspects of the network environment. The central theme of this discussion is the requirement that the various information technologies be integrated with the business needs. As a part of this presentation, some of the history of communications and data processing is examined to put the current status and projected future requirements of information networks in their proper context.

The second companion book, *Information Networks: A Design and Implementation Methodology*, presents the basic concepts and requirements for any development methodology. It also defines an example methodology that contains design and implementation techniques specifically structured to utilize the structure and principles of the example network system architecture defined in this book. Each step of the methodology is carefully defined, and the reasons for its inclusion are explained in detail. This discussion is designed to ensure that the resultant procedures will provide the results necessary and will advance the implementation in an optimum fashion.

This book is devoted to explaining the fundamental concepts and requirements of network system architectures. Although many aspects of architecture design are, and will remain for some time, an "art," approaches and techniques to the specification process can be defined somewhat rigorously. This type of analytical process enables different approaches to be compared by generating suitable metrics. Therefore, the emphasis of the architectural development discussion is on providing as much rigor and structure to the architecture development process as possible.

In many cases, the theory involved results in such complexity that manual methods of use are not practical. A computer assist is needed in these areas. When computer help is necessary, traditional informal methods will be used as a fallback so that an example architecture can be developed for illustration purposes. However, even the results of the informal methods will be compared with the requirements of the theory. As far as I am aware, the presentation in this book is the first attempt to develop a theory of network system architecture design.

The presentation starts by explaining the need for an architecture and defining the type of information it must contain. An in-depth discussion of the architecture structure and its implications is then given. The basic requirements for the design of any architecture are discussed and used to design a specifc example architecture. To manage the considerable complexity required by a comprehensive architecture, seven separate but coordinated and integrated subarchitectures are defined for the example architecture after classification rules are established. These subarchitectures are: end user services, system software, data, servers, communications, network management, and application development.

A set of associated principles, consisting of strategies, standards, guidelines, and rules, are derived from the architectural structure. These principles, which are defined and illustrated through specific examples, are further partitioned into three classes according to the scope of the principle: architectural, design, and operations. For additional ease in application, the principles are further classified according to the subarchitecture from which they are derived. The use and implications of the architecture can be ascertained clearly when this approach is used.

An extensive introduction is provided to establish the network system environment, including the system development characteristics that mandate the use of an architecture. The first chapter is devoted to determining the requirements and concepts for a system architecture and defining the overall structure of an example architecture. The remainder of the book devotes a chapter to each of the example subarchitectures to assure that sufficient detail is presented. In these discussions, several new results are presented, and they contribute greatly to the ability to design practical information networks and systems. The material is designed to illustrate the basic principles involved in the design of an architecture. Although a specific architecture is developed as an example, the fundamental goal of the presentation is to give you the knowledge necessary to design a comprehensive architecture suitable for your environment.

The information presented in this book has been designed to assist professionals involved in the research, design, and development of information networks and systems. It will also effectively serve the needs of students in a classroom or self-study environment. The method of use will be somewhat different in each case. In a business setting, the main uses of this series will be (1) to provide an organized approach to the design of an information network and services that will serve the specific needs and strategies of the organization; (2) to serve as a reference manual for those individuals responsible for providing network-based products and services; (3) to form a basis on which to direct the research and development of the concepts and structures needed for new information networks and systems; and (4) to provide a mechanism by which technical and business people can communicate more effectively.

Although no study questions are given at the end of each chapter, this book is also appropriate for classroom use in advanced courses in software engineering. A three-semester sequence, one semester for each volume, would be necessary to delve into the subject matter in some depth. This book would form the basis of the second course in the sequence. If a two-semester sequence is desired, only the major concepts and results could be covered. I have taught a course based on this latter sequence at the University of South Florida with excellent results. In either type of sequence, assignments would consist of example designs and possible alternatives to the procedures and methodologies presented. As in actual practice, most questions that can be posed have few single or simple answers, and the instructor must look for the validity of the approach and conclusions reached in determining the absorption of the material. In this regard, I must give special thanks to Dr. Murali Varanassi, chair of the computer science and engineering department at the University of South Florida, for giving me the freedom to experiment with new ways of providing students with an understanding of the needs of modern software engineering and practice.

I would like to express my deep appreciation to Don Peeples, former president of GTE Data Services, Dan Lawson, former vice president of information sciences, and Jim Hamrick, my current vice president. They provided the opportunity and environment that enabled me to research and develop the concepts presented in this book. Their encouragement and aid are gratefully acknowledged.

Thanks and recognition are also richly deserved by several of my current or former associates on the technical staff of GTE Data Services, who contributed in diverse ways to the formation of the information in this book. They participated in many discussions, arguments, and brainstorming sessions that greatly helped to solidify the concepts and ideas presented. The many late nights they spent reading and proofing are also appreciated. These individuals included Bill Livesey, who kept me honest in the data engineering area and who insisted that proper attention be given to modeling; Bill Berry, an expert in software engineering, who contributed much to the discussion of applications development; Scott Schipper, the human intelligence on fifth generation artificial intelligence; and Pat Jordan, who thinks technology planning should take over the world.

I would also like to thank Ed Daly, former director of technology management, our chief "devil's advocate," who wouldn't take "it's obvious" for an answer. Bob Staretz, my director at GTE Data Services during the start of this effort, deserves considerable credit for steering me in the right directions.

Recognition is also due Paul Yamashita, who helped with the important gateway discussion, and Rick Ahlgren, who served as the large computer system expert. Scott Shipper also contributed significantly to early versions of the architecture definition and structure, as did John Janis, a former colleague. Other staff members who should be mentioned are Paul Heller, who kept me focused on the end user, and John Ruble, the organization administrative specialist who kept things flowing smoothly. All of the above individuals, as well as the many I am unable to mention by name, are dedicated hard-working professionals. I am proud to have been associated with them in the writing of this volume.

I would also like to give a special thank you to Evelyn Banks, who was my secretary and administrative assistant as the writing progressed. Without her skill and dedicated effort, there would be no book.

Robert B. Walford
August, 1989

INTRODUCTION

Information network systems can be classified according to their historical evolution generation, the size of the organization required to produce a finished system, and the philosophy of the process used in their development. The specific characteristics associated with these environmental attributes determine the need for an architecture in the development process. Unless these characteristics are understood in detail, the definition, use, and structure of an architecture cannot be ascertained. Lack of this understanding is the main reason that there is no universal agreement by practitioners in the field as to the need, contents, and role of a system architecture.

Therefore, before a system architecture can be considered, the range of the three environmental areas given above must be examined to determine the inherent development requirements associated with different approaches. Once this has been accomplished, the definition and use of an architecture can be determined easily.

Currently, three generations of computer systems are of interest: the third, fourth, and fifth generations. First- and second-generation systems did not require networks and are of little interest in this discussion. A summary of the basic characteristics of each of the remaining generations is shown in table I.1. Because of the limitations of the third generation,

TABLE I.1 NETWORK SYSTEM GENERATION CHARACTERISTICS

Attribute	Generation		
	Third	Fourth	Fifth
Focus	Development professionals	End user	Network intelligence
Network scope	Centralized processing, dumb terminal to mainframe, switch	Distributed processing, intelligent workstation	Cooperative processing, multimedia workstation
Media	Data only, voice only	Unintegrated data/voice/image	Integrated data/voice/image
Development tools	Comprehensive, unintegrated, manual	Comprehensive, integrated, manual	Intelligent, automated
Development methodology	Waterfall	Rapid prototyping	Knowledge engineering
Data	Application-dependent	Shared databases	Shared knowledge bases
Human interface	Application-dependent/single skill level	Application-independent/multiple skill levels	Application-independent/adaptive
Processing	Function/data resident on single computer	Function/data may move from computer to computer	Function/data split across multiple computers
End user services	None	Office/decision support/ad hoc query	Comprehensive
Language	Procedural (COBOL, FORTRAN)	Nonprocedural (SQL, IDEAL)	Natural language
Deployment infrastructure use	None, except for the processor	Necessary as a basic part of system development	Most services/functions supplied by the infrastructure

it will be assumed that network systems are developed using the fourth- or fifth-generation characteristics. Note that these generations place a heavy emphasis on common data and functions as well as the sharing of network facilities. This emphasis will be an important aspect in determining the definition and need for an architecture.

The size of a system development project is usually reflected in the type of organization that is utilized for its implementation. The two basic types are "development in the small" and "development in the large." Development in the small utilizes one person, or, at the most, a small number of people (typically five or fewer). The procedures are mostly informal, and no approvals from outside the group are necessary. Because all development knowledge is contained within this small group, decisions can be made quickly and implemented without a great deal of documentation or communication. Systems can be constructed and deployed rapidly. The deficiencies of this type of organization, however, are significant: testing is usually inadequate, as is documentation; decisions concerning interfaces and software structure are not sufficiently discussed or reviewed; little attention is given to training and support; and the effects of future changes usually are not taken into account. The chief programmer team concept of the 1970s was an attempt to utilize the advantages of development in the small while minimizing the deficiencies.

Most network system products require development in the large because of the sheer size involved. Organizations of significant size are used, and the resultant systems are quite complex and large enough that no one person, or even a small group of people, understands all of the system. The development process must successfully accommodate the implementation of large-scale systems by reducing the overhead and inefficiencies usually associated with this type of organization.

On the plus side, it should be noted that development in the large usually produces systems that undergo rigorous quality control in terms of testing, documentation, and training programs. Entire teams of people are typically assigned to these functions, and in many cases a negative result from their efforts can stop the entire development until the problem is resolved. To some extent, because of the large number of people in separate organizations involved with development in the large, enough separation of "powers" occurs to ensure that all needs are met.

Unfortunately, because of the inefficiencies inherent in this type of organization, most large-scale software and systems development projects result in long delays, cost overruns, and user dissatisfaction with the delivered product. Most network system developments tend to be complex and large. Thus, the emphasis of this book is on development in the large. This is not intended to downplay the usefulness and effectiveness of development in the small where appropriate, but only to recognize the realities of today's large-scale development needs.

The development process can be partitioned into three areas, as shown in figure I.1. The specific characteristics chosen for each of these areas determine the way in which system development will be accomplished. Through the proper selection of these characteristics, a suitable process for network system development can be defined. As a natural consequence of this selection process, the definition and use of an architecture will be derived.

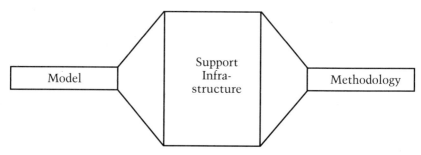

FIGURE I.1   DEVELOPMENT PROCESS CHARACTERIZATION

Three basic models of system development have found wide acceptance in manufacturing and similar areas. Applying them to software development requires that their original definitions be changed slightly, but the respective philosophies remain intact. The characteristics of each of these models is shown in table I.2, and a brief discussion of each follows.

The most widely utilized model is that of the job shop. In this model, each project is treated as a totally original development, with all application software coded from the beginning. Except for selection of the processing platform (hardware and software), little use is made of software or equipment that already exists (a deployment infrastructure). Systems that result from different developments are not intended to work together and are not required to follow the same design philosophy. The advantages of this structure are that the organization has total control of all aspects of development, the financial and accounting methods are relatively simple, and different systems may be optimized in different ways quite easily. The disadvantages are that a great deal of duplication exists, previous work is not utilized even when it is applicable, available equipment is not used to its fullest capacity, and little room exists for development productivity improvement.

At the other end of the spectrum is a product development philosophy that relies on a single product. This standard product is altered to meet specific market and/or customer demands. Although it may be argued that this model is less a development model and more a manufacturing model, it is nevertheless possible to modify a standard product to satisfy a variety of needs. The standard product model is extremely efficient, because all of the expertise and experience of the organization is concentrated on a single entity. The disadvantage of this model is its highly restrictive nature.

The final product development model that is considered here is that of a custom shop. A custom shop utilizes standard components and assembles them in such a way that the resulting product meets the needs of the customer or market.

TABLE I.2 DEVELOPMENT MODEL CHARACTERISTICS

Attributes	Job Shop Model	Standard Product Model	Custom Shop Model
Number of product classes	Large	One	Variable
Project size	Variable	Low (change only)	Large
Utilization of existing software/hardware	Low	Low	High
Cross-project interaction	Low	—	High
Intraclass variability	High	Low	High
Change frequency	High	High	High
Product utilization consistency	Low	High	Medium
Client expectations	Different	Similar	Different
Development efficiency	Low	High	Medium/high
Expertise applied	General	Product-specific	General and specific integration methods
Standards defined	Few	Many internal	Many internal/external
Financial arrangements	Customer-financed	Developer-financed	Developer/customer combination

To some extent, it is a combination of the job shop and the standard product models.

The major function of an organization using the custom shop model is integrating standard components that are already available to form a wide variety of products. The number of new components that must be developed to produce a specific product is kept to a minimum. The custom shop model requires that an organization decide which standard components are necessary for its product line(s). The design and implementation of these standard components must be completed before the components can be used in new products. The advantage of this model is that it produces highly leveraged development that has the potential of being used in multiple systems. The disadvantage is the need for a highly sophisticated engineering and financial organization that can define and finance the standard components independently of a specific system development. In addition, this model will probably not be economical for small projects. Because the orientation of this book is toward moderate- to large-scale projects, this restriction is not significant.

Because of this model's potential for large increases in development productivity and its inherent consideration of existing hardware and software in an established deployment infrastructure, this model offers the most flexibility and potential for developing large third- and fourth-generation systems. Further discussion will center on the use of this model for development.

Before the custom shop (or any) model can be used, it is necessary to define a set of activities and structures which are required to implement the model and employ it as a guide for development process. This set is referred to as the *development infrastructure*. It should not be confused with the deployment infrastructure referred to earlier. Although both are infrastructures (for example, shared sets of enabling resources), their purposes and places in the development process are different.

The development infrastructure has four parts, as indicated

by figure I.2: domain knowledge, available product set, deployment environment, and implementation environment. These parts differ in content and structure for each of the models. Only the definition that is applicable to the custom shop model is discussed here A brief explanation of the purpose of each part follows.

Domain knowledge is that knowledge which is required to produce products in accordance with the model. In the custom shop approach, the domain knowledge that is required in addition to general technical expertise is embodied in an architecture. This architecture provides the structure and principles (strategies, standards, guidelines, and rules) needed to assemble complex systems from standard components. In a very real sense, it is an extension of human expertise.

Integrating the above definitions with the network system requirements previously determined results in the definition of a network systems architecture:

The knowledge base containing the knowledge required for development in the large of fourth- and fifth-generation systems using a custom shop model.

This knowledge, along with the other parts of the development infrastructure, will be used by the development methodology in the actual implementation process. Although

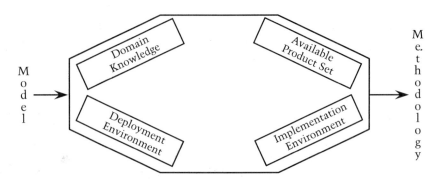

FIGURE I.2 DEVELOPMENT PROCESS
SUPPORT INFRASTRUCTURE ELEMENTS

the definition of architecture is simple when placed in the context of the entire development process, the definition of its structure and content is complex. The theory, techniques, and procedures for defining system architecture structures and content is the subject of this book.

For completeness, the purpose and use of the other parts of the development infrastructure will be described. Additional information concerning the entire development process is contained in the companion volume, *Information Systems and Business Dynamics*. The development methodology is discussed in detail in the companion· volume, *Information Networks: A Design and Implementation Methodology*.

The "available products" part of the development infrastructure (see figure I.2) is a set of products that can be utilized as part of a new system (or deployment infrastructure) development in order to produce a usable result. The products may be hardware or software or a combination of both. Product resources are usually acquired independently of any specific development process. In the custom shop infrastructure, available products are of two types: first, the hardware and software used as part of the deployment infrastructure, and second, the standard components (assets) from which the system is constructed. The two types of available products are differentiated because different methodologies and organizations are usually used to manage each activity.

The deployment environment is the current or anticipated environment in which the products must function. Two aspects of this environment must be considered. The first (and most important) is the deployment infrastructure. It consists of any existing deployed set of entities through which the system under development will operate. Existing networks, computers, specific software functions, and other products that have additional capacity and that could be used by the new system are examples of this type of entity. In general, the deployment infrastructure entities are shared physical or operational resources put in place for the purpose of serving current and future products/services. This particular part of the infrastructure is especially critical from an economic viewpoint.

The second important aspect of the deployment environment consists of the operational characteristics that are imposed on systems by the enterprise and that form a set of constraints that must be followed for the product to meet the requirements of the enterprise. These constraints arise from a need to use specific existing or anticipated facilities or to follow a corporate deployment strategy. If developers do not have a knowledge of this aspect of the environment, a product cannot be successfully implemented.

As an example of a corporate deployment strategy that would affect product implementation, consider the following example.

A corporate data processing strategy restricts the type of communications allowed. A workstation is allowed only to send data to a departmental processor, where it will be checked for accuracy before being sent to a corporate processor.

Although the facilities (deployment infrastructure) may be in place to allow other types of interaction, this corporate policy must be followed when developing the operating characteristics of deployed systems. Failure to do so will result in an unacceptable system even though it operates correctly from a technological point of view. This again points out the need to integrate technical and business needs in any development effort.

The implementation environment provides the tools and management structures utilized by the development methodology. Although the tools are not part of the architecture or development methodology, they are closely associated with it. The specific set of tools that can be used effectively depends in large measure on the requirements of the architecture and the methodology chosen. The tools currently are grouped and marketed under the heading of Computer Aided Software Engineering (CASE) tools. Because of their complexity, these tools cannot be discussed in detail in this book.

The management structures include personnel organization, project management, contractual requirements, etc. Successful system development is, in large measure, a function of how well these activities are organized and controlled. The architecture must reflect these needs, and they must be stated explicitly in the architecture as required. A comprehensive discussion of this area, however, is outside the scope of this book.

Although much of the development infrastructure is currently implemented through manual activities and proce-

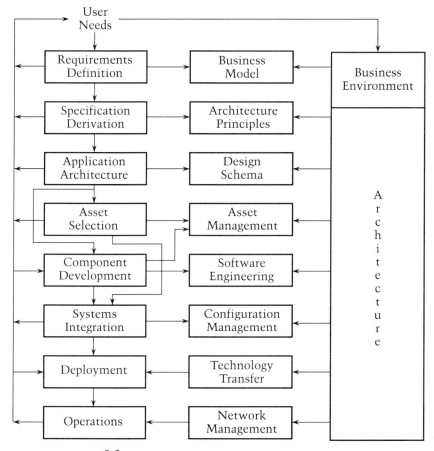

FIGURE I.3   COMPLETE METHODOLOGY STRUCTURE

dures, significant progress toward automation is being made with the aid of the fifth-generation techniques of artificial intelligence (AI). The complexities and size of current and future network system development require that these AI techniques continue to be emphasized in the development process. Without the effective utilization of AI technology, the network systems that will be needed in the future will not be viable.

The development methodology must interact with all of the components of the development infrastructure, and it must at the same time consider the vagaries of the real world. Because current methodologies are, in general, third-generation methodologies and do not utilize an architecture or consider the network environment, installed base, and deployment infrastructure, they are not adequate for the network system development process.

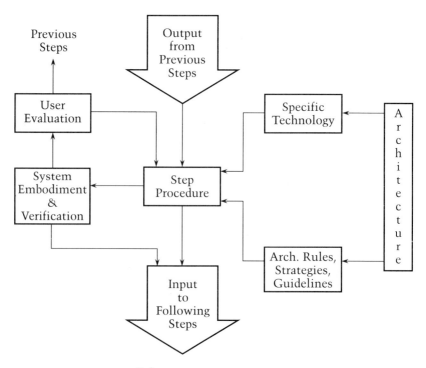

FIGURE I.4   COMMON STEP STRUCTURE

An example of a fourth/fifth-generation methodology that is constructed to consider all of the necessary infrastructure areas is shown in figure I.3. This methodology interacts closely with the architecture, is based on the use of prototypes, and requires user verification as indicated by the common step structure shown in figure I.4. Although it is beyond the scope of this introduction to discuss the methodology further, it is described in detail in the companion book, *Information Networks: A Design and Implementation Methodology.*

NETWORK SYSTEM ARCHITECTURE

O   N   E

ARCHITECTURE OVERVIEW

INTRODUCTION

As was discussed in the introduction, the custom shop model provides the most powerful and flexible foundation for the development of software used in networks and network systems. Also discussed in the introduction was the fact that the necessary domain knowledge for this development model is contained in an architecture. As such, the construction and use of this architecture is central to the efficient and effective development of networks and network systems. The architecture is only one component of a complex development process. It can be effective only when all of the other components are in place and functioning properly. The discussion in this chapter will make that implied assumption.

Because of the architecture's importance in the development process, this entire book is devoted to a detailed discussion of the design and structure of a suitable architecture. This architecture then forms one of the major inputs to the development methodology. The term *system architecture* will be employed to refer to an architecture in this context. This is necessary to differentiate this type of architecture from other architecture definitions and environments, both within the confines of the development process and in general usage. Some of these are mentioned as the discussion contin-

TABLE 1.1   EXAMPLES OF ARCHITECTURE CONTEXT

Field	Context 1	Context 2	Context 3
Construction	Building architecture	City plan	Structural engineering
Medicine	Anatomy	Genetics	Biology
Networks/systems	Application architecture	Portfolio architecture	System architecture

ues. As is noted in the next section, *architecture* is a common word that requires some qualification in order to clarify the context of its use.

ARCHITECTURE IN CONTEXT

The word *architecture* usually has one of three meanings:

1. The method by which an entity is designed or constructed
2. The principles that determine what entities should be constructed
3. The principles for constructing an entity

The word *entity* is used to indicate that the construction may involve physical or intellectual items. Although these three contexts seem to be similar, because they all deal with the construction of entities, they are, in fact, quite different. The correct interpretation as to which of these contexts is meant when references are made to an architecture is crucial to understanding the offered information. Because the differences in these contexts are not clear in most instances, a great deal of confusion has resulted from the use of the word *architecture*. This confusion has been increased by the use of analogies that are intended to provide guidance in interpretation.

Table 1.1 provides some examples of an architecture in each of the three contexts for some diverse fields. In most cases, the unmodified use of the word *architecture* is apt to bring up visions of tall buildings, stately homes, and, for the technically inclined, rolls of blueprints. This is clearly a context 1 case as applied to the construction industry. Because of this close association with the construction industry, many analogies have tied the concept of building architecture to software and system architecture. If the analogy is not carried too far, this association can be useful in discussing some of the overall purposes, because both building architecture and system architecture are concerned with organization, structure, and framework. If the analogy is pressed, however, the differences in context make the comparison a liability rather than an advantage.

Building architecture is concerned with a product (for example, the building), including its appearance as well as the structural details that are used in support. System architecture is concerned with the principles behind all system products rather than the details of a specific product. As shown in table 1.1, the term *application architecture* is sometimes used to describe the structure of an individual system. In this case, the term is directly analogous to the building architecture. Application architecture is important and is discussed in the companion book, *Information Networks: A Design and Implementation Methodology*. In this book, however, this type of architecture is not of interest.

In the zeal to maintain the construction analogy for system architecture (sometimes labeled *information engineering*) while overcoming the disadvantages of talking about building architecture, the "city planning" comparison is sometimes used. This is a closer analogy because it is more focused on enablers (for example, zoning) for the ultimate products (buildings), but the contexts are still different and this analogy too is inadequate if carried too far. A much more accurate comparison that maintains a tie to the construction industry would be with the knowledge of a structural engineer. This type of knowledge is concerned with the principles behind the construction of any structure without defining the structure itself. This knowledge also includes the use and limita-

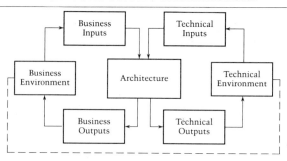

FIGURE 1.1   ARCHITECTURE DEVELOPMENT ENVIRONMENT

tions of the infrastructure, including zoning, roads, economic conditions, materials, etc. These have a significant impact on what the engineer (architect) is able to design and build. Any structure can be built as long as it follows the applicable engineering principles and practice. This is not unlike the development of a software system. Any system can be built as long as it follows the principles of the system architecture.

Although it has probably belabored the point, the above discussion is necessary because of the confusion in the industry concerning the definition and role of software architectures in general and system architectures in particular. The widespread use of the construction analogy also makes it imperative that the proper contexts be used and communicated.

ARCHITECTURE DEVELOPMENT

The development of the system architecture must consider the business environment as well as the technical environment. The architecture, in turn, will influence the way in which the enterprise conducts its business and will help assign priorities to the technical investigations that need to be performed. This dual responsibility is shown schematically in figure 1.1. Technology management provides one of the most important ways in which the business and technical environments are considered in the specification and alteration of the architecture. This process is discussed briefly in the following section. A more complete discussion is presented in the companion book, *Information Systems and Business Dynamics*.

Technology Management

Technology management is a process that utilizes a specific methodology for technology-related coordination, planning, and decision making. The major purpose of the process is to use the proper technologies at the proper time:

- In the products and services produced by the enterprise, and
- In the tools and methodologies used to develop those products and services.

Many possible methodologies can be effective in the technology management process. Each organization must determine what procedures will work with its particular culture, marketplace, and industry. However, the basic principles and objectives will remain the same.

The technology management methodology is shown in figure 1.2. The inputs to the methodology come from the major areas that influence the activities of the enterprise:

- Current technical environment
- Sources of technology
- Business strategies of the enterprise
- Products and services produced by the enterprise
- Market and competitive environment

These inputs include the two views of technology that are necessary for a comprehensive technology management process. The first is a technology-based view as to what the technology is capable of providing. The available technology may then influence changes to the enterprise's products and services and/or the fundamental strategies followed by the business. The second is a business-based view as to what the

5

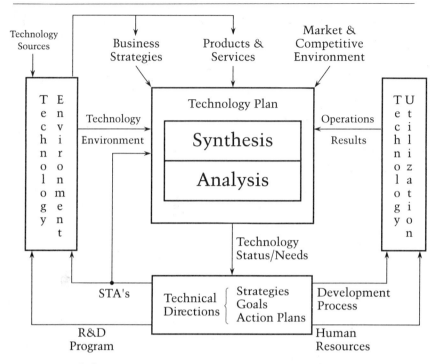

FIGURE 1.2 TECHNOLOGY MANAGEMENT METHODOLOGY

enterprise needs from technology. This will influence the specific technologies of interest and the manner in which the technologies are made available.

The outputs of the process are not all indicated explicitly in the figure because of their large number and diffused nature. Outputs occur at every step of the process and in many cases represent "soft" rather than "hard" information. The knowledge of the state of the art of a given technology may cause a specific product to be altered slightly with far-reaching results, or nothing specific may occur immediately. It is difficult to predict what the outcome of the knowledge may be. The major "hard" outputs occur as a result of the technical action plans whereby the enterprise defines specific steps to be taken to better utilize the technology available.

The process forms a closed loop that usually completes a cycle in about one calendar year. Although the timing could be changed, experience has taught that this planning period is quite acceptable and fits in with the natural planning cycle of most organizations.

There are four major activities in the technology management methodology:

- Technology plan development
- Development of technical strategies, goals, and action plans
- Technology environment determination
- Technology utilization

The technology plan is central to the technology management process. It forms the central database through which the enterprise can assess its uses and needs for technology and make appropriate decisions as to future directions. The technology plan consists of two stages, synthesis and analysis. The activities of the synthesis stage are designed to present the input data in a form suitable for making the required comparisons. The analysis stage utilizes the data from the synthesis stage to develop a set of charts that contain the data in a form that can be used for developing required action plans.

The information developed in the technology plan — which in a sense represents the technology status and needs of the enterprise — is now used to formulate technical directions that will provide more effective use of the available technical resources. This technical directions generation process is used to define the technical strategies for the enterprise and to develop associated goals and action plans which will implement those strategies. The specification of strategic technical areas (STAs) is an important part of this process. The STAs represent the fundamental technical needs of the organization.

Understanding and creating the technical umbrella under which the enterprise operates is the purpose of the technology environment function. This function contains all of the activities designed to provide technology to the enterprise. Some of these activities are shown in the following list:

7

- Research and development
- Technology transfer
- Technology assessments
- Product/vendor assessments
- Interactions with technology providers
- Technology-driven opportunities

Technology utilization performs two basic functions. The first is to monitor the effectiveness of the action plans with respect to the goals and technical strategies of the enterprise. In addition to alerting management to potential problems with the action plans, the utilization function also accumulates the quantitative data required for the start of the next planning period. Without the utilization function to provide feedback to the process, it would be impossible to determine if or how well technology management was performing.

The second function is to effect the transfer of technology to the development process through the architecture. As mentioned previously, this transfer is the major mechanism by which new technology is made available for use in the future products and services of the enterprise. The technology utilization function should be performed on a continuing basis, with full-time personnel assigned to the activity.

Pseudo-architectures

Some enterprises have defined a system architecture that merely envelops a collection of current products and services. This may be done for several reasons:

- To imply a product consistency and uniformity within the marketplace when none exists
- To satisfy an internal or external desire to compare new offerings with current ones in some type of framework
- Because of a fundamental misunderstanding as to what an architecture is and what it is designed to accomplish

These structures may have the superficial appearance of a system architecture, but on close examination they are found to lack one or more required characteristics (for example, design rules). You should be aware of the possibility of this type of misapplication and be prepared to identify it when it occurs.

Specification Process

The remainder of this chapter is concerned with the basic concepts required for the definition and use of a system architecture that is oriented toward the development of networks and network systems. The derivation of the architecture organization is considered first, followed by some examples that illustrate the concepts. The major architecture interfaces are then characterized and used to demonstrate the use of the architecture in the development process. The remaining chapters contain the more detailed information necessary to continue the process of specifying an effective architecture.

Although the results obtained are specific to the network environment, the specification process formulates and uses general approaches that could be adopted to provide system architectures for other environments. The determination and use of formal methods for the development of system architectures is not widespread. Because of the increasing importance of the architecture in the development of systems and the rate of change to which the architecture is subject, however, the definition, manipulation, and utilization of the architecture must be as formal and rigorous as the state of the art will allow.

The determination of the form and content of the architecture is currently an engineering process that requires a great deal of expertise and experience. Currently no known methodology can produce an architecture automatically. Because the specification process is essentially subjective, a high initial probability exists that errors will be found in the result.

9

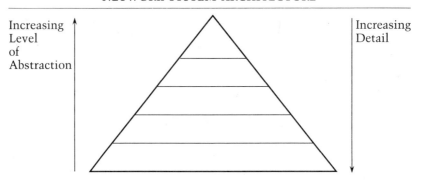

Increasing Level of Abstraction

Increasing Detail

FIGURE 1.3   PYRAMID STRUCTURE

These can be errors resulting from omissions, conflicts, and/ or incomplete or inadequate directions. The feedback from the implementers and other users of the architecture is critical in strengthening the architecture and making it more effective and efficient.

A robust architecture will have a relatively complex structure. Determining how and where the architecture impacts a given methodology area and/or a specific design situation is a difficult process under these conditions. In general, a computer assist using some form of intelligent database is necessary to make effective use of the architecture. Because this type of system is still in the research stages it would not be productive to pursue this area further at this point. Advances in this technology area must be tracked closely so that new results can be implemented quickly to make the use of the architecture as effective as possible.

PYRAMID STRUCTURES

The process of defining a highly abstract concept or need and adding detail in successive steps occurs in many areas of the architecture. This process can be modeled by a pyramid structure, as illustrated in figure 1.3.

Pyramid structures consist of levels with different amounts

of abstraction and detail. The greatest level of abstraction and conversely the least detail is contained in the top level. Successively lower levels become less abstract and contain greater detail. Because of their importance to many areas of the architecture, the general principles and properties of such structures are examined in this section.

Although the pyramid structure form is well known and is used frequently for a number of purposes, the methods for defining the contents of a lower level based on the information contained in the level above are not generally discussed explicitly — with one exception noted later. The definition and use of these methods, along with the specification of the interfaces between adjacent levels, are discussed here. Without knowledge of these subjects, it is impossible to understand the characteristics of any process or definition that is based on a pyramid structure concept.

Detail can be added to an existing level to obtain a lower level in four fundamental ways:

• Decomposition
• Assignment
• Augmentation
• Discovery

In a decomposition process, the contents of the existing level are partitioned and detail is added to each part, forming the lower adjacent level. This is the classical method of adding detail and is the stated basis for most of the attempts at defining a system architecture. It is also the method specified by the current major system development methodologies (assignment also plays a significant role, but it is usually not explicitly identified). Because the content of the lower level springs directly from that of the higher level, the process that interfaces them is generally called a *mapping process*. Specific content in one level can be mapped directly to that in the adjacent level. This process is illustrated in figure 1.4.

In an assignment process, the contents of the lower level

11

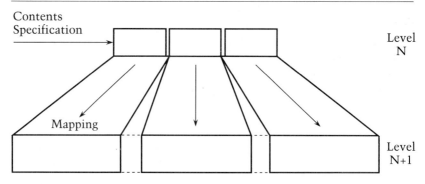

FIGURE 1.4   DECOMPOSITION PROCESS

are derived independently of those of the higher level. Contents of the higher level impose requirements on the contents of the lower level. Determination of the suitability of the lower level for supporting the higher level is obtained by assigning the higher level contents to the lower level contents. The applicability of this assignment is then determined through a verification procedure. This process is shown schematically in figure 1.5. An example of this type of process is the development of a physical network that will support the needs of the business as expressed by the definition of a specific service. The physical network is generally developed according to specific engineering principles and the applicable tariffs and regulatory requirements. It does not spring directly from the service definition. The usefulness of the physical

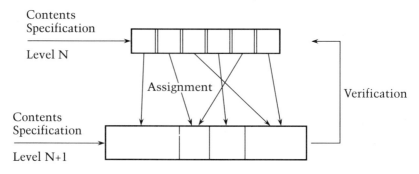

FIGURE 1.5   ASSIGNMENT PROCESS

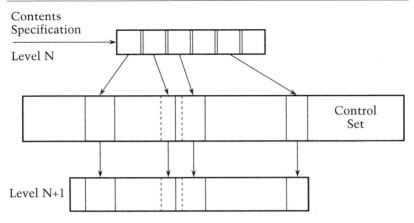

FIGURE 1.6 AUGMENTATION PROCESS

network is determined by assigning the requirements and structure of the service to the various physical elements and verifying that these components can produce the results desired. If either the assignment or the verification fails, the physical network design must be changed and the process must be repeated. The key to determining whether the relationship between the levels is that of assignment is in verifying the independent design of each level.

The augmentation process requires an independent source of detail information called a *control set*. The lower level is a subset of the information contained in the control set and is selected by using the contents of the higher level as the selection criteria. This process is illustrated in figure 1.6. An example of this process is the use of architectural principles (the control set) to supply technical specifications for a system under development. The business requirements are the contents of the higher level and serve as the guide by which the principles of the architecture are selected. The relevant principles become the nucleus of the specifications. This process is developed in detail in the companion book, *Information Networks: A Design and Implementation Methodology*.

The discovery process is similar to the assignment process. The major difference is that the proposed contents of the

13

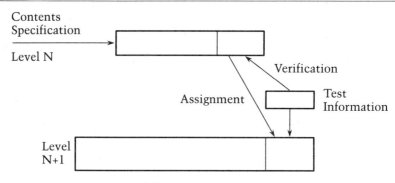

FIGURE 1.7   DISCOVERY PROCESS

lower level do not result from a development process but come from a trial-and-error process. Instead of the relationship between the levels being one of assignment then verification, the process is reversed and becomes verification then assignment. This reversal is desirable because the presumption of the discovery process is that the result is not appropriate. This process is illustrated in figure 1.7. An example of the use of discovery is in the selection of software assets for use in a system under development. A selected asset is placed in a verification process to determine if it meets the requirements of a component specification. Most of the assets tested will not be appropriate and will be eliminated from consideration. Those that survive verification are assigned a component. If this assignment cannot be justified (economically or technically), the asset is also eliminated. Although a comprehensive selection methodology can be defined, as discussed in the companion book, *Information Networks: A Design and Implementation Methodology*, the selection process still retains some of the characteristics of discovery.

Explicit identification and/or selection of a suitable method (or methods) for adding detail is important to the understanding of any development process. If this is not done, or if an inappropriate method is selected, the effectiveness of the results will be compromised.

ARCHITECTURE ORGANIZATION

The specific system architecture organization used as an example of applying the theory developed in this book is one with which I have had some experience, so the discussion is based on actual observations. It is also an example that adheres to the requirements set forth in the introduction concerning the needs of the network systems development process. It is an effective structure to exemplify the concepts and information requirements of a system architecture.

There are many possible alternative ways to approach and specify an effective architecture. Different enterprises have diverse needs and priorities, which can result in totally different architectural organizations that are successful in their environments. Most, however, will have certain requirements in common:

- They must allow new systems and services to be implemented quickly
- They must provide compatibility with industry and regulatory requirements
- They must allow the efforts of multiple organizations within an enterprise to be integrated effectively
- They must allow the effective introduction of new technology
- They must allow the "value chain" concept of automation to be implemented so that customers and suppliers can be accommodated
- They must provide the flexibility necessary to meet changing business conditions

The key to a successful system architecture is in adhering to the general philosophy and specific requirements as developed in this and the following chapters.

For simplicity, the word *example* will be dropped from the discussion that follows, as will qualification of the word *architecture* unless some confusion can result.

15

The architecture that is developed in this discussion is a "stretch" architecture. It is designed to encompass the emerging technologies and business use of a network as a strategic weapon. Although at times this may result in systems that initially do not conform completely to the architecture because of implementation difficulty, the desire to remain at and push the state of the art is one of the intangible drivers of this architecture design.

The architecture is divided into two fundamental parts, the internal structure and the output principles. The internal structure provides the framework through which the output principles are developed. These output principles are then used to control the design and implementation aspect of the development process. The large amount of information that must be contained in an architecture requires that both parts of the architecture be organized in a manner that makes their use and update relatively efficient. This can be accomplished by a decomposition process that partitions the internal structure and output principles into categories that reflect the major interface needs.

The internal structure partitions chosen must meet four conditions:

- They must be mutually exclusive
- They must cover the entire architecture
- They must reflect basic needs of the enterprise
- They must be selected from predefined classes

If these conditions are not met, the resultant architecture will be difficult to use and evolve and it may not adequately fulfill its function. The stated conditions are not difficult to achieve, as is illustrated in the following discussion.

In general, the partitions can be constructed to be mutually exclusive. Methods for accomplishing this will be evident as the discussion proceeds. If some need of the architecture is not met by one of the partitions, a new one must be defined or a current one redefined to include the need. This is an

16

TABLE 1.2   ARCHITECTURAL DECOMPOSITION
APPROACHES

Approach	Category Examples
Technology decomposition (Information technologies)*	Human factors Artificial intelligence Communications Software engineering Servers
Industry decomposition (Network provider)*	Network design Network operations Service specifications Security Customer service
Product class decomposition (Network services)*	End user services Network management System software Data Application development

* Information in parentheses indicates the area from which specific examples are drawn.

iterative procedure, and the architecture must be continually examined to ensure that the second condition in the list above is met. The determination as to whether the partition definitions meet the third condition must be made by examining the business vision, mission, and strategies. This is a judgment decision, but obvious inconsistencies will probably be evident if the analysis is performed carefully. Most of the classes used for partition selection should be available as a result of the technology planning process. Any relevant classes may be utilized, however.

For the example architecture, the appropriate partition classes are considered to be technology, industry, and product. Examples of the categories that result from each of the types of partitions are shown in table 1.2.

17

The advantage in using a decomposition approach is that the complexity can be handled more easily. The disadvantage is that the interactions between partitions tend to be ignored and not utilized as necessary. This latter difficulty can be partially overcome by explicitly defining the partition inter-actions.

Internal Organization

The organization of the subarchitectures is used in determin-ing and developing specific output principles, providing a mechanism for managing the complexity of these principles, and serving as information of "last resort" when none of the output principles seem to apply.

A workable structure may be obtained through formal or informal methods. To illustrate the techniques involved, a combination of these approaches is presented, beginning with a formal approach using synthesis techniques. This process, although general, is used only for specifying the high-level subarchitecture structure. An informal approach is used for further decomposition. Because of the heuristic nature of the informal procedure, an analysis must be performed after the structure is specified to ensure that the result covers all of the known requirements.

The first step of the formal procedure requires the decom-position of the overall architecture into a set of mutually exclusive subarchitectures, each of which is responsible for a specific aspect of a network system. For the architecture un-der development, a combination of the technology and prod-uct approach has been utilized as most representative of the needs of the enterprise. I am also familiar with architectures that use other combinations (such as industry and technology) that have proved successful. You are invited to examine var-ious combinations to determine which would be the most useful in your area of endeavor.

The specific subarchitecture set selected for the example architecture is as follows:

- End user services
- System software
- Data
- Servers
- Communications
- Network management
- Application development

A brief description of the purpose and content of each of these subarchitectures is given here to provide some of the background necessary for the remainder of the architecture discussion. It should also give an intuitive feeling for the scope and content of a system architecture and, as such, should provide some subjective information that will be useful in determining whether or not complete coverage has been obtained. No formal method exists to perform this particular verification. It must be approached through experience and engineering judgment.

The end user services subarchitecture controls the design and implementation of those aspects of the network and associated systems which directly interact with the end user. This architecture represents the user's view of the network and its services. Its purpose is to ensure that end users need not know any details about the network to utilize it effectively in their environment. It is also intended to enforce the "single view" of the network philosophy. Wherever the user is physically located, the network and its services should "look and feel" the same.

The system software subarchitecture determines the characteristics of the software support available for the applications and services on the network. The system software includes the server and network operating systems, security, and integrity. It can also be defined to include network management. However, because of the importance of that aspect of the architecture, network management has been assigned to a separate subarchitecture. The specified characteristics of this software must allow the network to be utilized efficiently

19

for all its defined purposes. It must permit distributed processing, cooperative processing, batch processing, distributed data, and a heterogeneous mixture of network and system components. The system software must also provide for 100-percent availability of the network during any changes, updates, or additions to any network facilities or functions in conjunction with network management. The architecture must allow for a wide variety of uses while maintaining the means for interoperability and resource sharing among the various functions.

The data subarchitecture determines how data is defined, stored, and utilized in the network. It provides for structures to ensure end user access, high-efficiency use, and integrity regardless of the location in the network of individual pieces of information. It must provide for the management of data as a separate and distinct function that is independent of the uses of the data. The architecture must (1) enforce designs that eliminate unnecessary duplication of data, (2) allow for transaction, ad hoc query, and batch operations, (3) allow data to be stored in many forms as suited to the operational needs, (4) encourage structures that can be repaired and that permit the necessary audits, and (5) provide for updates that allow 100-percent availability of the data.

The server subarchitecture determines the allowable types, functions, and interactions of the network servers. These servers provide the processing necessary to produce the services and functions available on the network. The server architecture must provide for multiple logical server connections and type definitions in order to accommodate the needs of different organizations. Specific server types must be able to be defined. The architecture should provide for servers to be self-defining to the network and their intended user group.

The communications subarchitecture determines the way in which network entities communicate with one another. Included in this architecture are the permissible network communication models and standards, permissible and mandated protocol conversions, gateway and bridge uses, physical

20

facility uses, and application-to-application communication principles.

The network management subarchitecture contains all aspects of network design, administration, operations, and planning. This architecture is responsible for ensuring that all networks are well behaved and have the proper capacity, services, functions, and availability to provide for the user needs. Under fault conditions, the network management architecture must provide for timely trouble identification and recovery of the network. The architecture must enforce the notion of end-to-end service regardless of the number of subnetworks or functions involved in the communications process. As part of this requirement, the architecture must require network operations designs that give the network user "single-stop service."

The application development subarchitecture determines how network applications are to be designed, implemented, modified, and replaced. It specifies the implementation methodology principles, directions, and tools; determines the network characteristics of the deployed system; and defines the way in which the deployed system interacts with the deployment infrastructure. It is the repository of the software engineering principles that will be used in the creation of new networks and systems.

Each of these subarchitectures is considered a complete entity in itself. To ensure that these subarchitectures form a unified whole, their interfaces and interactions must be defined and utilized as an integral part of the overall system architecture. This next step in the formal specification is accomplished by means of a structure graph, as shown in figure 1.8. The arrows indicate the flow of requirements from one subarchitecture to another.

For example, examine the system software subarchitecture. As shown in the figure, it places requirements on the data subarchitecture, network management subarchitecture, and server subarchitecture. In turn, the system software subarchitecture must satisfy requirements placed on it by the net-

21

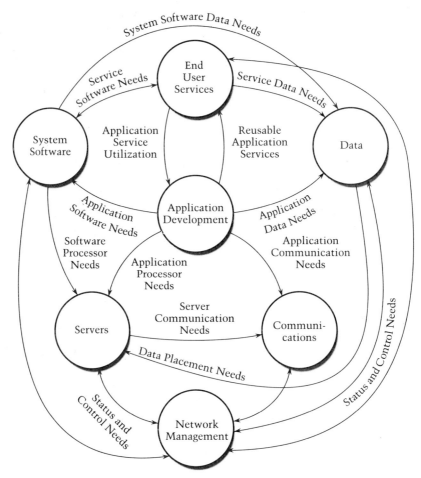

FIGURE 1.8   NETWORK SYSTEM ARCHITECTURE
STRUCTURE GRAPH

work management subarchitecture, application development
subarchitecture, and end user services subarchitecture. Consider the requirements placed on the data subarchitecture by
the system software subarchitecture. These might include the
following:

• Log data architecture
• User profile data architecture
• Directory architecture

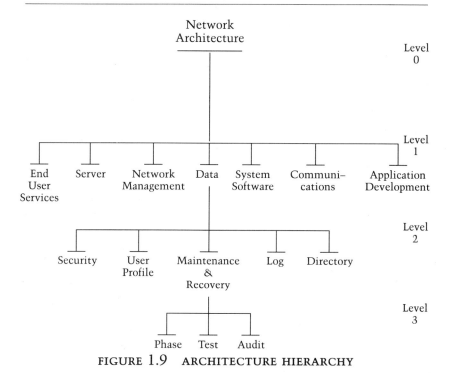

FIGURE 1.9   ARCHITECTURE HIERARCHY

• Data security architecture
• Data maintenance & recovery architecture

These architectures are subarchitectures to the data subarchitecture. If necessary, they could be further partitioned by the same process as described above. The network system architecture will thus consist of a hierarchy of architectures, as indicated by figure 1.9. Notice the similarity to the pyramid structure defined earlier in the chapter.

In general, a specific subarchitecture, SA, is constructed by the following steps:

1. Define child architectures of SA that satisfy the requirements of all of the other directly interfacing architectures of the same and higher levels of SA

2. Define a child architecture that satisfies the intrinsic

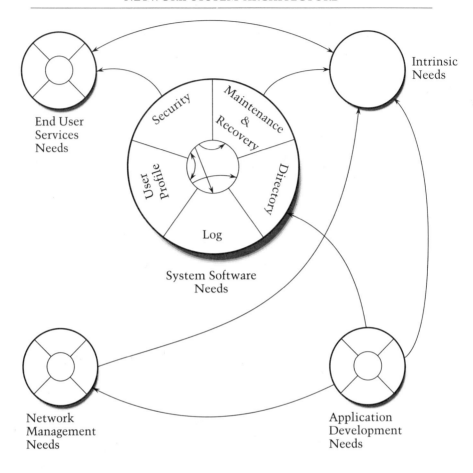

FIGURE 1.10   DATA ARCHITECTURE STRUCTURE GRAPH
(LEVEL 1)

needs for the particular system area the SA architecture is designed to address

3. Develop a structure graph for the contents of the SA architecture

The result of this type of synthesis process is illustrated in figure 1.10. This procedure can become complex rapidly and in practice cannot be specified manually much beyond the first level. Computer-aided tools are necessary. If desired, however, it is possible to partition the architecture structure down to whatever level of detail is necessary.

For the purpose of this discussion, the synthesis formalisms will be used only for the initial level. As stated, informal methods will be used to determine the next level of detail using the assignment process instead of the decomposition process. The resultant structure will then be analyzed to determine whether it has the appropriate coverage. Because of the awkwardness of the continued use of the "sub" prefix, it will be used in the future only if confusion can result as to where a particular architecture exists in the hierarchy.

An example of the type of results produced by the informal definition method is shown in figure 1.11 for the data architecture. Notice that a structure graph is present, but in a more implicit form than that shown previously. This implicit form (or a similar one) could also be obtained directly from the structure graph of figure 1.10 by including the appropriate detail in the diagram. Adding detail to the architecture by assignment instead of decomposition can sometimes provide additional insight into the information contained, because assignment allows more degrees of freedom in the definition process and because the result is in a more function-oriented arrangement.

Either approach may result in the definition of similar components in more than one subarchitecture. This duplication represents an interaction point between the two architectures and does not indicate a specification error. For example, a user profile component may appear in multiple subarchitectures. This indicates that many functional areas are concerned with this specific aspect of the system and the resultant design must satisfy all of them.

Output Principles

As shown in figure 1.12, the output of the architecture consists of four types of principles: strategies, standards, guidelines, and rules. Each of these has a specific purpose in deter-

25

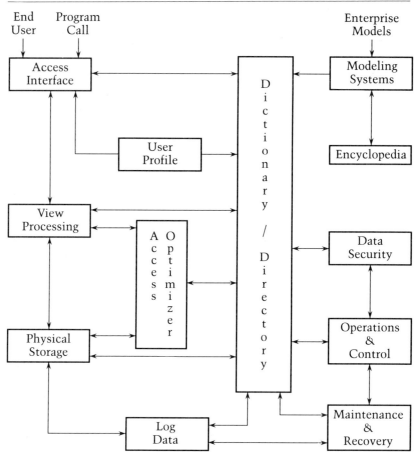

FIGURE 1.11   DATA ARCHITECTURE (INFORMAL STRUCTURE)

mining the implementation of a network or network system. Architectural strategies provide fundamental criteria that must be followed for compliance. These types of strategies are not the same as business strategies or technical strategies. In their specific environment, however, architectural strategies have a purpose similar to that of any strategy: providing the means through which the enterprise vision and mission can be implemented. Architectural strategies usually are limited to those areas which are deemed especially important to the enterprise. Unlike other strategy types, these strategies

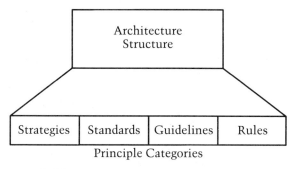

Principle Categories

FIGURE 1.12   OUTPUT PRINCIPLES PARTITIONING

are not intended to provide complete coverage for all areas of the architecture.

Standards reflect the necessity to perform some development procedures and activities and obtain certain results in a uniform manner. Standards can be of a number of different types and can be obtained from several sources, as shown in figure 1.13. The most important distinction from an architectural point of view is the difference between internal and external standards. External standards are developed by recognized standard bodies or the dominant enterprise in an industry and agreed to by a majority of the businesses in the industry. These standards are generally required when prod-

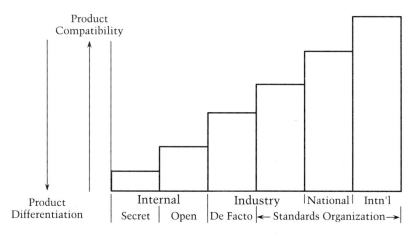

FIGURE 1.13   STANDARDS TYPES

27

ucts and services from different vendors must interoperate in some fashion. By necessity, the use of external standards will reduce the competitive advantage of a company, because all manufacturers in that industry have access to that standard.

The most important and usually the largest number of standards, however, are internal standards. These standards are selected by an enterprise as effective for use in its products and/or development process. Internal standards may include the specification of external standards if appropriate, but they may also include proprietary standards used only by the enterprise, as well as any type of standard between those extremes. The importance of standards to the architecture is reflected in the dedication of one principle category to standards requirements.

Architecturally enforced standards can insure that the resultant products/services can interoperate with others from the same enterprise or with those of competitors. Because of the high degree of agreement, definition, and documentation required, internal standards also ensure that appropriate attention is paid to those areas in which standards are specified. The determination as to which standards (internal and external) are required is usually a joint effort between marketing and technology management.

Not every aspect of architectural use can be predicted completely in advance. Interpretations of intent must be made when there is no specific direction available. Aiding this interpretation process is the function of the guidelines. The guidelines should be broad statements of intent that can cover a significant portion of the architectural area in which they exist. If information is required that is not covered explicitly, one or more guidelines should be available to provide some amount of direction. It should be remembered, however, that because guidelines are intended to be general, different interpretations can result from different individuals even under the same set of circumstances. In addition, although not desirable, it is possible for guidelines to conflict with one another because of the wide scope of their coverage. Usually, this is not fatal, because the guidelines require expert interpretation in any case. Conflicting guidelines just require additional effort to resolve. Although they are useful to cover areas for which no other direction exists, guidelines should be used minimally for the reasons specified above.

Rules are specific directions that must be followed if their enabling conditions occur. The rule and its conditions must be unambiguous and deterministic. Because of the rigid constraints imposed by rules, it is important that rules not conflict. When such conflicts occur, it is impossible for the user of the architecture to continue unless the situation is resolved. This resolution usually requires an update of the architecture. Removing such conflicts is a time-consuming process that should not have to occur often. The more areas in which rules can be specified, the more effect the architecture will have. The more rules that exist, the harder it becomes to avoid conflicts. Thus, the rules must be crafted carefully to prevent conflicts. Some of the techniques that have proved useful as approaches to truth maintenance in artificial intelligence may be applied to this problem in the future. It is important to remember that the rules *must* be followed when their conditions are met.

Each of the four output classes is further subdivided according to the scope and/or intended use of the principle. These divisions are as follows:

• Architectural principles
• Design principles
• Operational principles

This type of division is an aid in determining under what circumstances the principle is applicable. Because of the potentially large number of principles that will result from the architecture, any type of classification scheme will help. This is true for both manual and computer-aided approaches for applying the architecture. An additional classification structure will be discussed a little later in this chapter.

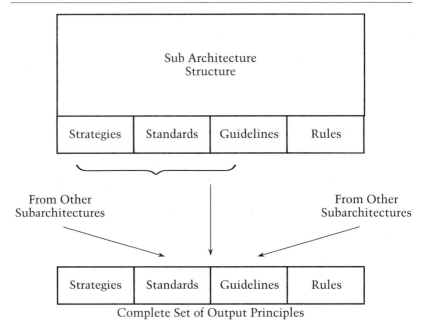

FIGURE 1.14 OUTPUT PRINCIPLES INTEGRATION

Combined Organization

The definition of a complete set of output principles (strategies, standards, guidelines, rules) is obtained by using the internal organization as developed previously. A partial set of output principles is developed for each subarchitecture. The principles are then combined at the next higher (parent) level. The process continues until the highest level is reached. The integration at this level is illustrated in figure 1.14. At this level, the output is usually stated explicitly for its subarchitectures. Although there will be some overlaps if the integration is not performed, these overlaps are usually not a significant problem.

The advantage in not performing the final integration is twofold. First, additional knowledge is obtained by explicitly identifying the general area from which an output principle is determined. Second, if the high-level partition is kept, it is easier to identify and apply the specific principles needed for the system under development. An example of how the specification of output principles is approached is presented in the next section.

The appendix contains an integration of the principles developed for each level 1 subarchitecture as presented in the remaining chapters of the book. Although not nearly complete, this set of principles can serve effectively as an illustration of the size, scope, and complexity of a set that could control the development of practical network systems.

PRINCIPLE SPECIFICATION

Once the structure of the architecture has been established, the specific output principles must be defined. This is accomplished by filtering the information coming from technology management through the architecture structure. As was shown, it is possible to define an architectural organization in a rigorous and structured fashion. Derivation of the output principles is a somewhat more heuristic process, is indicated in the following scenario:

In the last planning period, technology management has determined that it is time to allow the use of supercomputers in new systems. Supercomputers are computers that employ a number of processors to execute portions of a program in parallel, thereby increasing the effective execution speed considerably. The areas in which supercomputers are effective are currently quite restrictive, so the architecture must be able to direct their utilization effectively. The R&D organization initiated a technology transfer program, which has been in progress for about six months. The program is designed to ready development personnel to utilize the technology independently. Preliminary discussions have been held with the architecture control organization to include the technology in

31

the architecture and to develop a preliminary set of associated output principles.

The architecture control organization has determined that the addition of supercomputers directly affects the following subarchitectures:

- End user services
- System software
- Data
- Servers
- Application development

The structures of each of these subarchitectures have been altered to accommodate this new technology, and the preliminary output principles have been defined. The areas in the data architecture (developed in detail in chapter 4) which must be updated are indicated in figure 1.15, and examples of the additional output principles are shown in tables 1.3 through 1.14. Because the examples shown reflect only a small portion of the entire set of structures and output principles, it is difficult at this point to determine the usefulness of the information in guiding the development. As the architecture structure is developed in detail and additional output principles are determined in the following chapters, this uneasiness should be eliminated. Classification of some of the output principles may be subject to challenge, and depending on circumstances it is possible to place them in categories other than those shown in these examples. The important point is that the principles are presented explicitly. Their exact location is of secondary importance. Some of the new principles may be the same as those produced by other technologies and/or subarchitectures. In this case, only one principle need be stated along with the enabling conditions (for example, the specific processor classes for which it is true).

32

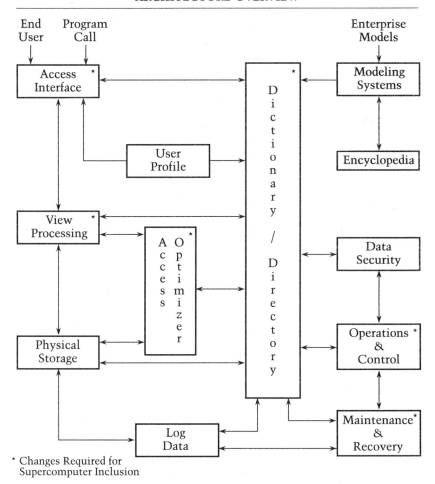

FIGURE 1.15   DATA SUBARCHITECTURE (SUPERCOMPUTER CHANGES)

In this scenario, the addition of the supercomputing technology did not require changing or eliminating other principles that allow the use of another technology. The main thrust of this supercomputer technology was to solve problems that could not be solved with current technologies and techniques. This may not have been the case if the technology being added was, for example, a new graphics technology. Elimination or

TABLE 1.3 END USER SERVICES ARCHITECTURE
SUPERCOMPUTER STRATEGIES

Aspect	Strategies
Architectural scope	Supercomputers may be used in systems to provide insight into the operation of complex systems. Whenever possible, the output for this usage should consist of video tape sequences to show the solutions of complex system equations. (Type I processing)
	Supercomputers may be used in (pseudo) real time systems in which multiple input streams must be processed independently to extract relevant information before combined processing can take place. (Type II processing)
	Multi-skill-level access shall be provided.
Design scope	The "look and feel" of all interactions between humans and supercomputers should be the same for all services.
	Supercomputers should not be used as the direct user interface into the system.
Operations scope	For type I processing, supercomputer access should be scheduled in advance, indicating the amount and duration of resources required.
	For type I processing, batch operation is preferred, but if necessary, transaction-oriented operation can be utilized.
	For type II processing, system operation must be continuous.

restriction of the older technology would have been probable, and the enabling principles would have had to be removed or restricted.

Many observations should be made concerning these principles. The first and most important is that enough information is contained in them to provide a rather detailed indication of the environment and conditions under which supercomputers should be used for network systems. Second, and almost as important, is the observation that you will want to add, delete, change, and move one or more principles

TABLE 1.4 END USER SERVICES ARCHITECTURE
SUPERCOMPUTER STANDARDS

Aspect	Standards
Architectural scope	The enterprise's standard human interface procedures must be followed for all software development using supercomputers. Standard graphics, windowing, and menu packages shall be made available for use by all supercomputer application and system services.
Design scope	Supercomputer applications must be designed for the particular machine to be utilized. Applications written for other computers should not be retrofitted for use on a supercomputer. Formatting of small amounts of output destined for the primary user interface server should take place in the user interface server using a standard package designed for this type of presentation. Bulk information should be transferred to the supercomputer by high-speed datalink rather than through removable media (tapes, etc.).
Operations scope	Supercomputers shall use the enterprise's standard message sets for initialization, operator interaction (removable media mounts, restarts, error indications, etc.).

depending on your experience and knowledge. For this reason, architecture principles must be subject to the examination and suggestions of all persons and organizations in the enterprise that are subject to the constraints and conditions imposed by the architecture. Agreement should be obtained from all concerned enterprise areas on the output principles (initial and changes) before they are used to design and implement systems.

Another important observation is that with current technology not all principles as stated are possible to observe in

TABLE 1.5   END USER SERVICES ARCHITECTURE
SUPERCOMPUTER GUIDELINES

Aspect	Guidelines
Architectural scope	For type I processing, natural language access should be utilized as one access method whenever possible. For type I processing, graphical input is encouraged where practical. For type II processing, a wide range of operating statistics should be made available.
Design scope	For type II normal processing, any user-related tasks have lower priority than standard processing tasks.
Operations scope	Outputs from the supercomputer to operations personnel should be in one of the following formats in order of preference: natural language, image, and graphical. For type II processing, under recovery conditions operator input must be able to override any automatic recovery sequences. Output to operator must clearly show state of recovery and planned phase sequences.

practice (remember that this is a stretch architecture). For example, it is not possible to obtain standard enterprise-wide message sets for all areas of operation across different classes and vendors of machines. This is a worthy goal that certainly deserves an architectural principle. That principle may need to be marked in such a way that it is excluded from immediate consideration by means of a waiver of some type. Immature technology is one of two reasons that a waiver of compliance may be needed. Even though the paperwork may increase as a result, requiring explicit examination of principles involving immature technology helps to apply some pressure toward an eventual solution through an internal research and development program or through interactions with one or more universities.

If a proposed system does not meet the requirements of the

TABLE 1.6 END USER SERVICES ARCHITECTURE
SUPERCOMPUTER RULES

Aspect	Rules
Architectural scope	Users submitting batch jobs to a supercomputer will be provided with periodic updates as to the status of the job. Transaction-oriented users of a supercomputer will receive highest priority for all needed resources, both internal and external to the supercomputer. Type I and type II processing must not be performed simultaneously on the same machine except for test purposes.
Design scope	End-user services must include on-line "help" facilities, on-line accounting information, on-line exception submission, on-line configuration information, on-line status information, and on-line schedule information from some server on the network, but not directly from the supercomputer.
Operations scope	For type I processing, assignment of all machine resources to a specific user must be available upon request, consistent with scheduling considerations. For type I processing, the supercomputer will not keep user data on-line for long periods of time. All data will be moved to another network processor at the end of a 24-hour period. For type II processing, the operator must not shut down the system without approval from the application manager except in case of life-threatening emergency.

architecture (other than for the technology-related reasons discussed above), there are three possible courses of action.

• Change the characteristics of the proposed system to meet the requirements of the architecture. This may be difficult if the proposed system contains a product that is a standard offering from an outside vendor.

TABLE 1.7 SYSTEM SOFTWARE ARCHITECTURE
SUPERCOMPUTER STRATEGIES

Aspect	Strategies
Architectural scope	Operating systems should intrinsically support all supercomputer features. System software should support complete unattended operation with full recovery and power restore capability. Supercomputers should be used for system functions only when no other processor is capable of satisfying the requirements.
Design scope	Direct operating system calls should not be made from application software.
Operations scope	Operational characteristics of the system software should be similar to other computers used by the enterprise. Training programs should be available for system software operation on a personal computer. System software updates should be made infrequently, except to fix major exceptions as provided by the vendor. No local alterations to the operating system should be made.

TABLE 1.8 SYSTEM SOFTWARE ARCHITECTURE
SUPERCOMPUTER STANDARDS

Aspect	Standards
Architectural scope	Commercially available operating systems should be used.
Design scope	Interfaces to the operating system will be made using the enterprise's standard techniques and/or software packages.
Operations scope	Exception-handling should be the same as that for any other enterprise processor type.

TABLE 1.9 SYSTEM SOFTWARE ARCHITECTURE
SUPERCOMPUTER GUIDELINES

Aspect	Guidelines
Architectural scope	For type I and type II processing, natural language access should be utilized as the access method whenever possible. For type II processing, a continuous graphical readout of the statistics of all processors should be available.
Design scope	System software should follow the major industry trends and commercial practice whenever possible.
Operations scope	Outputs from the supercomputer to operations personnel should be in one of the following formats, in order of preference: natural language, image, and graphical.

- Change the architecture to allow the inclusion of the proposed system. This should be done only after careful analysis and investigation. If this type of accommodation is undertaken too often, the purpose of the architecture will be undermined and it will no longer serve its intended purpose.
- Allow the nonconforming system to be used and to remain nonconforming. This should be done only as a last resort when neither of the first two options are possible. The only justification for this action is a unique nonrecurring situation that has significant economic or technical implications. This situation is the second reason a waiver may be used.

The decision as to what course of action to take must be made by the development organization in consultation with technology management personnel and senior management, because company-wide interests are involved.

The architecture output principles, as defined in the above discussion, form the major source of information for use by

TABLE 1.10   SYSTEM SOFTWARE ARCHITECTURE
SUPERCOMPUTER RULES

Aspect	Rules
Architectural scope	All supercomputers will run the same operating system.
Design scope	For type II processing, facilities for software interrupts and binary operations on interrupts must be available. For type II processing, at least 10 interrupt levels must be available. For type II processing, the operating system must be able to detect errors automatically and to recover without human intervention. For type II processing, the operating system must be able to reconfigure dynamically and operate on half of the normal number of processors.
Operations scope	For type I processing, data remaining after 12 hours will be deleted automatically by the system software. For type II processing, an audible alarm must sound when the processor enters a recovery state.

the interface activities (development methodology, assets, standard products). Examples of this usage are given in the next section. The structure of the architecture is also important as a source of information, although it is more general and indirect.

ARCHITECTURE USAGE

To set the context for the use of the architecture, its major interfaces with other development activities must be examined. Through these interfaces, the architecture provides the necessary information, controls the design and implementation procedures, and motivates the specification of standard components and the use of the deployment infrastructure.

40

TABLE 1.11   DATA ARCHITECTURE SUPERCOMPUTER
STRATEGIES

Aspect	Strategies
Architectural scope	For type I processing, data should not be kept resident on the supercomputer. It should be transferred in when needed and transferred out or erased when no longer required. Each on-line request to a supercomputer should behave as a single transaction. Successful completion should not depend on any other servers in the network. Dictionary/directory information should not reside on a supercomputer. For type II processing in which the supercomputer is configured as a database machine, the above strategies do not apply.
Design scope	Supercomputer data must adhere to the enterprise data model. When used as a database machine, a supercomputer must use the relational data model.
Operations scope	For type I processing, output devices should be channel attached (or equivalent) to the supercomputer. Large amounts of output should not utilize the network.

The major interfaces with other enterprise functions are shown in figure 1.16. Only the final flows are indicated, although each flow involves a two-way interaction prior to the final transfer of information. In addition, paths lead from each of the functions shown in the figure back to technology management. These feedback paths indicate how well the current technologies and procedures are serving the needs of architecture, asset management, and standard product management. As a result of this information, technology management may need to investigate replacement or alternative technologies in order to make these functions more effective. Although this is certainly an important part of the process,

41

TABLE 1.12   DATA ARCHITECTURE SUPERCOMPUTER
STANDARDS

Aspect	Standards
Architectural scope	Dictionary/directory information about supercomputer data should follow the same standard as that defined for other types of processors. Standard graphics, windowing, and menu packages shall be made available for use by all application and system services. The internal data format should be converted from the enterprise's standard data format before it is transmitted to the supercomputer. The internal data format should be converted to the enterprise's standard data format after it is transmitted from the supercomputer.
Design scope	When used as a database machine, the access language shall be SQL and the output shall be relational tables.
Operations scope	All data transfers from/to the supercomputer should follow enterprise standards for data transfers.

TABLE 1.13   DATA ARCHITECTURE SUPERCOMPUTER
GUIDELINES

Aspect	Guidelines
Architectural scope	The internal data format used should be that which makes the most efficient use of the specific architecture of the machine.
Design scope	For type I transaction-oriented processing, data views containing data resident on a supercomputer should be limited only to data on that machine.
Operations scope	None currently defined.

TABLE 1.14   DATA ARCHITECTURE SUPERCOMPUTER RULES

Aspect	Rules
Architectural scope	For type I processing, all data transferred to a supercomputer will be in the form of data files.
Design scope	Ad hoc queries against supercomputer resident data are not allowed.
Operations scope	All type I processing data used in a supercomputer must be removed within 12 hours of use. For type I processing, the supercomputer will not keep user data on-line for long periods of time. All data will be moved to another network processor at the end of a 24-hour period. For type II processing, all applications data necessary to reinitialize and restart the system will be kept permanently resident in the supercomputer.

the current discussion is confined to those paths indicated in the figure.

Although all of the interfaces shown are important to the effective use of the architecture, only those which directly interface to the architecture are discussed in this section. The other interfaces are discussed in the companion books referred to earlier.

Technology Transfer

Each of the information flows associated with the architecture is a form of technology transfer. A full (or complete) technology transfer is one that enables the receiving organization to perform independently original work in the technology. This type of transfer requires that a number of activities and events be satisfied. A list of these requirements is shown in table 1.15. If all of these occur in a timely manner,

43

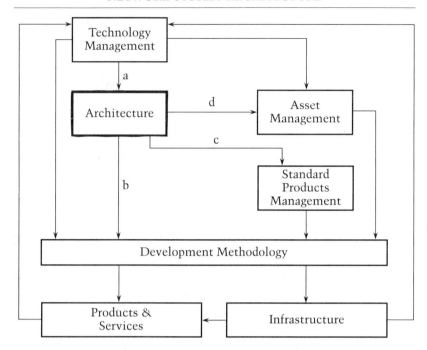

FIGURE 1.16 ARCHITECTURE USAGE ENVIRONMENT

a full technology transfer is said to take place. Transfers that involve only a subset of these components are said to result in a partial technology transfer. Each of the four interfaces of interest require a full technology transfer. Problems will occur when a full transfer is needed but not all of the components are present.

Training or education in a technology is most often incorrectly identified as full technology transfer instead of merely one of the components. Further, training is itself only one aspect of a comprehensive education program. (The same is true of documentation.) Education in the technology must also include a knowledge of the past and future of the technology, its operational behavior, and some of the "tricks" necessary to make use of the technology.

Even an excellent education program, however, does not constitute full technology transfer or provide the means to begin independent development and application of the tech-

TABLE 1.15   TECHNOLOGY TRANSFER
COMPONENTS

Area	Components
Environment	Equipment Tools Techniques
Education	Assessments Training Technical support Consulting
Experience	Apprenticeships Prototype construction
Commitment	Planning Resource allocation
Needs	Proposed uses Desired characteristics Acceptance criteria

nology. A person who is educated in the technology certainly is aware of the theoretical capabilities and projected uses of that technology. However, without actual experience, proper equipment, and resources, there can be no immediate application. This experience can be gained in many ways, such as through an apprenticeship or through the acquisition of experienced personnel.

The final component of the technology transfer has little to do with technology as such but instead deals with the commitment of the receiving organization to accept the transfer and make use of the capability. The transferring organization cannot by itself effect the transfer, although there is ample precedent for its trying to do so simply by "throwing it over the wall" at the intended receiving organization. If this intended receiving organization does not want the technology and does not formulate plans to use it effectively, no real transfer can take place regardless of the state of the other transfer components. The receiving organization must plan to incorporate the technology in its work program and products/services as appropriate, and it must allocate sufficient resources, both financial and human, to the task. Because this can involve significant effort, it is the final true test of the resolve to receive a technology and thereby effect the transfer.

Technology Management Interface

Two somewhat separate types of information flow from technology management to architecture. The first is concerned with new technology that is of interest in the development of future systems and that is reflected through the contents of the architecture. The second is concerned with changes to the structure and organization of the architecture itself. Obviously, the architecture is closely coupled to the technologies and to the product/service classes of the enterprise. The development and utilization of an architecture is a technology unto itself and, as such, is of considerable significance to the technology management process.

Because this entire book is an example of architecture development, there is no need to discuss such development as a separate topic within this section. The presentation on the interface between technology management and architecture is limited to the content required for new technology to be utilized in future system development.

The most significant component of the information flow is the availability of new technology for exploitation in future systems. In addition to this full technology transfer information, other needed data consists of interfaces with other technologies, commercial products that incorporate the technology, and other environmental information that could influence the introduction of the technology (for example, experiences of other companies with the technology).

As an example, consider relational database technology. This technology was in the development stage for about 10 years before it was considered mature enough for commercial exploitation. During this time it would have been tracked by

46

the technology management process. When the technology was deemed to be ready for use in future systems, the architecture would be updated to include this technology along with the older technologies of hierarchical and network organizations. Relational technology would then be available for use as the database organization for new systems, as would the older technologies. In addition, commercial relational database products that could be utilized would have been identified and would be evaluated as to their conformity with the architecture (qualification). The availability of suitable commercial products usually helps determine when a new technology will be used in place of an older one.

After inclusion in the architecture, the technology may be used in new system development because it is now in conformity with the architecture. It does not have to be used. Other alternate technologies can also be used as long as they are still contained in the architecture. In the example, new systems could use relational, hierarchical, or network database organization. The choice would depend on the technical and economic characteristics of the system under development and the selection of other standard products or assets. The procedures of the development methodology would be responsible for the selection.

At some point, if it is economically and technically justified, the older technologies may be removed from the architecture and made no longer available for use in new systems. Alternatively, as a migration aid, old technologies may be severely restricted in usage rather than completely eliminated. Thus far in our example, only relational database organization could be used for new systems. In actual practice, hierarchical and network database organization will be restricted in use to those cases in which their specific characteristics are needed by the systems under development. Currently, this includes cases in which the volume and frequency of accesses are extremely high and cannot be met by current relational technology. When this characteristic is no longer an advantage because of the improvement in relational tech-

47

nology, the nonrelational database organizations will be removed from the architecture entirely.

When the new technology has been included in the architecture, new assets and standard products will be implied by the new constructs and principles. After development, these will be available for new systems. Because of the possible long lead time to produce and/or acquire these new standard components, any changes in the architecture should be examined immediately for candidate standard components. Conversely, the removal of previously approved architectural constructs and principles may eliminate the future use of some assets and standard products.

In this way, the architecture becomes the mechanism by which technology change is implemented. The architectural format of technology information depends on the particular technology of interest and the area of the architecture in which it resides. This will become evident as the discussion continues.

Development Methodology Interface

As with the interface between technology management and architecture, that between architecture and development methodology has two main flows: organization and content. The organization flow results from the architecture's responsibility for specifying major aspects of the methodology (such as the use of network management procedures as contained in the output principles of the network management sub-architecture). Multiple methodologies or alternate steps of a single methodology may, of course, be allowed through the architecture as necessary. The characteristics of the proposed system would then dictate which alternatives would be selected by the development process control organization.

The content flow consists of architecture structure and principle information used by the development methodology in the actual design and implementation of the new system. The final structure of the system generally depends on the

48

methodology used and the specific architectural information. Unless these entities are properly defined, it is unlikely that the resultant system will be effective.

Standard Products Interface

Standard products are those which have been designated as preferred candidates for selection when their function is needed in a system under development. Other products may be used if any of the standard products are not appropriate (economically or technically). Because the characteristics of all products used in systems must be consistent with the architecture, products on the standard product list (or for that matter any alternates) must be qualified against the architecture. These qualification conditions are the major part of the information flow in the interface between architecture and standard product.

Another part of the information flow concerns the type of products that should be included on the list. Through suitable analysis, the architecture, as a direct result of its organization and knowledge, should provide direction as to the types of functionality that are generally needed in most networks and network systems. Products to provide these functions are then candidates for the standard product list.

From the example of the previous section, it is obvious that a supercomputer class should be established and that one or more supercomputers from specific vendors should be placed on the list. Closer examination of the example output principles indicates that video output packages for tape, operating system types and vendors, etc., could also be added to the list. The selection of a set of these products must follow the principles developed by the architecture.

Whenever the architecture is updated, this analysis process must be invoked to insure that all needed product types are represented and that the specific products included meet the requirements of the architecture. As an extension of the architecture, the use of standard products is an orderly way of

49

introducing new technology into the system development process.

Asset Management Interface

The interface between architecture and asset management is similar to that between architecture and standard products, as discussed in the previous section. The line between assets and standard products is fuzzy, because each can be considered to be part of the other depending on definitions. For the purposes of this book, it will be assumed that both assets and standard products are part of a category called standard components.

Standard products are those which are marketed as products (by either the enterprise or an outside organization) in their own right. They are not combined with another entity during the sales process. Assets are entities that must be incorporated as part of a larger entity in order to be marketed. These definitions are generally consistent with current usage, although local variations do occur. Although it is subtle, a distinction between assets and standard products is necessary because their management is generally handled by two different organizations, and their use and needs for architecture information tend to be different. A large majority of assets will be developed in-house, whereas most standard products are purchased. The enterprise can exert much more control over the characteristics of the assets than over standard products.

Several assets can be defined from the example architectural principles. These include on-line "help" facilities, on-line accounting information, on-line exception submission, on-line configuration information, on-line status information, and on-line schedule information for each type of supercomputer that is allowed in the architecture. Other candidate assets could also be defined by examining the requirements of each of the principles. Whether they should be implemented as assets will depend on an economic analysis of their potential use.

FURTHER SPECIFICATION

The remainder of the book is devoted to the additional specification of the internal organization and output principles for all of the first-level architectures. As stated previously, it is assumed that an informal approach has been used to arrive at the structure, and no formal method will be presented. However, justification for the result will generally be provided during the discussion.

SUMMARY AND CONCLUSIONS

Through the use of suitable structures and output principles, system architectures are able to contain a large amount of technical knowledge concerning the development of networks and network systems. This knowledge base is the primary source of guidance for the design and implementation phases of system development. As with any type of knowledge, great care must be exercised in the formats used to store the knowledge and in the way in which it is utilized. New knowledge must not be allowed to contradict what is already in place. Either the current or the new information must be changed to remove any contradictions before the architecture is updated.

Although they require resources, formalisms in the architecture should be encouraged, because they tend to insure that candidate information has been adequately considered before it is made a part of the architecture. Formalisms also remove the tendency to cut corners in the application of the knowledge or to apply it inconsistently. Overburdening the process with too much "red tape" should also be avoided, because of the waste of resources and the increased tendency to find ways around the system. Careful engineering is required to specify and apply these somewhat conflicting con-

51

straints so that they provide effective guidance to the implementation process.

As the investigation into architecture development continues in the remaining chapters, you should return constantly
to this chapter to make sure that the role and place of the
information being presented is known. Without this continu-
ity, much of the value of the discussion will be lost. As an
exercise, you are also encouraged to participate in the active
development of the example architecture by adding information that seems to be lacking and correcting areas that do
not seem to match your background and experience. In this
way, you can make the architecture a more real and useful
entity for you.

T W O

END USER SERVICES ARCHITECTURE

The human end user is the fundamental reason for the existence of an information network. Because of the widespread use of the term *end user* to include nonhuman users, such as computer software and terminal equipment, the restriction of the meaning of *end user* to indicate a human is made explicitly for the purpose of this chapter. The discussion is therefore oriented from the viewpoint of a human consumer of services. In the end user services architecture, the emphasis on end user services is on *what* is needed rather than *how* it is to be provided. The methods of providing the services are addressed in other chapters of the book.

The object of this architecture is to provide for systems whose end user interface is as efficient and effective as possible. This requires interfaces that exist simultaneously on a number of different levels. One level must allow for simple, easy-to-use operation, and other levels must allow the end user to control any complexities inherent in the system, if desired. The architecture must be able to specify how these requirements can be translated into the design parameters of individual systems.

When the human interface is considered, there is always a discussion as to whether the human is part of the network or external to the network. Although this is certainly an interesting question from a philosophical point of view, it need not be answered in order to develop an architecture for the interface between the human and the network. The more pressing problem is how to allow for the many innate characteristics of humans that make the inclusion of their needs in the network complex and difficult. The structure of this part of the architecture must be formulated to provide for the management of complexity while giving realistic guidance for the end user needs of the network and its associated systems.

The term *human factors* historically has been used when referring to the human-machine interface. This use has two major problems: the association with human physical characteristics (ergonomics) and the emphasis on creating one interface design that will fit all human operators. Human physical characteristics are certainly important, and the original goal of human factors — to identify the most important physical characteristics and design machines accordingly — was a significant step. However, other important human characteristics which should be considered:

- Personal preference
- Skill level
- Fatigue level
- Inherited characteristics
    Lefthandedness
    Color blindness
    Eyesight
    Personality
- Emotional state

When possible, these characteristics should be considered in designing the interface between human and machine. The term *presentation technology* is sometimes used to refer to this new way of viewing the interface between human and machine, and an overview of this technology was given in chapter 4 of the companion book, *Information Systems and Business Dynamics*. Presentation technology requires a change in the interface philosophy. Instead of the human operator adjusting to the design of the machine, presentation technology necessitates the machine to adjust to the needs of the human operator. Because some of these characteristics can change from day to day, and even hour to hour, the interface system must be dynamic so that it can immediately accommodate the changed conditions. A static system would require a design change to accommodate most deviations from the original design and would be unacceptable in the above context.

For example, consider the fatigue level of an operator. In the morning, when the operator is fresh and alert, the size of the characters on a CRT screen could be of a size and font pleasing to the operator. In the late afternoon, when the operator is tired, the system could detect that state, automatically increase the size of the characters by 20 percent, and change the font style. Farfetched? Perhaps! But it does illustrate the extent to which the end user architecture as espoused in this chapter adapts the concepts of presentation technology. The interface must adapt to the needs of the operator — preferably automatically, but certainly on request.

Some amount of interface redesign to fit the unique characteristics of handicapped persons has been accomplished, but it is usually very specialized and static in nature. It is generally useful only for the person it was designed for, and if the needs of that person change, the interface has to be redesigned; it cannot change dynamically.

Now that the philosophy of the end user architecture has been established, the next step is to characterize the environment of the end user. When this has been accomplished, a structure that can accommodate these needs will be proposed and evaluated as to its effectiveness. Finally, based on the structure and supporting information, a number of output principles will be derived for the end user architecture.

ENVIRONMENT

In the context of this book, the overall environment of the end user is considered to be that of a network user. Although this definition of environment can be used to help shape the required architecture structure, it is too broad to provide the detail necessary. A further definition of the environment can be accomplished by realizing that there are many other environments that impact the end user. These include:

• Job-related environment
• Physical environment
• Network functions
• Enterprise policies
• Personal needs

Each of these must be individually addressed and the results used to form an overall environment that can be used to develop and evaluate an end user architecture structure.

Job-related Environment

The work-related needs of the end user are determined broadly by the type of job assigned to the user. Examining the needs of each of these types can establish the requirements of this area of the environment. Job function types can be classified as shown in the following list:

• Clerks
• Knowledge workers
• Executives
• Customers
• Suppliers
• System developers
• Network administrators
• Network service personnel

The first three user types use the network for the exchange of information with other users or with data contained in the network. The next two user types are similar to the first three except that they are external to the enterprise. The last three types are concerned with administering and managing the network so that it can continue to meet the needs of the other user types.

Clerks are sometimes referred to as *power users*, because their job function is directly tied to the utilization of one or more enterprise applications, such as data entry or general ledger. These users have little time or need to change their interface characteristics, beyond a few characteristics that fall into the personal preference category (for example, background screen color).

Knowledge workers are professionals and middle management personnel who rely on the information contained in the network for decision-making and technology advances. These people include:

- Engineers
- Accountants
- Lawyers
- Architects
- Planners

People in this job type must have a great deal of flexibility in how they access and manipulate information, because their needs cannot be predicted in advance.

Executives rely on the network for summary information concerning the major aspects of business operation. Their time is limited, and they need access to a large amount of information shown compactly. The type of information needed usually does not vary much from day to day.

Customers and suppliers use the network to exchange information with their counterparts in the enterprise for the purpose of making the interactions between the different organizations more efficient. This type of exchange includes placing orders, making status enquiries, invoicing, etc. Because they are not part of the enterprise owning the network, such users usually have very limited access.

TABLE 2.1   JOB-RELATED ATTRIBUTES AND VALUE SETS

Attribute	Value Set
Utilization time	1% to 90%
Functions needed	Enterprise application
	Decision support service
	Office service
	System development service
	Service request
	Access change
	Network change
Formal training needed	Low, medium, high
Access restriction	None, type
Problem resolution	Contact point
Format control	Low, medium, high
Priority	Low, medium, high
Availability	Low, medium, high

Developers, administrators, and network service users are responsible for maintaining, upgrading, and operating the network for the benefit of the other users. These users need direct access into many of the network functions in order to monitor the operation of the network and provide any changes necessary because of malfunctions or the need for additional facilities.

Once the definitions of the various types of end users are known, the next step is to develop a set of attributes and associated values that can be used to categorize each of these user types. One possible set is shown in table 2.1. Table 2.2 shows specific values for the various user types. These values are representative and may change with the particular circumstances involved. The architecture structure must be able to satisfy the characteristics of each of the job types, including the delivery of the functions needed. This argues strongly for a loosely coupled set of subarchitectures, each of which con-

TABLE 2.2 JOB CLASS CHARACTERISTICS

Attribute	Class							
	Clerks	Knowledge Workers	Executives	Customers	Suppliers	System Developers	Network Administrators	Network Service
Utilization Time	80%	30%	10%	15%	15%	65%	90%	95%
Function								
Enterprise Applications	✓			✓	✓	✓		
Decision Support Services		✓	✓				✓	
Office Services		✓	✓			✓	✓	
System Development Services						✓		
Needed								
Service Request		✓		✓	✓			
Access Change		✓						✓
Network Change							✓	✓
Formal Training	High	Medium	Low	Medium	Medium	High	High	High
Access Restriction				Yes	Yes			
Problem Resolution	Supervisor	Network Service	Staff	Network Service	Network Service	Self	Self	Developers/Administrators
Format Control	Low	High	Medium	Low	Low	High	High	Medium
Priority	High	Medium	High	High	High	Medium	Medium	High
Availability	High	Medium	Low	High	High	Low	Low	High

59

trols a specific interface area. The validation procedure will be outlined after the architecture structure is developed.

Each of the functions listed in table 2.2 represents a class of services that are available to end users. The architecture must allow each of these functions to be made available to end users. When multiple services are employed to solve a particular problem, it is possible for the services to interact in a way different from that intended by the designer or user. This is commonly referred to as a *feature clash*. The architecture must be able to control the design of the function services in such a way that the occurrence of a feature clash is rare. This will be discussed further in chapter 8, which deals with the application development architecture.

Because the functions listed in table 2.2 are crucial in meeting the users' needs and expectations, a brief description of each function is given below.

Enterprise Applications   Enterprise applications are functions that have been developed to automate parts of the business operation. They are specifically designed to complement the business of which they form a part. The applications may automate some functional aspect of the business, such as accounting, inventory, order entry, etc.; such automation has been the traditional method of using computers in business applications.

The applications may also automate across function lines to allow an entire business activity to be computerized. This is the "value chain" approach, in which value is added to the process at every step. An example of this type of automation is an application that allows a customer to place an order using a workstation directly tied into the enterprise network. The order automatically goes to the warehouse to be filled and shipped, inventory is updated, the proper accounting records are updated, and an invoice is generated and sent to the customer via his/her workstation. In addition, statistical and other business information is updated to reflect the sale. Each of these steps represents increased value to the enterprise.

Regardless of the type of automation utilized, enterprise applications represent those functions which are integral to the operation of the business on a day-by-day basis. They are generally utilized by clerk-level personnel whose job it is to perform the function addressed by the application.

Decision Support Services Decision support services are features and functions that assist knowledge workers in the decision-making process. These services give users the ability to flexibly extract data from databases and quickly manipulate it in different ways. Individuals or departments can create their own views of the data, perform calculations on this data, and generate appropriate graphics and charts. These services allow the creation of summary data and the utilization of detail when necessary. Bulky and unchangeable management reports are often replaced with personal computer files that can be manipulated, scrolled, and modified and that permit all manner of "what-if?" calculations.

Office Services Office services are features and functions that assist office workers in the performance of their varied duties. Studies have shown that most of the possible gains in productivity within an organization can be obtained by concentrating on the needs of professional and managerial employees (knowledge workers) through the use of services that make the office environment more efficient and friendly.

The office environment can be viewed as an information processing and communications center where virtually all functions performed by office workers (professional and managerial employees) fall into one of the following categories:

- *Analysis and decision making*: Reading, calculating, planning, scheduling, and "think time"
- *Report preparation*: Writing and proofreading (by pencil or computer)
- *Typing/data entry*: Keying in previously prepared documents or data (not including data entry of a document by

61

its author or data entry by professionals in their own ana-
lytic work)

- *Copying/information entry*: Conventional copying and
publication for mass distribution; information entry is document entry using cameras or scanners
- *Information handling/storage*: Mail handling, document
retrieval, filing, and distribution, including both paper and
electronic documents
- *Telephone time*: Obtaining a number, dialing, wait time,
missed connections, and actual conversation
- *Interpersonal communication*: Casual face-to-face conversation, formal meetings, conferences, and travel for these
purposes

The network needs of knowledge workers in performing the
above tasks require the architecture to support end user services such as document generation (word processing, image
scanning, etc.), distribution, and storage; scheduling; and conferencing. Providing these services by themselves is not
enough. They must be integrated to form a coherent system
that provides for uniform access from a single workstation.

Information created by each service should be available for
other services. For example, mail should provide both voice
and text messages. In addition, because communication is
important to these functions, special attention must be paid
to the movement of documents and other information between otherwise incompatible workstations. This latter aspect will be covered in detail in the section on the communications subarchitecture.

To support interpersonal communication in the office environment, the architecture must provide for teleconferencing services. The technology is becoming available to allow
personal teleconferencing from individual workstations. Because of the importance of face-to-face conversations and
meetings in the office environment, teleconferencing is discussed in some detail here. This is not meant to minimize
the other aspects of the office environment but to give proper

attention to an aspect that is somewhat neglected in current practice.

Teleconferencing is defined as an interactive electronic meeting between two or more persons in separate locations. It makes doing business easier and more efficient by moving ideas rather than people. Faster decisions can be made because needed information is received quickly and directly. Better decisions can be made because all sides of an issue are discussed on the spot. Communication is improved through increased contact. In addition, travel costs are reduced and valuable time is better utilized.

There are several forms of teleconferencing: audio conferencing, audiographics, and freeze-frame and full-motion video conferencing. Audio conferencing allows more than one person per location to conference with more than two locations. The addition of graphics transmission (for example, electronic blackboards, slides, and textual material) to an audio conference is termed audiographic teleconferencing. Freeze-frame video conferencing allows for the transmission of still images and graphic materials. All of these forms have their place and must be supported by the architecture.

The most complex form of teleconferencing is full-motion video conferencing, which allows participants at two (or more) different sites to see and be seen by one another. Graphics transmission is usually integrated with a full-motion system.

As with all other aspects of workstation use, video conferencing services must be integrated with the other services, from both access and information transfer perspectives. This integration must be provided for through the architecture.

System Development Services   System development services are intended to allow new applications and systems to be designed and implemented. The architecture must provide these services for both the professional software engineer and other knowledge workers. The services would be somewhat different for these two groups, because their job requirements are fundamentally different. System development services would include the following:

- Compilers and assemblers
- Debuggers and testers
- Design tools

Tools would be needed to support development for the third through the fifth generation, although the use of the third-generation tools would not be great. Software engineers would need access to all of the tools, although they could be provided to others based on need and knowledge. The architecture must support the wide range of these services as well as the delivery to all those end users that need them. Additional discussion of these types of services is provided in the companion book, *Information Networks: A Design and Implementation Methodology.*

Physical Environment

The human–machine physical environment has historically received the most attention through the study of ergonomics, or the fitting of human to machine. The physical environment is much broader than that, however. A large array of entry and presentation devices, as shown in figure 2.1, must also be included. Each of these devices can be used to translate human actions to machine-resident data or vice versa. In current practice, the decision as to which devices may be used is determined by the system designer or implementor. Whenever possible, however, the specific devices used should be the decision of the operator, and the architecture must be able to ensure that systems will adhere to that requirement.

To accomplish this, a separate control function for the interface must be defined that is independent of the operation of the network and application systems. This control function is responsible for translating the needs of the human operator to the needs of the network or application system. The exis-

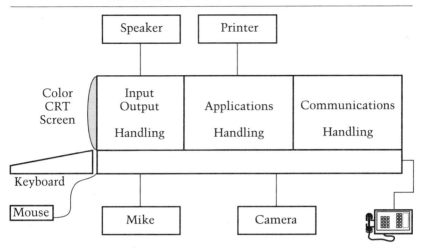

FIGURE 2.1   WORKSTATION FUNCTIONALITY

tence of such a control function must be specified as part of the end user architecture.

Network Function Environment

Three aspects of network systems (functions) impact the end user directly. The first consists of the actions necessary to be granted use of the function, the second is the access procedure necessary to make use of the function once permission has been obtained, and the third is the impact (cost, effectiveness, execution characteristics, etc.) of the function performed. All of these activities require some knowledge of the end users' characteristics (type, personal preferences, restrictions, etc.) and current status. Much of this information can be contained in a user characteristic database usually known as a *profile*. This profile can be altered by the user as well as through the use of network actions. Thus, the profile must be accessible by all network functions. A user profile must be specified as an integral part of the end user architecture.

Obtaining permission to use a particular function requires interacting with one or more of the network administration activities as defined previously. The end user should be able to perform this interaction automatically by interfacing directly with the appropriate database and associated control functions. This authorization process would be responsible for updating the network security, administration, and profile data. Obviously, use could be denied for appropriate reasons (for example, because the maximum number of authorized users has been reached) or restricted (for example, according to the time of day). Automatic authorization must be provided for in the end user architecture.

Assuming that permission to access a network function has been granted, the user profile must be updated with information concerning the function. This information would include:

- User specified access name(s)
- Training access linkage
- "Operational help" access linkage
- Problem-resolution access linkage
- Restrictions
- Possible feature clashes
- Level of service

This updating would be performed automatically by the appropriate network administrative function and would not require any action on the part of the end user. The architecture must accommodate this process.

Because the user profile contains only the access names, the access procedure function must also include a directory to hold the actual address of the function being accessed. If the function location on the network changes, this address must be updated. This process is the responsibility of network administration and must be transparent to the user. The directory will also be used for other purposes than the end user interface. These will be discussed in the appropriate architecture presentations.

Access procedures for individual or integrated functions should be simple, requiring the user to know only an access name that is provided by that user for initial function access.

Architecture support for efficient integration of individual functions will be discussed in chapter 8, on application system development.

Associated functions, such as training and "help" facilities, will utilize some standard variation on the user-assigned function name. The function may also require that some standard security information also be supplied by the end user. Depending on the level of security needed, this additional information may also be placed in the user profile. The system application should rely on the user profile for all of the needed initialization information. The end user should not be required to perform complex "hand-shaking" activities in order to begin the application function. The application development architecture must rely on this part of the end user architecture for services of this type.

The third aspect of the function environment that is of interest to the end user is the impact of using the function. Cost, time, results, etc. are all of significant interest. Except for cost (if any), which will show up as a bill of some sort, the other impacts are somewhat qualitative in nature and cannot be directly addressed by the network. If desired, the architecture could certainly provide for a comment facility in the user profile for that function, so that any unsatisfactory (or satisfactory) experiences could be sent back to the developers. Although the architecture does not have to account for all possibilities, the more robust it can be made, the more guidance can be given to the system development process.

Enterprise Policies

The formal and informal policies of the enterprise form an environment of considerable importance to the network end user. To a large extent, they dictate how and when the end user can utilize the network and the associated functions. The architecture must provide support for incorporating this information. Security-related issues have already been discussed, so this presentation will consider only other areas.

One of these areas is an overall limit on the amount of resources that may be consumed by a given end user in a specific period of time. Once the limit has been reached, the end user must apply for and receive additional resources or refrain from using the network until the new period begins. Another policy might determine whether an end user can access the network remotely (for example, from home). Still another might limit the personnel who can be contacted directly by the end user.

In these cases, the architecture must contain structures that allow the enterprise policies to be automatically enforced by the network. Future changes in policy must also be able to be accommodated by the architecture without altering the architecture itself significantly. It would be wise to have alternate structures that could accommodate a variety of possible future policy directions. Although this would not necessarily accommodate all possibilities, the amount of architecture change would be minimized.

Personal Needs

What has come to be called an individual's "personal space" has a large bearing on the productivity and attitude of the end user. Although much of what constitutes this "personal space" environment is out of the range of system architecture (office design, furniture, temperature, etc.), some aspects can be influenced as a part of system design, and these aspects require architectural control. This area is broadly concerned with the direct interaction of the operator with the network interface. Some of the attributes associated with these needs are shown in the following list:

- Amount of equipment needed
- Interface devices and characteristics
- Keyboard layout
- Screen format
- Screen size, brightness, glare

- Type and volume of sounds produced
- Response time
- Error recovery
- Response message intelligibility
- Repetitive operation
- Printer location and noise

Most of these factors, among the many others that constitute the operator's personal environment, greatly influence the effectiveness of the end users and need to be somewhat under their control. An amount of compromise is necessary in this area so that the needs of the operators, system, and enterprise are all met satisfactorily.

Some of these attributes, such as the repetitiveness of the operator entries, cannot be controlled by the end user but can certainly be addressed by the system designer. Manufacturing organizations have discovered that giving assembly line workers a variety of tasks instead of a single simple operation enhances the workers' concept of the job and results in more efficient operation. Likewise, system design should allow for the network end user to perform a variety of tasks and not be limited to a few simplistic operations. This will enhance the end user's comfort with the system and produce a more comfortable feeling of personal space and environment. The architecture should produce this type of end user system interface.

Currently there is widespread concern over the health aspects of network operators. So intense is this concern that various laws regulating the amount and type of usage have been passed or are being considered by various governmental bodies. This has occurred to a large extent because little concern has been paid to these personal environmental issues. People resent being treated merely as an extension of a machine or software system and will react negatively. Health problems are a very human way of coping with the perceived inhospitable environment.

Everyone has differing personal environmental needs, and

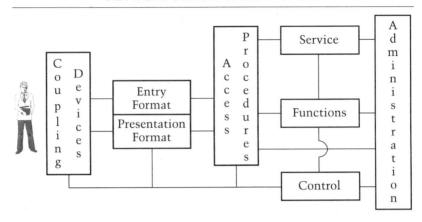

FIGURE 2.2   END USER ARCHITECTURE COMPONENTS DIAGRAM

no one solution will fit everybody. The architecture must provide for systems and devices that allow each end user to personalize their environment to their individual needs without sacrificing the intent of the system or the needs of the business. This requires a great deal of thought and engineering effort, in addition to inputs from psychologists and other health care personnel. Increasing both personal happiness and business efficiency is well worth the effort.

ARCHITECTURE STRUCTURE

The previous discussion has indicated explicitly a number of areas that need attention from the architecture. A construction (decomposition) technique similar to the one presented in the previous chapter could be postulated to develop the constructs required to meet these areas. However, it is much easier to formulate a candidate structure and determine by analysis whether all of the specified needs are met (assignment process). This approach will be taken in the development of this and all of the other subarchitectures.

The candidate structure for the end user architecture is presented in figure 2.2. It consists of eight components (subarchitectures) that are interconnected through twelve two-way paths. The word *component* will be used to avoid any confusion with the other uses of the term subarchitecture. Some of the components also have counterpart components in the other level 1 subarchitectures. These include the service and administration components, which interconnect with the network management architecture; the functions available component, which interconnects with the system software, data, and application development architectures; the control component, which interconnects with the communications architecture: and the remainder of the components, which interconnect with the server architecture. Only the major interconnections are named; many others also exist but are not needed to present the concepts.

Each of the functions addresses a set of issues as determined in the previous discussion. The paths indicate services required from one function by another in the same way as was defined for subarchitecture interconnections in the previous chapter. The following presentation discusses the definition and major functions of each of the components and identifies which of the stated needs they cover. For consistency, all of the component definitions use the following basic structure, although deviations will be made as necessary:

- Purpose
- Major functions
- Services required

Coupling Devices

The purpose of the coupling devices component is to allow the transfer of information between the end user and the network. This information is transmitted through one of the human senses, including touch, sight, hearing. Although it would be possible to use the smell or taste senses to transfer information, I am not aware of any devices that have been developed to do this. A specific coupling device may transfer information in one direction or both, depending on its design.

71

TABLE 2.3   POPULAR COUPLING DEVICES

Category	Devices
Current	CRT screen (color, monochromatic) Keyboard Telephone handset Speaker Mouse Tactile sense pad Printer Plotter
Emerging	Television camera Microphone Scanner and optical character reader (OCR) Liquid crystal screen
Past	Teletype Light pen Track ball Touch screen
Special purpose	Eye movement sensors Body location sensors Muscle voltage/current sensors

Many types of coupling devices have been developed over the years, either to meet a specific need or as an attempt to provide a general coupling function. The most prevalent ones are listed in table 2.3.

The development of coupling devices is one area of technology that has seen rapid change and that will continue to evolve rapidly, although the rate of change seems to have slowed in recent years. A standard interface needs to be specified in the architecture for each type of information — data, audio, and video. Devices or their drivers would then contain the conversion function to convert this standard protocol into the specific format needed by the device. For example, to enter character data, the user could choose among a keyboard, tactile pad, or scanner with optical character reader functions, without affecting the operation of the system. The choice should be made locally and should not require network re-

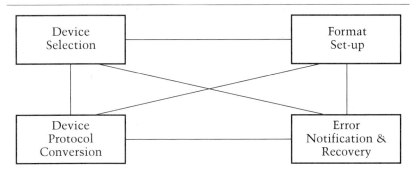

FIGURE 2.3   ENTRY/PRESENTATION FORMAT
SUBARCHITECTURES

sources. Currently, many systems allow the end user to select one of two alternatives, such as keyboard or mouse, to control a cursor. However, this automatic transfer of coupling devices is the exception rather than the rule, and the use of alternatives must be extended to most other types and combinations of coupling devices.

The coupling devices component requires cooperating services from (1) the control component, which provides for the selection of different devices either automatically or on a manual basis, and (2) the entry/presentation format components, which provide for the device-specific format based on the needs of the user and the application system requested.

Entry/Presentation Format Components

These two components are similar in function, except that one reacts to input coupling devices and the other reacts to output coupling devices. Their purpose is to provide a suitable interface to the end user. This interface is the result of the user's desires, the particular coupling device selected, and the needs of the system function(s) being accessed. Both manual and automatic adjustment methods must be made available in the component. The major functions of this component can best be understood through the diagram shown in figure 2.3. The four component subarchitectures are responsible for

73

ensuring that all relevant factors are considered in the determination of the system interface.

The device selection and protocol conversion functions are self-evident. They provide the criteria as to how and when coupling devices are to be selected and the means that must be present to perform protocol conversion. The format set-up function provides the criteria for developing manual and automatic set-up procedures required to obtain the proper interface formats. The error notification and recovery function provides the criteria for monitoring the operations across the interface and determining if any errors have occurred. It also provides the principles for designing the end user notification of the problem, if necessary, and developing recovery procedures so that the end user may continue operation.

These functions must interact (receive and give services) with cooperating functions in other subarchitectures so that any system built under the architecture will receive consistent advice as to what is necessary in each aspect of system operation. The most critical of these functions is the error notification and recovery function, which must closely interact with the network management and application development architectures.

Access Procedures Component

The purpose of the access procedures component is to provide the principles necessary to allow functions to be acquired and utilized automatically. End user systems built using this architecture should require only a minimal effort for the end user to obtain access to a function and begin to make use of it. The major functions of this component are shown in figure 2.4 in block diagram form.

The user profile subarchitecture contains the principles for structuring and using the information specific to the end user and the type of interface available (equipment and software). The user profile information must be accessed by the end user, the interface environment, and any network function,

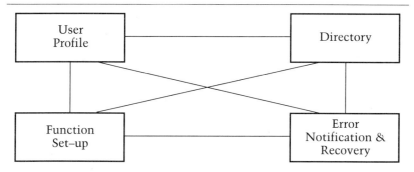

FIGURE 2.4   ACCESS PROCEDURES SUBARCHITECTURES

within the constraints of security and operations considerations. The principles derived from this area must support that broad access need.

The directory contains the addresses of all network functions, or alternatively, the means to obtain the addresses. The subarchitecture that provides for this need must specify the exact method that this function will employ, because it must be standard throughout the network. If more than one directory is to be allowed, the directories must be placed in a specific relationship with respect to one another (such as a hierarchy), so that the role of each directory is clear. The directory subarchitecture must be the same in any place that it occurs. This implies a strong relationship between the end user architecture and all of the other level 1 architectures that contain a directory function.

The function set-up subarchitecture contains the allowable protocols and procedures for obtaining access and utilizing any network function. Its purpose is to provide the principles that govern the access of any network function by the end user. This subarchitecture should also govern how the results of different functions may be combined into a single result for presentation to the end user. Network functions may be partitioned into classes depending on their characteristics and the different access procedures used for each class. The architecture must allow for this possibility.

This subarchitecture must interact closely with the application development and system software architectures to ensure that systems contain the proper protocols for use in the end user systems.

The error notification and recovery subarchitecture is similar to that required by the function set-up architecture. Their allowable structures and principles must be similar while allowing for differences in the system activities covered. As before, this type of function must interact closely with the network management architecture.

Control Component

The purpose of the control component is to provide the principles for the coordination and interaction of all of the other end user functions. Because the amount of direct intervention of the end user in the system processes should be minimized, the control function must provide for intelligent systems that can make routine decisions without relying on the operator.

The control function must interact closely with the network management and system software subarchitectures to ensure that status information concerning the end user is available to other network functions as required and that the end user system has information concerning the status of the network and systems.

Service and Administration Components

These components provide the principles for the use of services from the network and system providers. These principles include the following:

- Systems operation help
- Permission to access network systems and functions
- Inquiries as to system status
- Inquiries as to end user status (billing, resources used, etc.)

These components are tied closely to the components of the network management architecture, and an expanded discussion of their needs and requirements is provided in chapter 7.

Functions Available Component

The functions available component provides the principles that govern how the end user can identify all of the available functions, as well as providing a description of their capabilities and characteristics. For networks with a robust set of functions, the identification of those which will meet the needs of the end user can be complex. For this reason, the functions available component must provide for an intelligent search and identification process to provide availability information.

This component must interact closely with the system software, application development, and network management architectures so that it can provide for timely information content.

COVERAGE

The major purposes of the structure, as defined previously, are to (1) make sure that the architecture covers all of the needs as expressed during the definition process and (2) motivate and classify the specific principle statements that will be used by the methodology during the system implementation process. Coverage is determined by a validation process that examines each of the needs defined explicitly during the definition process and then identifies a specific architecture function whose definition includes that need. If such a function cannot be identified, the architecture structure must be altered. When all needs have been validated, the structure is considered complete.

When new needs are identified during the course of normal business operation, the validation process must be used for these needs and the architecture structure must be altered as necessary, as discussed in the architecture overview of chapter 1.

PRINCIPLES

This section, like the principles sections of the remaining chapters of this book, lists a set of principles that are derived from the structures and requirements of the architecture. As discussed in chapter 8, a subset of principles may be misleading. To partially overcome this problem, the entire set of principles from all of the level 1 architectures is listed in the appendix.

Principle Presentation

The principles are presented according to the classification discussed in the architecture overview chapter. In addition, they are grouped according to the function or component from which they evolve. For simplicity, categories for which no principles are defined are not listed explicitly. In actual practice, it might be wise to list all possible categories to ensure that all possibilities for principal statements have been considered. So that the maximum amount of information is presented, no attempt will be made (outside the appendix) to integrate the principles up through the level 1 architecture.

Because of space limitations, a demonstrably complete set of principles cannot be provided. The set presented in this section is indicative of the different principle types, scopes, and contents; an architecture robust enough to guide large development projects would of necessity contain many more statements than those shown in the next section.

In addition to space limitations, the discussion omits the many principles that must be included to reflect business strategies, policies, and other enterprise-specific environ-

78

ments. Obviously, these will vary considerably from organization to organization, even when the architectural philosophy presented in this book is followed closely. Although examples of some of these principles will be provided, they can make complete sense only in the context of a real organization.

Principle Statements

I. Strategies
  A. Global
    1. Architectural
      a. All end user interfaces will be based on intelligent workstations containing at least one user-accessible processor.
      b. Only one physical workstation will be provided per end user. All necessary functions must be available on that workstation.
    2. Design
      a. A single end user system will be designed and used for all network functions. Changes to the end user system may be made as required for new systems.
      b. The "look and feel" of all functions should be identical.
    3. Operational
      a. All workstations will be connected to a physical or virtual LAN through direct coupling or via a remote access facility. Gateways will be utilized for access to other networks.
      b. All network functions should have 100-percent availability.
  B. Coupling devices
    1. Architectural
      a. Each workstation will be able to support text,

voice, graphics, and image interfaces through appropriate coupling devices.
  b. Enterprise-standard interfaces for all coupling devices will be defined and implemented.
C. Entry/presentation format
  1. Architectural
    a. Multiple skill levels will be supported.
  2. Operational
    a. End users will be allowed to change their workstation characteristics to meet their individual needs.
D. Access procedures
  1. Architectural
    a. Default user profile, directory, and function set-up data will be provided automatically by the network functions. No end user intervention will be required. The end user will have the ability to alter this information if desired.
E. Control
  1. Architectural
    a. Each workstation will have a control function that maintains the state of all other functions in process and coordinates their execution.
  2. Design
    a. The workstation control function will be designed as an integral part of the network operating system.
F. Administration
  1. Architectural
    a. Network function access permission will be obtained automatically through the network administration function.
G. Service
  1. Architectural
    a. Queries may be made using any of the supported media forms (such as text, voice, image, etc.).

H. Functions available
  1. Architectural
      a. All network functions should be made available to every end user unless there is a specific reason to deny access. Users may be required to explicitly subscribe to a function in order to utilize it.

II. Standards
  A. Global
      1. Architectural
          a. Enterprise-defined interface standards should follow international or other industry standards when possible.
  B. Coupling devices
      1. Design
          a. X-windows standard will be used for all screen devices.
          b. NTSC video format will be used for image input/output.
          c. Provision will be made for 6 RS-232C auxiliary ports.
          d. Enterprise-standard interfaces for all coupling devices will be defined and implemented.
  C. Entry/presentation format
      1. Architectural
          a. Enterprise standards shall be defined for the design of each type of entry/presentation format.
  D. Access procedures
      1. Architectural
          a. Enterprise access standards will be defined and utilized for all systems.
      2. Design
          a. CCITT X.400 protocol will be used for electronic mail.

E. Functions available
   1. Design
      a. All user-accessible databases will be relational.
      b. The DIF format will be used for spreadsheet and word processing data.
      c. ACM SIGGRAPH will be used as the graphics standard.
      d. Standards for all user functions will be defined.

III. Guidelines
   A. Global
      1. Architectural
         a. Enterprise-defined guidelines should follow accepted industry practices whenever possible.
   B. Coupling devices
      1. Operational
         a. Users should be allowed to select the specific coupling devices that are comfortable to them.
   C. Control
      1. Design
         a. Control should be based on finite state machine concepts and should utilize AI knowledge structures when possible.
         b. Control should attempt to recover automatically from error conditions before alerting the end user.
   D. Functions available
      1. Architectural
         a. End user presentation and application protocols should have the same look and feel.
      2. Design
         a. Some amount of stand-alone functionality should be provided for all remotely accessed functions so that processing may continue for a time if the remote function becomes unavailable temporarily.

3. Operations
   a. Function processing should be performed as closely to the end user as possible.
   b. Voice- and text-oriented electronic mail shall be interconnected and accessed using the same procedures.

IV. Rules
   A. Global
      1. Architectural
         a. The end user system will have the same interface regardless of the physical device or system software on which it is resident.
      2. Design
         a. The coupling devices, entry/presentation format, and access procedures components shall be resident on the workstation.
   B. Coupling devices
      1. Operational
         a. All workstations will support the following devices, and the end user system will be able to interface with them:
            • Keyboard
            • Color screen
            • Mouse
            • Speaker
            • Telephone handset
         b. Every person in the enterprise will have a terminal attached to the network.
   C. Entry/presentation format
      1. Architectural
         a. Additions only can be made to the format set. No existing format may be eliminated or altered unless the network functions for which it was used is eliminated.
      2. Design
         a. A default format will exist for each system.

      b. Error notification to the end user must not disturb any other functions in process.

D. Access procedures
   1. Architectural
      a. The end user must not be required to know the network location of any function.

E. Functions available
   1. Design
      a. All workstations will have access to the following functions in addition to those specifically required to perform their job:
- Spreadsheet
- Relational database
- Word processor
- Desktop publishing package
- Network function directory
- Picture creation package
- Electronic mail
- Document storage and retrieval
- Calendaring

   2. Operations
      a. Voice- and text-oriented electronic mail shall be interconnected and accessed using the same procedures.

VALIDATION

Once the candidate set of principles has been developed, the principles must be validated against the stated needs of the organization from both technical and business standpoints. For example, consider the need for a user profile that contains knowledge of the specific characteristics of the user and associated environment. This was expressed in the earlier discussion in this chapter of the network function environment. Two of the principles in the set just described deal with this aspect:

- Default user profiles will be provided.
- The user is allowed to change the user profile.

If other principles are deemed necessary to fully meet the intent of the user profile, they should be added at this time. One possible addition would be a principle that sets forth the minimal set of information that must be contained in a user profile.

This example showed the validation of an explicit need. Implicit needs also must be validated. This is a much more difficult process, for two reasons: first, the need must be identified, and second, the validation process is more involved. For example, consider the needs expressed in the description of user characteristics presented at the beginning of this chapter. What principles address the need to provide for the skill level of the end user? An examination of the principles shows some that might address this area:

- Default user profiles will be provided.
- The user is allowed to change the user profile.
- Each workstation will be able to support text, voice, graphics, and image interfaces.
- End users will be allowed to change their workstation characteristics to meet their individual needs.
- Queries may be made using any of the supported media forms.
- All network functions will be made available to every end user unless there is a specific reason to deny access.
- Users should be allowed to select the specific coupling devices that are comfortable to them.
- End user interfaces should have the same "look and feel" for all functions.

There are other related principles, but these will suffice for the discussion. Although many principles seem to address this area, the real question is whether they provide sufficient guidance to system implementors so that the resultant systems really will allow for differing end user skill levels in the operation of the network. This is a subjective judgment, and more information may be needed before the validation process can continue. Some questions that may need to be asked follow:

- What constitutes different skill levels?
- How much inefficiency is tolerable in providing for this area?
- Should multiple skill levels extend beyond the workstation?

The answers to these and other associated questions will determine whether the principles as given are sufficient in this area. If not, more must be added. In the particular example given, more principles would probably have to be added to address this issue sufficiently. For example, no principles specifically address the skill level issue.

In the remaining chapters, it will be assumed that the validation process expressed in this section will occur and that you will be able to perform such a process using the same philosophy. It is not an easy process, but it is necessary if the architectural principles are to serve their intended function.

SUMMARY AND CONCLUSIONS

The end user architecture presented in this chapter was deliberately designed to encompass all of the current and foreseeable future needs for system design in a network environment. Because it is a stretch architecture, in some areas a technological advance is required to make use of the design and implementation techniques allowed. One example is the automatic selection of coupling devices and the associated alteration of the presentation format. This would be an excellent addition to any system and is allowed (and encouraged) by the architecture, but present technology will not yet allow its inclusion in system designs.

T H R E E

SYSTEM SOFTWARE ARCHITECTURE

INTRODUCTION

System software is common software that provides services for the network application systems and that, as such, is considered to be part of the network deployment infrastructure. Originally, system software was synonymous with computer operating systems. With the advent of intelligent workstations, interconnected processors, database management systems, graphics, and other specialized packages, the scope of system software became greatly expanded.

In the networking environment, many more services are required by applications systems, and these services are more complex than those resident on a single processor. As an example, applications may be split among a number of processors (cooperative processing), they may be moved from location to location (distributed processing), and/or they may require complex fault-detection and recovery procedures.

The management and utilization of these and other network-oriented services necessitates a further expansion of the concept of system software. The term *network operating system* (NOS) is sometimes used to refer to this expanded role in the support of network-based services and functions. Because of the importance of the concept, the basic concepts of a network operating system are presented in this chapter.

87

As an illustration of some of the possibilities, one possible model for an NOS is defined and analyzed. It should be noted that, as yet, no widespread agreement exists as to the structure and characteristics an NOS must have. Although some products are currently being marketed with that label, they are not necessarily considered to be true embodiments of an NOS. Although it is crucial to the development of an architecture, this discussion is given with the caveat that NOS technology is a rapidly developing area subject to considerable change in the future.

Once an explanation of the purpose and requirements of an NOS has been developed, a candidate structure for the architecture of all of the system software aspects is presented and discussed. The principles associated with this structure are then listed in the same fashion as that used in the previous chapter.

NETWORK OPERATING SYSTEM (NOS)

In a computer, the operating system is designed to allocate resources among all of the entities that have requested them and to make the use of these resources efficient and effective. The same basic philosophy holds for the network environment NOS, except that the scope is somewhat enlarged because resources can exist anywhere in the network. In addition, one major aspect of the network environment must be considered: many processors in diverse geographical locations must be served simultaneously by the NOS.

There are two approaches to producing an NOS. The first uses a single network processor on which all of the NOS functions reside. The major advantage of this approach is simplicity of design, implementation, and usage, because the NOS can be constructed and used much as is a classical operating system. All requests for network resources would be handled by this single-processor NOS, regardless of the source. The major disadvantage of this approach is that a bottleneck is created because all requests must be routed to the single processor. This bottleneck would severely limit the capacity of the network. For this reason alone, the disadvantage in this approach usually overshadows any advantage and, with a few exceptions, this structure is not viable.

If the size of the network can be capped, the single-processor NOS solution can work, assuming that a processor of sufficient size to handle the largest network can be obtained. Usually, however, any design capacity is eventually exceeded. Even if other parameters can be extended to accommodate the increase, it may not be possible also to accommodate the single-processor NOS in this fashion.

The second approach is to distribute the NOS functions throughout the network, utilizing the same processors as those providing network services. The advantage of this approach is that capacity is not limited by the throughput of a single processor. Theoretically, as network processors are added, the capacity of the NOS also increases. The disadvantage of this approach is that the complexity of the design and implementation of the NOS is increased considerably. Although the specification and architecture of this type of NOS has not met with widespread agreement, the approach seems to be the one that must be taken in order to meet the future needs of the network and its application systems.

In order to realize the distributed approach, an NOS operational model must be developed and used as the basis for the architecture. Such a model is shown schematically in figure 3.1; this model is used in the architecture presented here for network resource control and allocation.

The NOS model consists of two interrelated object-oriented systems (OOS). The first is a network of individual sections that act together to provide the necessary network resources and functions where and when they are needed. Each section must be able to perform the tasks shown in the following list:

• Identify node type and location to the other sections
• Distribute node status to the other sections

89

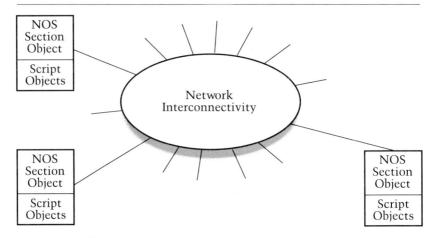

FIGURE 3.1   NETWORK OPERATING SYSTEM (NOS) MODEL

• Distribute available node network resources to the other
  sections
• Receive and store other NOS section information
• Locate network resources that will perform needed functions
• By establishing sessions with other NOS sections, make
  available any network resources requested by the node on
  which it is resident
• Obtain information using both polling and broadcast techniques
• Queue requests from other NOS sections and send periodic
  status messages to requestor section
• Integrate transaction, real-time, interactive, and batch processing as required by services in progress

All processors attached to the network have at least one
resident NOS section. Every NOS section is considered to be
an object, and the set of communicating sections is an object-
oriented system. Communications between NOS sections is
by messages. Taken as a whole, the NOS sections along with
their interaction capabilities become the NOS.

The interaction of NOS sections is controlled through the

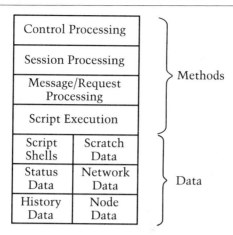

FIGURE 3.2   NOS SECTION OBJECT
DEFINITION

use of scripts. Scripts also form an object-oriented system through which the control aspects of the NOS are exercised. Each of these object-oriented systems is discussed in more detail in the following sections in order to foster an appreciation for the role and complexities of an NOS. However, a full treatment of the subject would be much too long to be included in this chapter. The overview that is presented discusses the major points and directions, which will be enough to allow you to understand the architectural implications of an NOS and to interpret the literature as it becomes available.

An understanding of the principles of object-oriented design is needed to fully understand the material in this discussion. If you are not familiar with this design technique, consult one of the appropriate references in the bibliography before continuing.

NOS Section Object Definition

Each NOS section object has the structure indicated in figure 3.2. There are six major data types and four major methods. The data stored in each node consists of the following:

91

- Node data — This is the data that describes the node, including hardware configuration, operating system, communication methods, functions available for network use, and similar types of information.
- Network data — This is the data that has been sent to the node by other nodes on the network, describing their configuration and status. Data may be obtained by receiving broadcasts from other nodes or by a specific request. In this area, the directory structure is specified. Because of the importance of the directories in the proper functioning of the network, additional discussion of this function is provided later in this chapter.
- History data — This is data that contains records of all node interactions with the network. This data is similar to log data for a conventional operating system, but it is oriented toward network interaction information. It is useful during error recovery and for statistical purposes.
- Status data — This data contains the current state of the node as a network entity, including information about service requests in progress, queue status, NOS sessions in progress, and any other data needed to convey the node status.
- Script shells — This data consists of scripts the node can activate and execute. Each script may be activated any number of times, subject to restrictions discussed later. Parameters may be inserted into the scripts before activation.
- Scratch data — This is volatile temporary data used by the NOS section in performing its function. This data is useful during error recovery and for statistical purposes.

This NOS data is used only when the node is participating as a network entity. Processing between elements of the same node does not affect this network information unless a physical node has been split into two or more independent logical nodes. In this case, the nodes would behave as if they were

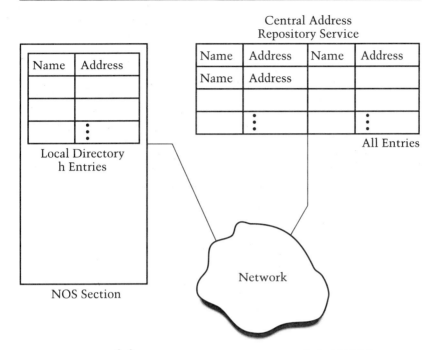

FIGURE 3.3   CANDIDATE DIRECTORY STRUCTURE

on different processors of the network, and they would interface through the NOS.

Directories are defined to be those data structures which contain the address information for all network resources, including services, data, end users, and facilities. This can amount to a large body of information that is impractical to duplicate in its entirety at every NOS section. A central repository would also be impractical because of the bottleneck problems discussed previously. One structure that avoids most of these problems is discussed briefly here to provide an indication of the problems and some of the advantages and disadvantages of proposed solutions.

Assume a structure as shown in schematic form in figure 3.3. In a sense, this information is analogous to the way a cache memory operates. The amount of information contained in each NOS section directory will be considerably less than the total amount of such information in the network. A directory request is first made to the local NOS directory. If the required information is found, its usage count is updated and the request completes. If the information is not found, the request is sent to the (logically) central repository service and the required information is returned. The least-accessed local NOS directory entry is replaced with the new information, the usage count is updated, and the process completes. This method has the advantage that global information is always available but the large majority of the requests should be satisfied on the node level.

If the location of a network entity changes, the central repository is updated and a broadcast is made to all nodes that the address information concerning that entity has changed. The new information itself is not broadcast because of the desire to keep broadcast messages short. The first time a node requires the new information, it must go to the central repository. The NOS structure in this chapter assumes the directory model as presented.

The four methods of the NOS section object are concerned with the following:

- Script processing — Executes scripts that have been activated. This method may invoke any of the other methods or may ask the node operating system for node-resident resources.
- Message/request processing — This method sends and receives all messages from other NOS sections. It handles message queues and error conditions. In the communications model discussed in chapter 6, it is at layer 7, the application layer.
- Session processing — Although much of the interaction between NOS objects will be in the form of individual messages and replies, some of the network resources will require longer-term relationships. Sessions are logical connections that reflect this need. NOS object sessions are

94

similar to those defined in chapter 6 for the communications model. The difference is in the number of nodes that can be part of a single session (greater than 2) and the level of the information passed.

- Control processing — This method determines how and when the NOS objects interact with one another. Control information is contained in scripts, and by activating different scripts, control is changed, passed, or deleted from one or more NOS objects. This will be discussed further in the following section on scripts.

Because all of the NOS section objects have the same basic structure, the inheritance hierarchy is only one level deep. For this reason, it is not necessary to discuss this aspect of the object system in any more detail. On the other hand, the script objects have a significant hierarchy, which is presented in the next section.

Although the amount of information in this section is sufficient for architectural purposes, a significant amount of additional information would have to be generated in the design phase during the implementation of an NOS.

Scripts

A script is defined to be a set of process and control statements that, when executed, perform a specific service or function utilizing building elements and other network resources.

Building elements are discussed briefly in the next section and in chapter 8, which is concerned with application development. For now it can be assumed that they are well-defined primitive operations that provide a specific function or service. Scripts were originally proposed as one form of knowledge representation for artificial intelligence. As such, their utility and flexibility is considerably greater than is needed in this presentation. However, it is possible in the future that scripts will be allowed to assume some of their original intent of knowledge representation in order to provide intelligent control. Although NOS sections could probably be implemented without the use of scripts, they seem to be the most effective way of providing the necessary flexibility and control. The architecture presented here will utilize the concepts of scripts as the mechanism by which NOS sections interact.

As mentioned in the initial discussion of this section, scripts can also be considered as objects. As such, they also follow all the tenets of object-oriented systems, some of which are utilized in the next section.

Script Types   Several different types of scripts exist:

• System
• Service
• Network
• Instance
• User
• Supervision
• Facility
• Error
• Recovery

Although all of these types follow the same basic principles, the differences are necessary to provide adequate NOS control of the network resources. The inheritance hierarchy of these types is of particular interest and is shown in figure 3.4. The existence of this hierarchy allows script objects to be created without having to specify the large number of characteristics that are inheritable. For example, all scripts will provide some linkage to the network management process. This linkage need be specified only in the design of the root script. It will then be inherited by all other scripts and does not need to be specified explicitly.

Inheritance can significantly reduce the number of errors and omissions that would occur if each script were programmed in its entirety. Each of these script types is discussed

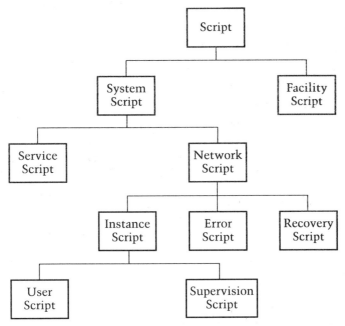

FIGURE 3.4 SCRIPT CLASS HIERARCHY

briefly to help you understand their role in the operation of the NOS.

System scripts define and control the operation of a software-defined system, service, or operation. They contain all of the information and knowledge necessary to utilize the network resources and functions in obtaining the desired results. They can exist at many abstraction levels and locations in the network and are the most prevalent type of script.

Service scripts provide basic control for high-level network services usually designed for use by end users. The terms *information provider* (IP) or *service provider* (SP) are sometimes used to describe the organization responsible for operating the service. These scripts control only the operation of the service and are usually executed by the NOS section resident in the same processor as the service. Although this does not have to be the case, it may provide for more efficient operation.

97

Network scripts are similar to service scripts except that they control network primitives that are used only as part of a more global service. Because they are concerned directly with network resources, network scripts can exercise additional control over network operations and interact more closely with the control scripts.

Instance scripts are temporary scripts that are created whenever a new request requires the particular function defined by that script. When the requested function has been accomplished and/or the requestor leaves the network, the instance script disappears.

Supervision scripts are instance scripts used to monitor the operation of a function or service when more than two NOS sections are needed. Supervision scripts can determine if the operation is aborted early for any reason, if processing has completed normally, and/or if any constraints on the operation have been violated (time, data amounts, etc.). The supervision script then takes the actions necessary to terminate the process.

User scripts are instance scripts that control the user's interaction with the network. They contain profile and other user-specific information to provide an effective user-machine interaction. Whenever the user is active, a user script is created and activated. When the user no longer is on the network, the script is eliminated.

Facility scripts are logically assigned to a physical piece of equipment and provide the network with any desired information as to the status and operational characteristics of that equipment. They are also used for local error control and to indicate the particular version or generation of the equipment.

Error scripts are invoked when other scripts detect error conditions that they are not equipped to handle. Error scripts try to isolate the condition causing the error. They may be attached to other scripts or they may operate independently, as the situation demands.

Recovery scripts are used in conjunction with error scripts

to recover network functionality when an error has been detected and isolated. Recovery is one of the most complex functions performed by the NOS, and these scripts reflect that complexity.

The issue of control will be addressed in additional detail after some examples of service and network scripts (the simplest types) are presented. These examples will provide a basic understanding of the definition and execution of a script. The purpose of most of the building elements used in the script examples is self-evident. However, brief descriptions for all the building elements used in the example scripts, as well as some other interesting ones, are given later.

High-level Service Script Example   First, consider a consumer-oriented network service. This service, called the Road Emergency Service (RES), is illustrated schematically in figure 3.5. A motorist is stranded along a road and needs assistance. Assuming that a phone is available (public or private) in the immediate vicinity, the motorist places a call to a toll-free number to reach the Road Emergency Service network node. This node may be located on the public telephone network or may be attached to a private network (illustrated in the figure) that is reached through the public telephone network. Through an automated dialogue with the motorist using voice and/or the dial key pad, the service obtains the following information:

- The credit card name and number of the motorist
- The telephone number from which the call is being placed (may be entered manually or provided automatically by the phone company if available)
- The nature of the problem

Using the telephone number obtained during the dialog, the location database of the proper telephone company is accessed and the approximate geographic location of the telephone is found. Based on the location information, the nature of the motorist's difficulty, and other needed data, such as the time

99

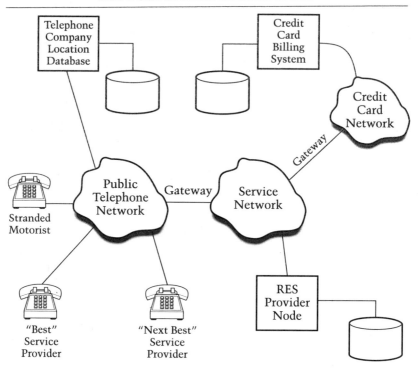

FIGURE 3.5   ROAD EMERGENCY SERVICE EXAMPLE

and day of the request, the RES service computer utilizes the information in its database about service providers (such as garages and towing services) to locate the most appropriate provider.

The RES service then contacts the provider and, through an automated dialogue, inquires whether it can meet the motorist's needs. If so, the motorist is connected directly to the provider for final instructions and information as to exact location, type of car, etc. If the service provider cannot handle the request, the next most appropriate provider is selected and the process is repeated until an available provider is found. Once this has occurred, billing information is sent to the credit card company.

This example shows a common condition in the definition of comprehensive user services: the need to utilize more than

100

RES_Script /*Activated by Incomming Call*/

```
    * Begin Script (Caller);                                Note:
      Obtain Caller_Info;              /*NBE*/              /*NBE*/ Indicates
    * Case Station_Type                                     a Network
      TT: Dialog (TT);                                      Building Element
      RD: Dialog (RD);
      WS: Dialog (WS);                                      /*PBE*/ Indicates
    * End Case;                                             a Private Building
      Obtain VH_Coordinate;          /*NBE*/               Element
      Select Provider (XYZ);         /*PBE*/
      Connect (RES, XYZ);            /*NBE*/
    * If Error Begin Recovery_1;
      Send (XYZ, Caller_Info);       /*PBE*/
      Disconnect (RES, XYZ);         /*NBE*/
      Connect (Caller, XYZ);         /*NBE*/
    * If Error Begin Recovery_2
      Bill Caller;                   /*NBE*/
    * End Script (RES_Script);
```

FIGURE 3.6   ROAD EMERGENCY SERVICE SCRIPT

one type of network. In this case, the public telephone network, the service network that contains the service of interest, and a third-party network that processes credit card billings are all involved. In most cases, these will be entirely different networks connected only through the use of gateways. Although an NOS that includes all three network types would be ideal, it is not yet possible. A great deal of standards work must be accomplished before this can be considered.

Some additional considerations involved in multiple network services are discussed in chapter 6, which deals with communications architecture, and chapter 7, which deals with the network management architecture. For now, the NOS that is being discussed must be restricted to the service network. This is not too great a restriction, because the gateways can be defined as service network building elements.

A script for this service is shown in figure 3.6. The syntax for this script is not difficult to discern. Each statement in the script either handles script control (CASE, IF) or calls a building element (SELECT, SEND). The building elements may themselves be implemented via scripts and may be located anywhere in the network. The NOS must be able to

```
DCN_Script  /*Activated by Request*/
Begin Script (Request);
Obtain Request_Info;
Monitor Request;
Profile Request;
Directory Termination;

Profile Termination;

Configure Bandwidth;
If Error Begin Recovery_1;
Partner Termination;
If Error Begin Recovery_2;
Send Data;
Disconnect;
Bill Request;
End Script (DCB_Script);
```

FIGURE 3.7   DATA COLLECTION NETWORK SCRIPT

locate these building elements and send the appropriate messages to them. This is accomplished using the NOS sections.

Notice the simplicity and power of a script. Very complex systems can be defined with a minimum of development, as long as the proper building elements are available.

Network Script Example   Another type of script is depicted in figure 3.7. This script defines a service that collects data from a node on the network. As a part of this collection, the characteristics of the remote node must be determined, and based on that information, network parameters such as bandwidth need to be set. This function could be used either as a stand-alone service or as part of another service that includes it in its script. There is no need to maintain a strict hierarchy of script communication. Any script can use any other script as a building element as long as it makes sense to do so.

From the designer's point of view, the type of service scripts we have discussed are relatively easy to use and understand. From an overall network control point of view, however, the definition and use of scripts are complex processes that require a sophisticated NOS control mechanism.

102

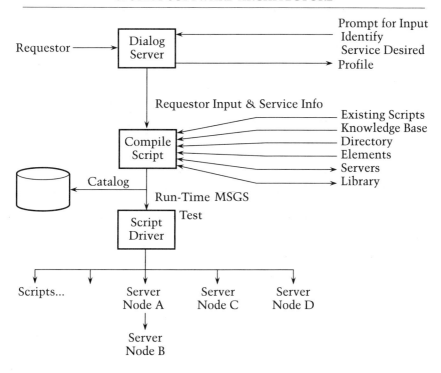

FIGURE 3.8   SCRIPT CREATION AND TRANSFORMATION

Script Building   In a sense, the language utilized to create scripts is a specification language. This language has as its scope the entire network, and the allowable constructs reflect that wide scope, as will be illustrated through examples presented later in the chapter. A script has some characteristics in common with a program, including the ability to be interpreted or compiled. The selection of execution type will depend on the type of the script and the development phase it is in.

The development of service scripts must be easy and effective. One possible architecture for this process is shown in figure 3.8. This process identifies the requestor through an appropriate dialog. The requestor enters the new script, and it is compiled by the system using information about the network and its services. It is then tested to make sure that

103

nothing in the script will cause a failure in the network. The testing does not necessarily ensure that the script will perform as the user intended. It is concerned only with potential harm to the network. The user can, of course, perform other tests to ascertain its functional correctness once the script has been approved for inclusion in the network.

Script Control   From a control point of view, scripts can be compared to the tasks of a conventional operating system, with the exception of the following characteristics:

- More than one script may be executing at the same time.
- Script execution is not based on the existence of "ready" or other queues.

The concept of script control of the NOS is based on two characteristics that can be assigned dynamically to any of the script types discussed above:

- Anchor
- Control

For a specific function or service, an anchor script is the base control script. Control always starts with and returns to the anchor regardless of the number of control changes involved in the overall control process. As will be noted later, the anchor property can be transferred from one script to another for a given operation. This can happen only under certain conditions and specific constraints. A script is given the control property for a given operation if it is performing some activity toward the completion of the operation in progress. Many control scripts can be active at the same time but there can only be one anchor script. The anchor script is always considered to be active.

For control purposes, the NOS always assumes that the first script encountered in a specific network request, usually a user or other instance script, is the initial anchor script. Some of the other high-level control aspects of scripts are

104

1. User is always interfaced to anchor script.
2. A non-network script can never be an instance anchor.
3. Anchor scripts must always have an associated error script.
4. Non-anchor scripts may have an associated error script.
5. Only one control script (in addition to anchor script) can be active at a specific time.
6. Many non-control scripts can be active or running simultaneously.
7. Anchor scripts may be user-dependent.
8. External ip's can build function scripts only.
9. The location of the anchor script may be anywhere in the network.
10. Every facility (hardware) will have a facility script.
11. The initial instance anchor script is located at initial network access point.
12. An anchor script can be transfered ONLY while it is running.

FIGURE 3.9   ADDITIONAL SCRIPT PRINCIPLES

shown in figure 3.9 to provide more insight into the control process. These statements could be considered to be design-level principles of the architecture, if desired. To avoid undue complexity, however, they will not be restated in the principles section of this chapter. The complexity of the control aspect of scripts is the price exacted by the requirement that the NOS be distributed.

As an example of script control where the original anchor does not change, consider the scenario illustrated in figure 3.10. A service request is received by an NOS section, and it activates an instance script, which also is given the anchor characteristic. The service requires a network connection, so the instance script activates a network connection script, which in turn activates a supervision script and an error script. The network connection script needs some specialized facilities and activates the proper facilities script to provide information relating to the needed equipment. Finally, the connection is made, and the service script is activated. When a script has finished its work, it deactivates itself. The network connection and facilities scripts deactivate when their work is completed without further input. The supervision and error scripts deactivate only when the service script is finished or the service request is terminated. Deactivation in

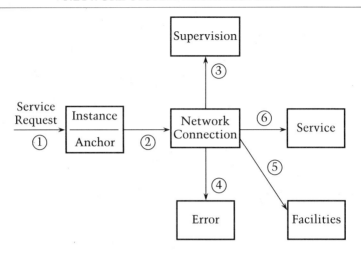

Note: This diagram shows only control activation;
data transfer and deactivation are not shown.

FIGURE 3.10 SCRIPT CONTROL EXAMPLE —
PERMANENT ANCHOR

this case occurs as the result of a message that places the script in a state such that its only remaining function is to deactivate.

A scenario in which the anchor changes is illustrated in figure 3.11. This case is similar to the previous one, except that the service is such that the original requestor is disconnected from the service and replaced with a new user. In this case, the anchor is transferred from the initial script to a script associated with the new user.

Building Elements

Building elements can be thought of as one type of standard component, as discussed previously. These components are network functions that can be accessed and utilized by any network user as long as security and other restrictions are met. As illustrated by the script examples in the previous section, building elements can be considered to be one of two types: network or private. Network building elements are part

106

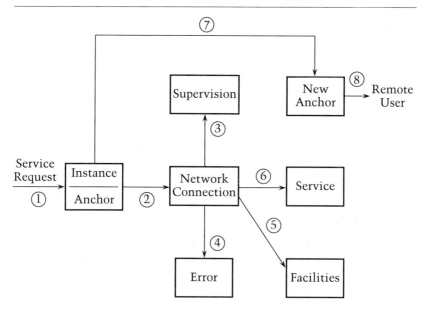

Note: This diagram shows only control activation;
      data transfer and deactivation are not shown.

FIGURE 3.11   SCRIPT CONTROL EXAMPLE — VARIABLE ANCHOR

of the deployment infrastructure available to every network system builder. Private building elements are restricted to an individual system implementer, or at most, a relatively small set. In many cases, they will be proprietary and guarded as a trade secret. Large application systems can be constructed using the building element and script technique. The architecture necessary for this type of development is considered in chapter 8, which deals with the application development architecture.

To provide some insight as to what constitutes a building element, some candidate network building elements (including those used in the script examples) are listed and described briefly below:

• Configure
• Monitor
• Partner

- Subscribe
- Directory
- Obtain
- Connect
- Disconnect
- Bill
- Profile

These network building elements will probably not be atomic; they will use other building elements in their implementation.

Deciding on an appropriate set of building elements is a difficult engineering task and must be approached with caution. One method for determining a usable set of building elements is to define a number of possible network services and then decompose the services into atomic components, using any of the available decomposition techniques (such as SADT). The elements (atomic and nonatomic) that were common to a significant number of services would then be defined as part of a candidate set of building elements from which a final selection could be made.

The configure element is invoked to change one or more of the network characteristics during all or part of a service use. These characteristics could include:

- Bandwidth
- Error rate
- Transmission media
- Time-outs
- Delay or echo parameters

The monitor element is invoked to determine when a particular condition has occurred in the network. This could be related to the network characteristics given above or to higher-level information, such as a specific address. Hardware status data could also be obtained using this element.

The partner element is used to establish a conversation between two unlike end users. The element automatically provides for the proper protocol conversions by interrogating the appropriate profiles and determining the required changes.

The subscribe element is used whenever an end user wants to use a service that currently is not available. Although this element could be used as part of a real-time system, it may be more suitable if used as part of a batch procedure prior to the need for the service.

The directory element is used to update information regarding the physical or logical network location (address) of an end user or service.

The obtain element is used to retrieve information located in network databases. This type of retrieval is generally limited to small amounts of information. Large data transfers would require a separate function designed for that transfer.

The connect element locates and implements a network path from the requestor to the termination point, consistent with any configuration data and the service desired.

The disconnect element removes a path from the network and returns the resources to the network.

The bill element sends appropriate billing information to the network billing service, where it is processed. Depending on the parameters given, this element can also be used to send data to other networks for use by third-party organizations.

The profile element is used to retrieve and update information from the profile of an end user or service. One of the statements in the script that implements the profile element uses the obtain element.

Messages

All object-oriented systems communicate through messages. These messages may be logical or physical in nature depending on the nature of the implementation. Because the object-oriented systems discussed in this chapter are implemented over a network, the messages that are used for object communication eventually are implemented as physical network

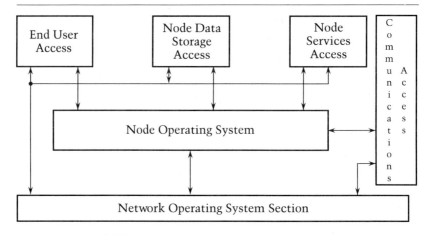

FIGURE 3.12   SYSTEM SOFTWARE SUBARCHITECTURE
COMPONENTS DIAGRAM

messages. If the volume of these messages is large, the performance of the network could be impaired. It is up to the
network and/or system designer to limit the number of control messages to a small fraction of the total network messages. Based on current investigations, this does not seem to
be a difficult problem to solve.

SYSTEM SOFTWARE STRUCTURE

Now that the structure of the system software architecture
that is directly concerned with the network aspects has been
determined, it is necessary to define the remainder of the
system software architecture. This software consists of the
classical processor-based operating systems as well as additional software, such as communication handlers and
database management systems. The candidate structure of the
system software architecture is shown in figure 3.12. The
subarchitecture has six components and nine interfaces.
The relatively small number of interfaces reflects the fact
that the node operating system tends to be central to the node
operation, resulting in a modified star pattern.

Three of the components are concerned with access to func-

110

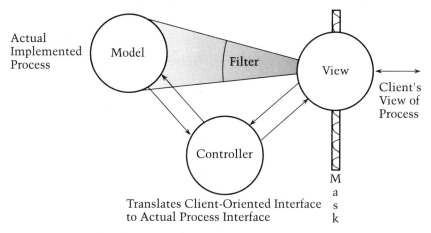

FIGURE 3.13   MODEL-VIEW CONTROLLER STRUCTURE

tions resident on the node. These are the user system access, node data storage access, and node services access. Other architectures provide for the functions themselves, and they are not discussed here. However, the access to these functions is defined to be a part of the system software architecture and as such is discussed in this chapter.

The access components are used to provide a buffer between the node services and other parts of the system software. These components should allow the functions to be used with different node operating systems, allow for expanded queueing strategies and transaction control, and provide an interface to the network management architecture.

This is made possible by using the structure shown in figure 3.13. This structure consists of three parts: model, view, and controller. It is sometimes known as a model-view-controller structure in recognition of its makeup. Because of its generality and power, this structure is applicable in a number of areas. It will also be used in the data architecture described in the next chapter. An application-level example is used here for clarity in the description of this type of structure. However, the principles are the same regardless of where or how the structure is applied.

111

The model is the entire process that has been implemented. It is designed to be as complete as possible so that the needs of all potential users of the process can be accommodated. In making the model general, a way must be found to customize its interface such that a specific user receives exactly what is needed in an effective and efficient manner. This is the function of the view. It can be considered to be a projection of the model onto the requirements space of an individual user and, as such, is the user's view of the process. Thus, the view consists of a number of individual views, each of which is tailored to a specific client. The controller is the part of the structure that translates the client's needs as expressed by its view into a suitable interaction with the model so that the required results are obtained.

The following is an example of that process as applied to the access component at an application level. Assume that a service exists on the node that provides a requestor with information as to the status of energy use in a building. The model would encompass all types of energy, including solar (window load), electrical, natural gas, heat (equipment load), etc. Further assume that a client service that makes use of this model is one designed to limit the total amount of electricity consumed during a one-minute period. The view of the process, and thus of the model, that the client needs is all current electrical consumption by equipment category as well as a projection as to future use. The amount of natural gas being used may be important in the model so that the proper parameters can be determined, but it is of no use to the client. The controller would formulate the interaction with the model so that the results are presented according to the view needed — the electrical consumption projection.

Node operating systems have been studied extensively and discussed in a large number of publications, some of which are listed in the bibliography. No discussion of node operating system architecture is provided here. However, the principles section of this chapter contains some specific entries relating to node architecture based on general operating system knowledge. The network operating system has been discussed in detail, and the proposed structure will be used to generate a set of associated principles.

The communications architecture is usually assumed to be a part of the system software. Because of its importance to network and system design, it has been given the status of a separate level 1 architecture and is discussed in chapter 6.

PRINCIPLES

The following statements are the principles derived from the structures defined for the system software architecture. In keeping with the practice established for this section, these principles are grouped according to the components of the architecture. For convenience, references to the network operating system are abbreviated "NOS," and references to the node operating system are abbreviated "OS."

I. Strategies
   A. Global
      1. Architectural
         a. All networks will have an explicit distributed NOS.
         b. Only one directory structure will be used in a network. All services and functions will utilize that structure.
         c. All system software should support unattended operation with full recovery and power restore capability.
      2. Design
         a. Access routines should be used for all network services. A network service that allows new views to be added to access routines must be available.

  b. Source code for all operating software must be available.

  c. All node system software and the network operating system must be designed such that they interact efficiently.

 3. Operational

  a. Training programs for all system software operations personnel should be available as a network service.

  b. All operations personnel should be trained on all operational software used in the enterprise.

  c. No local alterations to the operating system should be made except in emergencies. Any changes made should be backed out as soon as possible.

  d. System software updates should be spread out over time. Whenever possible, multiple updates should not be made simultaneously.

  e. Changes to the network operating system must be made without bringing down the network.

  f. All network system software functions should have 100-percent availability.

  g. System software operator messages should be minimal. An expert system should be utilized to handle most interaction with the NOS.

B. Network operating system

 1. Architectural

  a. The NOS should support simultaneous use of the network for transaction, batch, real-time, and interactive services.

  b. The NOS should support distributed and cooperative processing.

 2. Design

  a. The NOS should be based on object-oriented principles.

   b. Scripts should be used for NOS control and service definition.
   c. Messages between NOS sections should use the same network as the data. A separate control network should not be established.
   d. A robust selection of building elements should be developed and made available.
3. Operational
   a. The NOS should require only one operations point. That point should be able to be moved anywhere on the network.
C. Node operating system
   1. Architectural
      a. All OS should support simultaneous use of the network for transaction, batch, real-time, and interactive services.
      b. All OS should support distributed and cooperative processing.
      c. All processors used for the same network server class should use the same OS. (Server classes are discussed in chapter 12.)
   2. Design
      a. Every OS should be multitasking.
      b. Every OS should support remote operations.
   3. Operational
      a. Every OS should have the same core set of features and functions.
D. Service access
   1. Architectural
      a. All services will use an associated service access function.
      b. Service access interfaces will be programmable by the client.
   2. Design
      a. Service access functions will be built using the model-view controller structure.

3. Operations
   a. Access routines to the service interface should allow complete portability of the service between network nodes.
   b. If the same service exists on more than one network node, the service access routines must be able to spread the load among the instances of the service.
   c. Network service access permission will be obtained automatically through the network administration function.
   d. Service security is a function of the service access routine.
   e. The interface of a service to network management is a function of the service access routine.

II. Standards
   A. Global
      1. Architectural
         a. Enterprise-defined system software standards should follow international or other industry standards when possible.
         b. Commercially available system software should be used when possible.
   B. Network operating systems
      1. Architectural
         a. Enterprise-standard interfaces to the NOS will be defined.
      2. Design
         a. Any portions of the NOS developed by the enterprise will use object-oriented design.
   C. Node operating systems
      1. Architectural
         a. Commercially available operating systems will be used.

    2. Operational
       a. Enterprise-standard operational techniques will be developed and used.
  D. Service access
    1. Architectural
       a. Enterprise access standards will be defined and utilized for all systems.

III. Guidelines
  A. Global
    1. Architectural
       a. Enterprise-defined guidelines should follow accepted industry practices whenever possible.
       b. System software should be selected in the following priority order:
- From computer vendor
- From software vendor
- Internal development
       c. System software messages and commands should be based on natural language processing.
       d. System software should be able to recover automatically under fault conditions.
       e. System software functions should be placed where they will have the widest scope.
    2. Design
       a. All system software should be designed to detect and destroy any viruses that enter the system.
  B. Network operating systems
    1. Architectural
       a. Automatic interoperability between all users, functions, and services should be provided.
    2. Operational
       a. NOS updates should not remove any functionality; only new functionality should be added.

C. Node operating systems
   1. Architectural
      a. As few OS types as possible should be used in the network.
      b. Every OS in the network should be widely used under similar circumstances in the industry.

IV. Rules
   A. Global
      1. Architectural
         a. Documentation for all system software will be in machine-readable form.
         b. An enterprise expert must be developed for all purchased system software before the software is deployed.
   B. Network operating system
      1. Design
         a. The NOS will be optimized to support the network configuration defined in chapter 6.
      2. Operational
         a. The NOS will support gateways to the following network types:
            • Public telephone network
            • Public packet network
            • Cable TV
            • Private service networks
   C. Node operating systems
      1. Architectural
         a. Detailed criteria must be developed for selecting an OS.
      2. Design
         a. Every OS must be able to be updated without taking down the node.
         b. Every OS must be able to use the NOS directory structure.

3. Operational
   a. A software maintenance contract must be maintained on every deployed OS.
D. Service access
   1. Operations
      a. The service access function will not add more than 3-percent overhead to any service.

SUMMARY AND CONCLUSIONS

The system software architecture presented in this chapter was deliberately designed to encompass all of the current and foreseeable future needs for system design in a network environment. Because it is a stretch architecture, in some areas a technological advance must occur before the design and implementation techniques allowed may be used. One example is the explicit use of a distributed network operating system based on object-oriented principles, using scripts for control and messages for communications.

The use of access functions that allow network services to be distributed among any processor on the network and to be viewed by different classes of clients from their own unique perspectives is also an advanced concept. It is expected that network system software concepts and architecture will be the subject of intense research and debate as networks become more pervasive and integrated with the enterprise operations.

F   O   U   R

DATA ARCHITECTURE

INTRODUCTION

With the transformation of society from an industrial base to an information base, the role of data in the network environment rises to extreme importance. Being able to find, manipulate, store, retrieve, and utilize data efficiently and effectively is a fundamental requirement of the modern enterprise. The data architecture is a crucial tool in meeting that requirement.

Businesses that have an effective data architecture will have a great competitive advantage over those that do not. Through the application of a comprehensive model of the data needs of the enterprise, the data architecture provides a comprehensive framework for the development of a structured approach to the management of data. It determines how the data needed by the enterprise is defined; how the data will be generated; and how, when, where and to whom the data will be made available. In addition, the data architecture determines how the data will be protected from contamination; how the data will be kept secure from competitors, unauthorized use, operator errors, and equipment faults; how the data will be administered; and what kind of facilities are needed for the data. By addressing all of these areas in a coordinated integrated approach, the data architecture can

120

form a foundation for the entire enterprise as well as the network that serves it.

Obviously, the data architecture encompasses a relatively large domain that contains a tightly coupled mixture of business and technical considerations. This implies that the development of the architecture must be carefully motivated and that the philosophy behind each construct must be stated explicitly and must be consistent with the overall direction. To facilitate this level of understanding, a modified top-down approach to the development of the data architecture is used here. In addition, the meaning of each major concept as used in this chapter is defined explicitly to avoid confusion resulting from the lack of industry-wide standards in this area.

The architecture development task is complicated immensely by the many different ways of viewing data that have been adapted in the past and that are still in use. In order to fully explain the role of data, it is necessary to develop a modern structure to serve as a vehicle for understanding and utilizing data while keeping the historical methods in perspective. This requires the resolution of competing and conflicting terminology and processes. This will be one of the major goals of the chapter.

The result of the development of the data architecture may seem more a methodology than an architecture. Because part of the architecture does specify the major components in the data design methodology, it can be difficult to separate the architectural considerations from the procedural. However, although it specifies the major functions of the methodology, the architecture does not define how they are to be performed. This must be specified by the methodology selected. As far as I can determine, only architectural considerations are included in the presentation, unless the conditions are specifically identified as related to methodology or implementation.

From time to time, the presentation must differentiate between the data architecture, the data design methodology, and the network system that provides the data to applications and other network clients (end users or software systems).

This latter function will be called the *data system* and is defined to include the operational aspects of deployed data and its access.

BITS, WORDS, DATA, INFORMATION, KNOWLEDGE, AND WISDOM

In common usage, the word *data* has a wide variety of meanings. The words *information* and *knowledge* are used in a similar manner. This indiscriminate usage results in a great deal of ambiguity and confusion that must be controlled (or at the very least understood) if the data architecture is to be placed on a firm foundation. Unfortunately, the vagaries of the English language do not permit the complete elimination of the ambiguity problem. Later sections of the chapter fall back on historical terminology to simplify the syntax of the discussion and to explain how current practice fits in with the architecture. Explicit reference to this use will be made when it is needed.

This difficulty in adhering to new terminology does not negate the need for rigorous and nonambiguous definitions of the major terms and concepts of the architecture. This process will be the major focus of the section. Because of historical conditioning in this area, some of the discussion may seem to be artificial and needlessly constrained. This is unfortunate, but the restrictions are necessary if the development of the architecture is to continue in a reasonable way.

As a start, it is necessary to use some word to refer to any of the common euphemisms for data (data, information, knowledge, etc.). For the purposes of this discussion, the word *item* will be employed. An item is defined to be a fragment of intelligence. Thus, the architecture really can be considered to be an item architecture, because it encompasses a wide range of diverse intelligence fragments. Although this usage is inconsistent, because of the widespread use of the word, *data* will also continue to be used to refer to the entire range of intelligence and usage. You should be aware of the possibility for confusion.

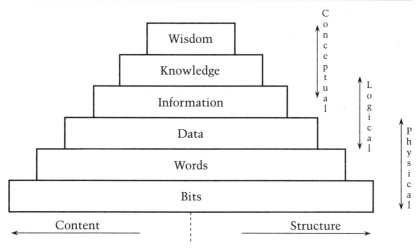

FIGURE 4.1 LEVELS OF INTELLIGENCE

The intelligence present in an item can be depicted in a hierarchical format, as shown in figure 4.1. The layers of this hierarchy form a pyramid structure, which was discussed in chapter 1. Some of the characteristics are also similar in nature to the layers of a communication model, which is discussed in chapter 6. Although there are significant differences in implementation, the data model and the communications model are based on the same philosophy: Physical media is required to implement the process; interfaces can be defined to allow interaction between different layers; and protocols can be defined to allow interaction between the same layers in different systems. The layered concept is also used in chapter 7, which is concerned with the network management architecture.

Four attributes are contained implicitly in the diagram of figure 4.1, each of which must be known before a specific item can be categorized:

- The level of intelligence
- The size of each level
- The abstraction level
- The level orientation

123

A bit carries the lowest amount of intelligence, and wisdom carries the highest. As the intelligence layer increases, the number of items generally decreases, as depicted by the decreasing size of the boxes. Items with lower intelligence content tend to be physically oriented, whereas those of higher intelligence tend to require higher levels of abstraction. For convenience, the amount of abstraction present in an item is divided into three categories: physical, logical, and conceptual. These categories overlap for two different reasons. First, no firm dividing point separates the categories. To a large extent these are qualitative descriptions rather than quantitative, measurable entities. Their descriptions can mean different things to different people. Second, some items are described using two different orientations, structure and content. At the same layer, each orientation may carry different levels of abstraction. This aspect will be discussed shortly.

For the purposes of this chapter, the three abstraction categories can be described as follows:

- Physical items are described according to their physical characteristics. Physical characteristics are those which respond to one or more of the human senses, even if tools must be used as an aid (for example, a microscope that allows humans to view the protrusions formed on an optical disk when the bit patterns are stored).
- Logical items are described according to their usage characteristics or content type but independently of any physical embodiment (for example, employee name).
- Conceptual items are described according to their underlying meaning (for example, business plan).

The orientation of the layers must be discussed and defined before abstraction levels can be assigned. A description of how items in a layer are related, grouped, identified, located, stored, associated, duplicated, administered, and audited is concerned with the structure of the items. Depending on viewpoint, a structure may be able to be described with different amounts of abstraction. If an item is referred to in terms of its structure, it may not be clear which abstraction level is meant. This is particularly true in the data layer. Data layer structures may be described in terms of records, fields, files, etc., which are physically oriented. They can also be described in terms of tables, networks, hierarchies, etc., which are more logical in nature. A description of the content of an item, however, can be accomplished with only one abstraction level.

If a data item is "employee name," it would be difficult to describe it in a physical context. If this item is referred to as the employee name field, the reference becomes ambiguous as to orientation and abstraction level. It is therefore necessary to understand the orientation and context of the usage when discussing items in a level. Without this understanding, it is difficult to assign the proper abstraction level to the item.

Constructs at the higher layers are supported by those at the lower layers. This is generally accomplished through the assignment of attributes to an item. The values of the attributes may exist at a layer that is lower than the original item. This support can also be accomplished in other ways, which will become clear as the presentation proceeds. To provide the final set of definitions, a discussion of each of the layers is given here, starting with the lowest layer.

Bits are a representation of the physical state of the machine. They are purely a physical quantity and carry little intelligence in and of themselves. Some additional definition as to what the bits represent is needed before they can be utilized. This is one of the functions of the higher layers. Bits can be used to determine a yes/no quantity, but higher-level structures usually perform even that chore. However, all of the structures at higher levels eventually must be represented as bits in order to obtain a physical representation so that they can be automatically processed. In addition, the method of storing these bits can have a large impact on the efficiency of utilizing the higher-level constructs. These methods in-

125

clude the storage media (magnetic disk/tape, optical disk, etc.) as well as the location and amount of redundancy needed.

Words are formed from groups of bits. Words can carry more intelligence than bits alone, because they can represent alphanumeric characters or numerical quantities. They seem to have more intrinsic intelligence than a string of bits. However, additional explanation as to the meaning of a word in its proper context is still required. Words are still considered to be a purely physical quantity. They provide a convenient structure for efficiently representing the intelligence of the higher layers.

Data represents the first layer in which the intelligence of the item can be such that the intent of the item is clear from the item itself and does not require additional explanation. As an example, consider the item *employee name*. The intent of the item is clear. It does not depend on how the item will be physically stored. It is clearly a logical entity. The construct of this item can be given in logical terms (table A entry) or in physical terms (field 4 of record type F). It is also possible to define the logical constructs of the layer in terms of the physical constructs.

Information is data placed in context. Taking the "employee name" example, it is unclear without further explanation as to the exact nature of the item. It could be any of the following:

- Competitor's employee
- Retired employee
- Employee on project X
- Employee of the month

When the context information is added, the item becomes much more valuable because its intelligence content is increased. Assume that the information item is a list of all retired employees. It is now necessary to determine the level of abstraction of the contents and the possible structures. The level of abstraction of the list of retired employees depends on how the list is obtained and used. If it was found in a straightforward manner and used as a mailing list, the abstraction level would probably be considered to be logical (the usual condition). If, as part of a proposal to fund a recreation plan for retired employees, the list was obtained to determine the number of years a retired employee lives beyond retirement, the list might be considered to be conceptual. Ultimately, the abstraction level is in the eye of the beholder. The structure could be given in terms of a pension fund statement (information structure), a table (logical structure), or a file (physical structure). The parentheses indicate the level of abstraction of the structure.

Knowledge is information arranged in a form suitable for inferring new data or information. This type of information is generally used in artificial intelligence systems. In these systems, the knowledge is used by a specialized computer program, called an *inference engine,* to determine additional data or information concerning the problem under investigation. This type of knowledge is almost always considered to be at a conceptual level of abstraction. Several constructs can be used for knowledge representation. Each of these is considered to be at a conceptual level because of the high degree of abstraction necessary in the inference process.

Finally, *wisdom* is knowledge arranged in a form suitable for generating new knowledge. This process is generally related to machine learning and as such is in its infancy. The necessary techniques and procedures are still in the fundamental research stage. Wisdom might require a higher level of abstraction for the inherent contents and structures. At present, no definitions are available as to what this level might be.

In the preceding discussion, explanations were needed as to how item contents were defined or what structures were utilized. In popular usage, such explanations fall under the category of data about data, which is termed *metadata.* This is an imprecise definition and is not used here. Instead, *metadata* is defined to be explanations that are intended to expand the understanding of the purpose, usage, or definition of any item. Metadata is an important concept that is used as an integral part of the enterprise data model and architecture.

The definitions and concepts presented in this section are referred to during the remainder of the chapter. Although different terminology systems are also employed, any possible areas of confusion are discussed and resolved. You should follow the same degree of caution in dealing with any aspect of data, information, or knowledge that arises in the normal course of work.

THE DATA PHILOSOPHY

The modified top-down approach to specifying the architecture structure requires the following procedure.

1. Articulate the philosophy that governs how the enterprise perceives data.
2. Determine the enterprise requirements for data.
3. Derive a high-level data model that reflects the philosophy.
4. Analyze the model to determine the overall constraints and requirements for the architecture.
5. Use an informal technique to specify the model in terms of the components and interfaces of the architecture.

The data philosophy is determined as part of the enterprise's strategic planning process. This planning process is designed to translate the business vision and associated mission into explicit, implementable programs and projects. The determination of the data philosophy must be one of the defined activities that result from this process. Formation of the data plan must involve the entire organization, because the decision will affect all areas of the organization. The results of one such planning session are presented in the following list (note the emphasis on treating data as an independent resource — asset — that exists to serve the needs of the enterprise):

1. Data is a fundamental corporate resource and will be treated as such.
2. Data must serve the needs of the business efficiently and effectively.
3. Data must be managed as a separate entity.
4. Data integrity must be maintained at all times.
5. Data locations will be distributed.
6. Data will be available on a continuous basis.
7. Data access will be controlled.
8. Data must be delivered efficiently to all requestors.

In the information age, data is an asset that is more important than the physical assets of the industrial age. Because information is intangible, and because its life is short compared to physical assets, suitable financial accounting for the value of information has not yet caught up with the technology. In some cases, organizations have made incorrect decisions because of overreliance on classical accounting information that does not give the proper weight to the value of information. This tendency must be noted and overcome.

The requirements for the data must be determined based on the statements of philosophy. These requirements are more detailed articulations of the philosophy statements. No specific methodology is available for this process. For this reason, the requirements specification is more of an assignment process than one of decomposition, although both processes may be present to some extent. At present, engineering judgment can best interpret the philosophy statements and specify the required detail. Some of the major requirements derived from the philosophy statements given earlier are presented below:

9. A chief information officer reporting directly to the CEO will be in charge of the data and will have full responsibility for safeguarding the resource.

10. Statistical data concerning the use of the data resource will be gathered and analyzed to improve the utilization.

11. The data definition procedures will be based on business requirements and will be an on-going process.

12. Data will exist as close to the client as possible.

13. Data will be made available in a form that is directly usable by the client.

14. Changes to the data must be made without compromising availability.

15. Response to a data request must be made in a timely manner.

16. Data audits will be continuously active.

17. Referential integrity will be maintained automatically.

18. Clients will not have to know where needed data is located in the network.

19. Clients will not have to know the format of needed data.

20. Financial and cost-accounting procedures will be put in place to accurately reflect the true value and cost of the data asset.

21. Clients must be allowed to construct their own views of the data and change them in an efficient manner when necessary.

22. Data must exist in a heterogeneous storage environment.

23. A distinction must exist between official and unofficial data.

24. Efficient methods of partitioning and merging data must exist.

25. Documentation pertaining to each data item and its use will be maintained and made available as required.

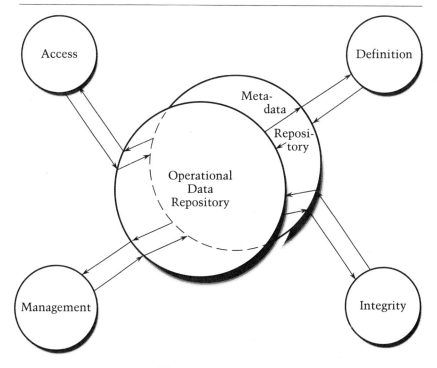

FIGURE 4.2 DATA ACTIVITY MODEL

Although many more requirements could have been stated, the ones presented are sufficient to develop the high-level model needed as a prerequisite to the architecture structure.

THE DATA MODEL

The data model (*data* is used in the global sense throughout this section) presented in figure 4.2 is an embodiment of the philosophy statements and needs as determined and presented in the previous section. Notice that the model has two data repository areas, which are connected together. One contains operational data, and the other is used for metadata. Although the metadata is not used directly in the operation of the business, it is of great importance in keeping the op-

131

erational data reliable and current. Each component of the model is discussed and related to the specific philosophy and requirements statements it is designed to address.

The access function provides the means for effective use of the data. It serves as a uniform way of specifying, locating, formatting, and returning requested data (statements 6, 7, 8, 13, 15, 18, 19, 21, 24). The access function is used to retrieve both operational data and metadata. This function is used by the end user and software clients to provide a view of the data that will serve their needs most efficiently. In addition to serving the direct needs of the client, this function is also used to control access to the data. The access to the data must look the same to the client regardless of the client's location on the network.

The data definition function provides the means for the enterprise to define the data items, their interrelationships, and the documentation that explains how the results were determined (statements 1, 2, 11, 25). In a dynamic business, data definition must be a continuous process. New data must be added, and obsolete data must be eliminated. The process is not unlike that associated with other aspects of network administration.

The data integrity function provides the means of maintaining data that is complete and correct (statements 1, 4, 16, 17). It is an independent function that operates under its own set of principles. Data integrity is concerned with the accuracy of each item of data, as well as with ensuring that changes are made in all areas that are affected. If the definition of a data item is to be expanded to accommodate a new use, all software concerned with that item must be examined to determine whether the new definition is consistent. This requires interaction with the metadata as well as the operational data.

The data repository function is the mechanism by which the data is physically stored in the network (statements 5, 12, 22, 24). It consists of the physical storage mechanisms, such as database management systems (DBMSs) and files utilized, the organization of the data in the DBMS or file, and the replication of the data in different network locations. Statistical information must also be gathered by the repository function to enable the function to be "tuned" to maximum efficiency with changing conditions.

The data management function is concerned with the effective functioning of the entire data process (statements 1, 2, 3, 9, 10, 14, 20, 23, 24). Like other management areas, this consists of operations, planning, and administrative functions. Each is required to ensure that the proper data in the correct format is available where and when it is needed.

An analysis of the philosophy and requirements statements covered explicitly by the model shows that every statement has been accommodated. Thus, it can safely be said that this model is a high-level embodiment of the data needs of the enterprise. A practical data architecture structure will require additional detail. The architecture structure is formed independently of the model, and their relationship becomes one of assignment.

DATA ARCHITECTURE STRUCTURE

Throughout this section, the word *data* and sometimes the word *information* will be used to refer to the entire body of items. Although this conflicts with the definitions given previously, I am deferring to common usage. When *data* or *information* is used in its narrower sense, this use will be stated explicitly or will be clear from the context.

The structure of the data architecture is shown in figure 4.3. It is a relatively complex structure, having 12 components and 18 interfaces. The dotted lines are a rough indication as to how the data model elements were assigned to the architecture components. As with all assignment processes, a one-to-one relationship seldom exists between the initial starting point and the result. Although this overlap is not

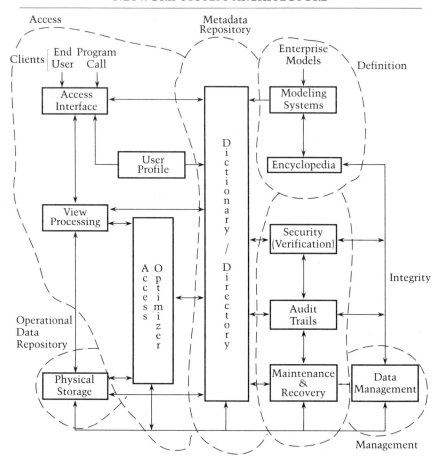

FIGURE 4.3   DATA SUBARCHITECTURE STRUCTURE

indicated in the diagram for simplicity, it is obvious that several of the model elements must also be assigned to physical storage, because that is the only way in which they can be implemented. You are invited to find the other overlaps that exist.

The function and interfaces of each of the components are discussed in detail to illustrate the effort and resources that must be expended in a comprehensive data resource architecture and program.

134

Data Definition

The starting point in a top-down specification must be the definition of the data that is needed by the business. The components involved in this process are the enterprise models, data modeling systems, encyclopedia, and a part of the dictionary/directory. Together they form a system for defining the information layer and part of the data layer of the hierarchy. No strictly physical quantities are considered in this effort. Because of this positioning, these components are sometimes referred to as the *information architecture*. The enterprise models are used to understand the fundamental operation of the business.

Outputs of the business model are also used to determine the types and characteristics of the network services needed by the enterprise, including functionality, personnel, etc. All aspects of the business model results are stored in the encyclopedia. For the purpose of this chapter, only the aspects of business modeling that are concerned with data requirements are used. That part concerned with the definition of network services is discussed in chapter 8, which covers application development. The use of the business model in the development methodology is discussed in the companion book, *Information Networks: A Design and Implementation Methodology*.

The data modeling subarchitecture has three parts, as shown in figure 4.4: the enterprise view of the data, the user view of the data, and the storage view of the data. In this case, the storage view is not physical. That can come only with deployment, which is not considered at this point. All of the information developed through the use of this model (metadata) is stored in the dictionary/directory. It will be used by other parts of the data system in the performance of their functions.

Before a detailed discussion of the data modeling process required by the architecture can be begun, it is necessary to

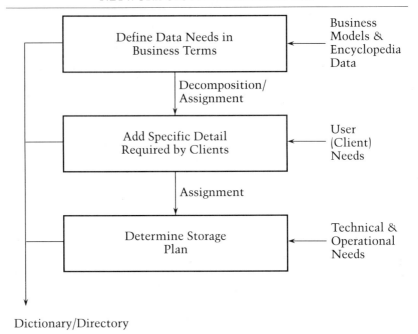

FIGURE 4.4   MODELING SYSTEM SUBARCHITECTURE

discuss the main technology that will be used in that process. That technology is known as *entity-relationship (E-R) modeling* or *diagramming*. The building blocks for this process are defined in the following sections. Although values are the ultimate goal of the process (in a usage sense), they are not really considered to be part of the development process except as a means to define the range of permissible entries.

Entities   Entities are persons, places, things, or concepts used in performing some business activity. Examples are customers, headquarters location, equipment, and accounts receivable. Note that entities cannot be stored in the computer memory (that is, a customer cannot be made machine-readable); they can only be defined.

Relationships   Relationships can be defined between entities and attributes. The present discussion considers only entity

136

relationships. A relationship can consist of any reasonable type. Examples are "ISA," "WORKS ON," and "USES FOR" (an employee WORKS ON project Q). Employee and project Q are entities. Like entities, entity relationships cannot be stored.

Attributes Attributes are specific qualities of an entity or relationship. Examples are ID number, color, salary, etc. Attributes can be stored, but, except for self-defining systems, they generally are not. Values for attributes can be stored if they vary, or they can be implicitly attached to an entity. RED, BLUE, and GREEN are values for the attribute color that would be stored depending on the instance. The attribute YEARLY for the attribute salary probably would be defined implicitly and not stored. The numeric value for the salary would be stored.

The above attributes were attached to entities. A relationship attribute attached to the relationship WORKS ON would be NUMBER OF HOURS when it is a function of both employee and project entities. These attributes also have associated values.

Relationships between attributes are usually NEEDS A relationships. If two attributes of the entity "employee" are ID and AGE, the relationship between the attributes might be AGE NEEDS A ID. If this relationship were not present, it would not be possible to attach an employee's age to the proper employee.

Values A value is an instance of an attribute and consists of a specific quantity or quality. As before, RED, BLUE, and GREEN are values for the attribute color. Not all values that could be assigned to an attribute are permissible. The permissible values must be defined during the data development process.

The connections among the building blocks of the E-R process are shown abstractly in figure 4.5. This type of diagram is required throughout the data modeling process. No-

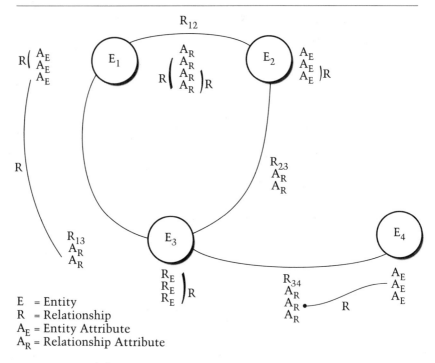

E = Entity
R = Relationship
A_E = Entity Attribute
A_R = Relationship Attribute

FIGURE 4.5   ENTITY-RELATIONSHIP DIAGRAM EXAMPLE

tice that the relationships can be quite complex. This complexity necessitates a highly structured approach to the data architecture. Without such a formalized structure, the data system can easily become inefficient and ineffective. This problem has been the downfall of many enterprises that otherwise had excellent procedures and tools.

Another aspect of E-R modeling is the use of inheritance, as depicted in figure 4.6. Entities can be decomposed into other more specific entities. The decomposition can continue for as many levels as desired. Attributes associated with parent entities are inherited by child entities. This simplifies the definition of the comprehensive E-R model. The determination of the proper entities for use in the enterprise depends on the development generation that is used (see introduction). This is illustrated in figure 4.7 for the third and fourth generations. A process using fifth-generation techniques that

138

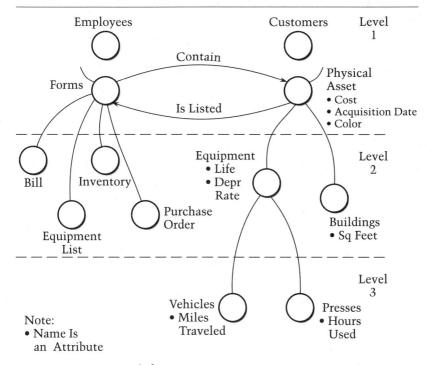

FIGURE 4.6 E-R INHERITANCE CONCEPTS

could be used as a base for all of the enterprise data needs has not yet been defined to the degree necessary and is not considered further. A great deal of research in this area is in progress and will eventually produce an acceptable process.

The third generation considers data only for one user at a time. There is no attempt to integrate the data needs of various users or to incorporate the overall needs defined by the enterprise. The fourth generation considers an integrated view of the data that incorporates the enterprise view as well as the view of each user. The union of all of these needs formed the basis for the enterprise data system. As in other areas, the architecture presented here assumes that the fourth-generation definition is used.

The architectural concept used in the data definition process is that of subject databases. *Subject databases* are the result of the conceptual abstraction level, shown in figure 4.8,

139

Third Generation

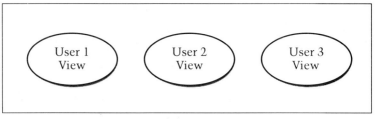

Aggregation of Disjoint User Views

Fourth Generation

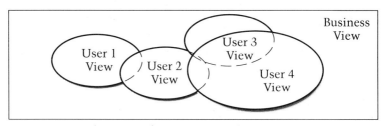

Combination of User Views and Business View

FIGURE 4.7   ENTERPRISE DATA VIEWS

and they contain the data needs of the enterprise as a whole. Through the use of the business model, high-level entities that are needed in the operation of the business are defined and relationships among those entities are specified as necessary. The relationships allow an affinity analysis to be performed on the entities, which are grouped into "subjects" according to this analysis.

An example of a subject database is shown in figure 4.9. Because of the way in which subject databases are depicted, this type of diagram is sometimes called a "tank farm." Subject databases provide a framework on which to develop the rest of the data system. More levels of entities than are shown in the diagram can be included.

In many cases, subject databases have been considered to be physical entities that required that the set of data in a particular "subject" be physically placed in the same location and storage media. Because of previous technology limita-

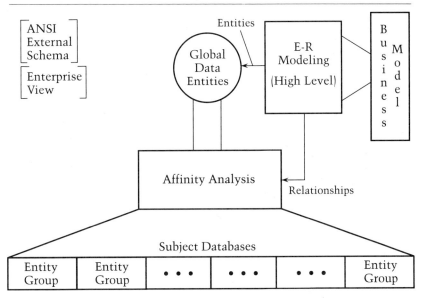

FIGURE 4.8   SUBJECT DATABASE DEVELOPMENT (CONCEPTUAL
ABSTRACTION LEVEL)

tions and the embedded base of data that resulted from the
third-generation systems already deployed, the use of subject
databases was severely restricted. Current technology and the
concepts presented in this chapter allow subject databases to
be utilized in their proper role as a design concept and logical
structure rather than a physical entity. This change in perspective should motivate developers to use this powerful concept in the development of network data systems.

After the definition of the entities is complete, global attributes that will define the overall properties of the entity
must be specified. One of the most important of these attributes is one that determines how the entity is to be considered from a data generation perspective. This attribute assigns
an entity to be *base data* or *transaction data*. Base data is
that data which is required by almost all activities of the
enterprise and which must be shared among many functions
and activities. Such data tends to be relatively stable and does
not change appreciably due to normal operations. Entities

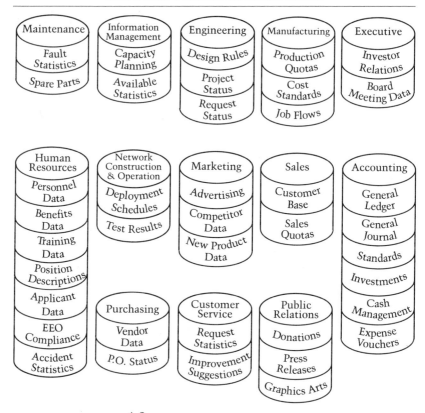

FIGURE 4.9   SUBJECT DATABASE EXAMPLES

such as customers, employees, factory locations, and stock shares outstanding are examples of base data. Changes to base data are typically made as a result of nonoperational conditions.

Transaction data is volatile data that is generated from the operational activities of the enterprise. It results from and is directly associated with a business event. It tends to be shared among a much smaller set of enterprise functions, and its life is generally much shorter than base data. Examples of this type of entity are orders, accounts receivable, inventory, and expense vouchers. Transaction data may be summarized or aggregated to form data that is then considered to be base data. Examples of entities resulting from this conversion

142

would be the enterprise's balance sheet, income statement, inventory statistics, productivity statistics, and customer service statistics. Classifying data in this manner is useful in several other functions required by the architecture. These include data integrity, physical deployment, and access.

Ownership is an associated global attribute that is also important from an organizational point of view. To some organizations in an enterprise, the ownership of the data implies control, which may be important from a political perspective. The architecture requires that the ownership of all base data be vested in the organization responsible for the data system. The intent is to require a single point of responsibility for all corporate-wide shared data. The ownership of transaction data may be assigned to individual organizations that have a vested interest from an operational or political viewpoint. However, the architecture does not give the owner of the data any special privileges with that data. All changes or other interactions must be in accordance with the tenets of the data management architecture. If these controls are circumvented, the data will remain unofficial and will not be allowed to be used by network systems and functions.

After definition of the entities and the assignment of global attributes, the next step in the data modeling process is to consider the specific needs of the users for data needed to run their individual aspects of the business. In its purest form this is an assignment process, although elements of decomposition will probably occur. The architecture component that is concerned with this area of data modeling is depicted in figure 4.10. The major result is the attachment to the entities of additional attributes that are user-specific. This is accomplished by aggregating the needs of the individual users for specific attributes and attaching them to the proper entity. Initially, this can be done on a user-by-user basis. Duplications and other problems should be removed during the normalization process.

The normalization process uses a series of rules to form the attributes into a set of attribute groups. There are different

143

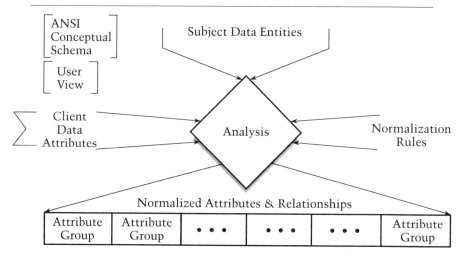

FIGURE 4.10   SUBJECT DATABASE DEVELOPMENT (LOGICAL
ABSTRACTION LEVEL)

levels of normalization, and although the process is relatively straightforward, it is too tedious to present here. Consult the appropriate documents listed in the bibliography. The result of the normalization process is a set of attribute groups that will be easy to implement and maintain. An example of some attribute groups is shown in figure 4.11.

The final step in the data definition process is the development of the storage plan. Because of the many engineering design factors that must be considered in this phase, the relationship to the subject database structure becomes one of assignment. The architecture of the storage plan determines how and where the attribute groups will be stored. Each group must be stored in a database management system or file system, taking into account the operational needs of the various clients that must use the data. This process is shown in figure 4.12. In order to meet the clients' needs effectively, the attribute groups may need to be denormalized, replicated, and/or distributed throughout the network. As stated previously, the attribute groups need not be placed together even though they are derived from the same "subject." They may

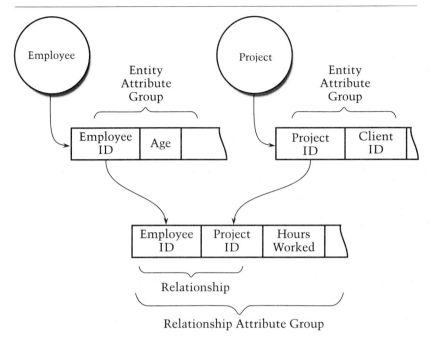

FIGURE 4.11   ATTRIBUTE GROUP EXAMPLE

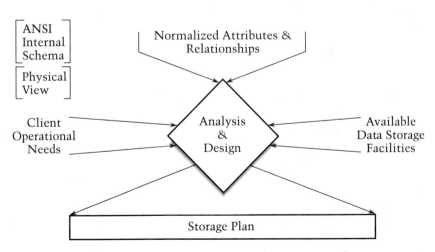

FIGURE 4.12   SUBJECT DATABASE DEVELOPMENT (PHYSICAL
ABSTRACTION LEVEL)

be placed as necessary based on the values of the global attributes, historical reasons, efficiency, or operational considerations.

The rules for performing this function are mainly qualitative and rest heavily on the skill of the engineer charged with this task. This engineer is usually known as a database administrator (DBA); this important function is discussed in more detail later in the chapter.

As with the previous two steps in the data definition process, the results of the storage plan development are stored in the dictionary/directory for use by the DBA as well as other network clients that need to know how the data was defined for implementation. The actual implementation of the storage plan is a separate function that must consider the network topology, user locations, and the anticipated amount of data traffic. This aspect is addressed in a later section concerned with data management.

A slightly different set of definitions and associated terminology was proposed and standardized by the American National Standards Institute (ANSI) CODASYL committee, which was charged with the development of data standards. Their result defined three views or schemas that identified different ways of considering the data.

The *conceptual schema* views the data as a complete normalized entity that contains all of the enterprise-defined entities as well as the user requirements. In a sense, it is the result of applying a methodology that is consistent with the first two parts of the data modeling architecture described here.

The *external schema* is the view of the individual users for their specific data needs. As such, it is similar to the second part of the architecture.

Finally, the *physical schema* is the view of the data as deployed and roughly consists of the results of the third part of the architecture and the deployment process, which is discussed later.

The CODASYL standard's emphasis on views or results

146

makes it appropriate for use in considering the ultimate outcome of a data design process but difficult to use in the definition of an architecture and methodology that would provide that output. For that reason, the development presented in this chapter deviates from the CODASYL standard — although many of the concepts, including E-R modeling and the separation of user and enterprise views, are the same.

Dictionary/Directory

The dictionary/directory contains all of the metadata resulting from the design process or operational activities. A dictionary is usually considered to contain definitional information, and a directory is usually considered to contain location and relationship information. Because these two types of information are inherently interrelated when applied to the enterprise data system, they are usually contained in the same repository; hence the composite name for this common area. The data contained in the dictionary/directory consists of the following:

- The results of the data definition process
- The use of each data item (each end user and software program that references the item)
- The geographical location(s) of each data item
- The physical aspects of the data layer
- The contents of the lowest two hierarchy layers, as required
- Usage statistics

By interrogating the directory/dictionary, a user can obtain a complete picture of the data system.

The directory/dictionary can be defined to be passive or active. An active directory/dictionary is one that is updated automatically when changes occur in the use, constraints, definition, location, relationship, or other context information of a data item. In addition, it automatically enforces any applicable usage rules. A passive directory/dictionary requires manual entry of the change information and manual verification of the usage rules. The architecture specifies an active directory/dictionary, because it is difficult to maintain the proper correspondence between the current context (users) of a data item and the directory/dictionary contents when a passive directory/dictionary is used. Maintenance of the proper relationship between an item and its context is called *referential integrity*. Referential integrity is an important part of the data system, because of the complexities of the data and the multiple ways in which it can be used. An active directory/dictionary will promote consistency of application for each area of the data.

Data Management

Data management is concerned with maintaining an efficient and effective data environment for use by the clients. It contains comprehensive planning, administrative, and operational activities, as shown in table 4.1. This type of activity is usually performed by a database administrator (DBA), as mentioned previously. Planning activities comprise the largest part of the data management function. These activities can be classified into three broad groups:

• Design
• Usage analysis
• Capacity planning

Although most of the design activities have been detailed in the previous section, the implementation architecture has been left to this section because physical database design is usually the exclusive function of data management. The other design activities are generally considered to be the responsibility of the modeling function. Ideally, all parts of the design process are the result of close cooperation between the data modeling and management functions, so that each effectively utilizes the expertise of the other.

The physical database implementation architecture is shown in figure 4.13. There are five parts to this architecture.

TABLE 4.1   DATA MANAGEMENT ACTIVITIES

Area	Activities
Administration	Security changes
	User permission changes
	Data location changes
	Training and education
	Data migration
	Planned configuration changes
Planning	Needs forecasting
	Simulation
	Disaster planning
	Standards enforcement
	Product qualification
	Usage pattern analysis
	Data integrity processes
	Change scheduling
	Database design
Operations	User interaction and problem resolution
	Availability
	Fault handling
	Performance analysis
	Emergency configuration changes
	On-line monitoring
	Usage control

Although the storage plan has determined how the data is to be partitioned into databases and what type of management system is to be used for each, specific network locations must be determined and appropriate products selected, procured, and installed.

After the physical data storage products are available for use, they must be populated with the appropriate data. This is usually necessary only for certain types of base data, because the transaction data will be populated automatically from operations. The results of the initial data population must be tested for accuracy and consistency, and the entire data system must be tested under operational conditions to determine if the system design is proper. Integrity issues that

149

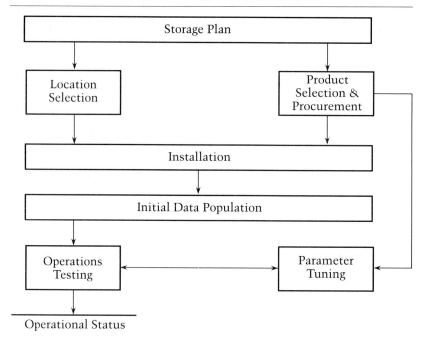

FIGURE 4.13   STORAGE PLAN IMPLEMENTATION
SUBARCHITECTURE

result from data population and generation are discussed shortly.

During testing, each management system is tuned for the most efficient and effective operation, both locally and as a part of the entire data system. Once the system has passed all of the tests, it is opened to production use. Additional detail on the deployment process as applied to software systems is provided in the companion book, *Information Networks: A Design and Implementation Methodology*. Much of that discussion applies to data also and will be of use in understanding the overall deployment process.

Although the design functions detailed above and in the previous section are certainly important, the other data management activities are equally as necessary to ensure that the design is translated into an efficient and effective deployed system that meets the needs of the clients. Usage analysis is necessary to detect changes in the way the data is generated, accessed, and utilized so that appropriate changes in the design or deployment characteristics can be made. Any design, no matter how well conceived and implemented, has a finite life. Leaving an obsolete data design in place will greatly reduce the effectiveness of the entire enterprise. The usage analysis should be a continuous process.

Capacity planning assures that enough resources are available so that every client can access the data according to the needed view and response in a cost-effective manner. Obtaining and deploying additional capacity is an activity with a long lead time, and it can greatly affect the physical design of the data system.

The administrative functions are needed to meet the client needs on a day-by-day basis. Change administration forms the largest part of this function, and efficient procedures for processing these changes without adversely affecting any client must be in place. In general, changes should be accomplished without restricting the availability or integrity of the data.

The operations activities of data management are generally related to problem detection and correction that cannot be handled by the data integrity function. Although this is an important aspect of data management, the use of this activity should be minimized if the requirements of the other components of the architecture are followed in implementing a data system. A problem may be related to a software or hardware fault or it may occur because the usage patterns have shifted from those which were expected. In either case, the data management function must have developed procedures that would enable the administrator to isolate and circumvent the difficulty. This process is similar to that of network management, and the two management functions are closely related. Close cooperation must be maintained between the data and network management function. The network management architecture is discussed in chapter 6.

Data Integrity

Data is a fragile and volatile resource. It is easily corrupted inadvertently or through intentional tampering. Computer viruses are dangerous for a number of reasons, but the most critical effect is their tendency to destroy and/or corrupt the data. Once lost, data is difficult to reconstruct, as many enterprises have discovered when their accounts receivable records or customer lists have been destroyed.

Misapplication of data can also adversely affect the integrity of the data. Misapplication in this context refers to the incorrect derivation of data that is presented to the data system as correct. This problem has been exacerbated by the proliferation of personal computers (PCs) that are not connected directly to the network and that are not placed under any direct or indirect administrative control. These PCs are differentiated from individual workstations that are connected directly to the network and that operate under the established management framework.

It is almost impossible to determine if the results obtained from a PC have used the correct data and have performed the claimed calculations correctly. The time-honored method of passing data by use of flexible disks effectively eliminates any possibility of monitoring and validating the data transfer. Although data validation is still a difficult problem with workstations, the architecture can provide some means of dealing with the issue, as discussed below. This is another reason that stand-alone computers are not allowed within the architecture.

Before derived data can be considered to be correct, it must pass a verification test that will determine if the data is suitable for inclusion in the data system. This requires that data be partitioned into official and unofficial data. Official data has been determined to be correct, whereas unofficial data may be correct or incorrect. Its status has not yet been determined. One way of providing for this verification

TABLE 4.2   MAJOR DATA ERROR CAUSES

Cause	Errors
Direct human problems	Initial population errors Poorly formulated data requests Entry errors Incomplete understanding Intentional destruction
Design problems	Poor system design Updates *not* applied to all copies of replicated data Error propagation Incorrect new data generation
Operational problems	Hardware faults Software faults Noise Acts of God

would be to tag each data item with an audit trail that would be updated each time it was used in a process or calculation. Although theoretically elegant, the state of the art does not yet lend itself to that level of identification. This type of explicit aid to verification will not yet be included in the architectural requirements; more indirect methods will be specified.

The data integrity architecture is intended to prevent any type of error from entering the data. In order for this task to be accomplished, the source of errors must be determined and classified so that an appropriate control for each type can be determined. Table 4.2 lists the major sources of data errors. A brief discussion of the type of controls required for each error type is given to help explain the data integrity architecture design.

Directly caused human errors are the most difficult to handle, because they involve a wide range of reasons and effects. Addressing these causes requires a four-pronged approach:

153

- Restrict the ability of any end user to interact directly with the data. Only those with a strong need to correct problems should be allowed to do so.
- Define value constraints and use them to screen any direct data input into the system. Expert systems that test the reasonableness of an entry would also be an appropriate direction.
- Define and enforce administrative controls similar to financial internal controls. These controls would limit the ability of any one person to make an undetectable error in entering or updating data.
- Educate end users in the proper use of the tools and systems that affect the data. This is needed for data input as well as for interpreting the results of any output data.

Although none of these protective measures are foolproof, their consistent use as required by the architecture should reduce the number of these types of errors to an acceptable level. Notice that the second two actions involve mainly business-oriented considerations. Error control must be addressed from both a technical and a business perspective.

Design problems are best addressed at the source. A set of requirements and specifications developed specifically to eliminate design-induced data errors must be added to all systems. If these fundamental constraints are observed, systems will always consider the causes and effects of data errors as an integral part of the design process and not as an add-on that attempts to address the problem in piecemeal fashion. Suitable requirements/specifications might include the following:

- All data accesses will be made through one access routine that will examine the data and determine its correctness.
- During initialization, and periodically thereafter, the system will interrogate the dictionary/directory to determine if the data needed has undergone any change that could influence the results of the system.

• The system will keep statistics of its data usage in a standard format for later interpretation.

Operational problems require the most additional investment in hardware, software, and people in order to provide an acceptable level of containment. Because it is difficult to predict the effect and time of occurrence of operational problems, continuous monitoring must be performed along with extensive contingency plans. These could include background audits of the data, functions that examine log data to determine if any unusual events have occurred, etc. Major catastrophes, such as losing a data center through fire or flood, must also be considered, and the proper plans must be developed for recovery. Such protections as backup copies of the data in geographically dispersed areas, along with the means for keeping them current, would be necessary.

Although the different error causes have been discussed individually, in reality they are all interrelated, and one cannot be considered without examining the effect on the others. The experience and expertise of the database administrators in conjunction with a comprehensive data architecture is usually invaluable in achieving a suitable approach to the error containment problem.

The data integrity subarchitecture is shown schematically in figure 4.14. These components are the same as those shown in figure 4.3, except that the verification component is expanded into multiple components that reflect different types of verification. The verification components must be satisfied before the data can make the transition from unofficial to official. The base data verification component must verify the consistency and accuracy of the values assigned to the shared data. This is accomplished by using the business model and the contents of the encyclopedia.

The transaction data verification component examines the characteristics of any transaction data that is to be made official and determines whether the requirements of the architecture and company policies have been met. These re-

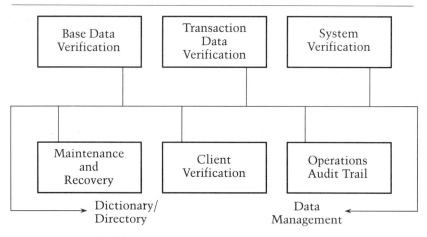

FIGURE 4.14   DATA INTEGRITY SUBARCHITECTURE

quirements may vary depending on the source of the data, the type of data, and the amount of data involved. As discussed previously, data received from individual workstations would be subjected to the most controls and examination. Other data, such as that received from automated billing services, might be accepted as tendered with only minor checks for consistency or reasonableness.

System verification is a complex activity that attempts to qualify a network system as having no adverse effect on the data with which it interacts. No attempt is made to perform any quality check on the system itself as far as its functionality is concerned. The only need is to ensure that the data interaction is not harmful. No standard architecture or methodology currently exists for performing that type of check. Extensive testing seems to offer the best chance of success at the current state of the art.

Client verification requires that all system users, whether end users or software program users, be positively identified. Once identification has been accomplished, this function controls what data resources the client may have access to and how client-derived data may be returned to the system, either in an unofficial of official capacity. Many client verification

156

schemes have been proposed and implemented with varying degrees of success. The architecture does not specify which of these are required in a specific circumstance. This is an economic rather than a technical decision. Enough security should be purchased to offset possible losses from a breach. The architecture does require that some client verification process be established for each system and network and that breaches be investigated thoroughly.

Maintenance and recovery is the function that is charged with the responsibility of maintaining data integrity in the presence of data problems. The problem may range from a wrong item value to a malfunctioning database management system. In any case, the problem must be identified and corrected as quickly as possible. Although automated methods such as background audits and on-line performance monitoring are valuable, many, if not most, problems will be identified through complaints of the users. An effective means of using information obtained in this way to identify and correct problems is a fundamental requirement of the architecture.

In many cases, the operations audit trail is required by the other integrity functions to identify and correct current or potential problems. This component could be as simple as the writing of a log containing the results of all data interactions; alternatively, the audit trail process could be able to perform more sophisticated operations. Some of the possible operations could be:

- Manage a checkpoint facility so that the data system can be returned to any previous state
- Manage an alarm function that indicates improper usage (volume, cost, frequency, access, etc.)
- Provide an analysis as to the effectiveness of the administrative and other internal controls
- Integrate the results of multiple network locations

The architecture will require an audit trail process, but the requirements of the specific network and systems will determine the extent of the functions included.

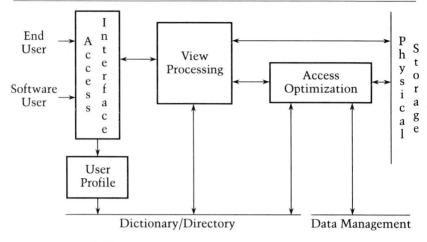

FIGURE 4.15   CLIENT DATA ACCESS SUBARCHITECTURE

Data Access

The data access subarchitecture consists of the access interface, user profile, view processing and access optimizer components, along with part of the dictionary/directory, physical
storage, and data management components, as indicated in
figure 4.15. These components determine how the data system will react to requests coming from the various clients.
The access interface and the user profile components were
discussed extensively in chapter 2, which dealt with the end
user architecture. For data access purposes, the functionality
of these components needs to be extended to include software
users. This is a relatively easy task and need not be covered
in detail. You are invited to perform this activity.

As discussed previously, many different ways of viewing
the same data are possible and desirable. Restricting the view
to what is needed results in more efficient and effective system designs. The architecture must provide for the network
functions that will make the development and use of the
individual client data views an efficient process. A view, in
effect, is a translation of the contents of the entire set of data
into a set that is directly usable by the client. The develop-

158

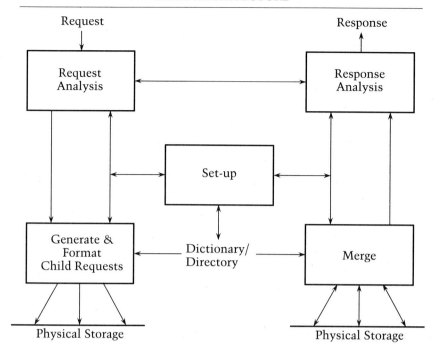

FIGURE 4.16 VIEW PROCESSING SUBARCHITECTURE

ment of the translation criteria should be derived automatically from the stated needs of the client for data. The type and specifics of the client information needed should be in the dictionary/directory, and a network system that can perform the necessary translations should be available. Manual adjustment of the view must also be available. The use of the translation should also be invisible to the client and, in addition, must be almost as efficient as direct access of the data. The degree of closeness necessary will, of course, depend on the client's needs.

A suitable subarchitecture for view processing is shown in figure 4.16 and consists of five activities, two concerned with the request process, two concerned with the response process, and one concerned with the set-up process. When a new client is added to the system, the set-up process should be invoked automatically to produce a default view. The parameters of the view will be placed in the dictionary/directory to facilitate further changes or coordination with other client views.

Three types of requests may be handled by the view system:

- Requests to change the view
- Requests for knowledge, information, or data
- Requests to update or add new knowledge, information, or data

One of the activities of the request analysis function is to examine each request and, depending on the parameters as provided by the set-up function, take an appropriate action:

- Deny the request with or without an explanation
- Tentatively accept the request but ask for more instruction before continuing
- Immediately accept the request and attempt to perform the desired actions
- Return status indicators

Client software systems must be designed such that each of these responses are handled correctly without terminating the function. End user clients must be taught how to respond to the various conditions when they occur. The user access system discussed in chapter 2 should be able to handle the large majority of these conditions automatically.

Another activity of the request analysis function would be to translate a request at one intelligence layer into a request at a lower layer. The user may request an item at the information layer, such as the total amount of the charges for the billing period. This is termed an "infological" request. Request analysis must then translate that request into other requests at the data layer, so that the appropriate storage facilities can be interrogated. These latter requests are called "datalogical" to reflect the changed layer of intelligence. The "logical" ending is added to reflect the fact that both of these are logical requests rather than physical ones. The "infological" request example for charge information could be translated into "datalogical" requests for individual service connect time, charge rates, special requests, flat fees, etc., drawn from wherever in the network they might reside. After receiving all of this data, the view processing function would have to assemble it into an information layer response for presentation to the client. This would be accomplished by the merge and response analysis functions, as discussed shortly.

In most cases, the translation from the infological realm to the datalogical and reverse currently is performed by the client. Use of an expert system to analyze the translation requirements is possible, and research along these lines is in progress, with some encouraging results. Although the process is not as well defined, the same discussion would hold for translation between other intelligence layers, such as the knowledge layer and the information layer.

The request analysis function is also used to infer and provide knowledge (at the knowledge layer) to the client. As an example of this process, consider an end user request for data. Knowledge that may be necessary, especially for large amounts of data, is the cost for executing the request. If the cost is above a preset factor, the requestor is notified as to the cost and approval is requested before the request can continue.

Once the request has been accepted, it is decomposed into its component parts by the format function. The optimum network location for each of the data components is then determined by the format function, and individual requests for each part are composed and sent. The decomposition process and acceptable network locations for the data must be allowed to change asynchronously. Changes may come from the dictionary/directory as necessary.

If the request is for information or data to be returned to the client, the required items or a problem explanation is sent to the merge function. If the request is for an update or for storage of new data, an appropriate response indication is sent to the merge function. In the latter case, the merge function is responsible for ensuring that the update to all the data has

161

occurred properly. This process is called the *commit function*, and it must be designed so that an error will cause the entire update process to fail. An incomplete update must be avoided, as it can lead to severe data errors. Commit processes can be quite complex, and considerable research is still underway to improve the efficiency and effectiveness of network-wide commits. See the bibliography for sources of more information on this process.

Once the merge function has been properly completed, the response analysis function is invoked. This function determines whether the received data accurately and completely fulfills the original request. If not, a new request is formulated and executed, if possible. During this process, the client may be asked to supply additional information. Again, software clients must be prepared for this eventuality. If the received data is deemed to satisfy the original request, the data is formatted and sent to the user access function. Appropriate statistics and summary information concerning the request and response is collected and sent to the dictionary/directory.

If a condition of use is the elimination of as much overhead as possible in the view processing function, most of the functions just described can be circumvented through the view processing mechanism itself. Of course, this will place a greater burden on the application system for error detection and handling. Depending on the application and client community, this may be an acceptable trade-off.

The access optimization component is necessary to monitor the operation of the data system from the clients' point of view and to determine when changes are needed to the view processing or physical storage parameters. The output of such a component would be relevant usage statistics or candidate changes in the parameters themselves. Depending on need, this type of adjustment could be performed automatically through the use of some type of knowledge-based system or adjusted manually by a DBA. The architecture recommends that this component be present in the data system but does not require it.

The physical storage component has been discussed thoroughly in other publications and as such does not need to be treated further in this presentation. However, some of the principles presented in the next section will follow from general knowledge of this area.

This completes the discussion of the structure of the data architecture. As with the other level 1 architectures, the next step will be to determine the principles that will be used to guide the development of systems for the network. In the case of the data architecture, the data system will be affected most directly. As was seen from the verification and access components, however, application systems also must abide by the principles of this architecture.

DATA ARCHITECTURE PRINCIPLES

The following statements are the principles derived from the structures defined for the Data architecture. In keeping with the practice established for this section they are grouped according to the components of the architecture.

I. Strategies
  A. Global
    1. Architectural
      a. The responsibility for the data will rest in an organization solely charged with that responsibility. The executive in charge of that organization will be given the title of Chief Information Officer (CIO).
      b. Data will be treated as a corporate asset, and the effectiveness of the management of the data will be audited periodically.
      c. All base data will be owned by the Chief Information Officer.
      d. All transaction data will be owned by the Chief Information Officer unless there are

163

compelling reasons to assign that responsibility elsewhere.

2. Design
    a. No one person should be able to alter substantial amounts of data. Approval for such changes must be built into the data system.
    b. At least two copies of all official data must be located in geographically dispersed areas.
    c. Heterogeneous environments for all aspects of the data system must be assumed.
    d. Data modeling is a continuous process, and the results should always reflect the current status of the enterprise.
    e. All entities should have a global attribute that contains the proper intelligence layer of the entity.

3. Operational
    a. All official data should have 100-percent availability.
    b. All procedures that assign official status to transaction data must be approved by a designee of the CIO.
    c. Only one copy of replicated data may be official.

B. Data definition
    1. Architectural
        a. All enterprise data shall be defined through the data modeling process.
        b. Subject databases will be used as the conceptual layer definition model.
        c. Normalized attribute groups will be used as the logical layer definition model.
        d. The storage plan will utilize only database management systems for official data unless the life of the data is less than one day.
        e. Unofficial data may use file structures for storage if desired.

2. Design
    a. The result of the data definition process shall be approved by all clients.
    b. An efficient process for updating the results of the definition process shall be implemented.
    c. All intermediate and final results of the definition process shall be stored in the dictionary/directory in a self-defining form.
3. Operational
    a. The definition of a data item shall be the same regardless of network location. Local definitions are not permitted.
    b. All defined data items must be available subject to verification requirements.

C. Data integrity
1. Architectural
    a. All transaction data shall be verified before becoming official.
    b. All network systems will be verified for data before being allowed on the network.
    c. The CIO will specify the client verification conditions for all official data. The owner will specify the client verification conditions for all unofficial data.
    d. Some form of operation audit trail will be implemented.
    e. Explicit data maintenance and recovery procedures will be developed and implemented in the data system.
2. Design
    a. End user verification for base data access will have a probability of circumvention of less than .01 percent.
    b. Changes to the operational characteristics of the data integrity functions must be approved by the CIO and verified by the internal auditing organization.

D. Client access
  1. Architectural
     a. At a minimum, view processing must be able to identify the network location of requested data.
     b. Enough usage information must be made available for the DBA to tune the data system effectively.
     c. Data access conditions should be independent of network location.
  2. Design
     a. Client access functions will have different efficiency levels available to meet diverse capacity needs.
     b. The client access function shall be designed as a separate system with well-defined interfaces to other data functions.
E. Data management
  1. Architectural
     a. The data system must provide the statistics and other information necessary to allow the planning, administrative, and operations functions to be performed effectively.
     b. Internal controls for the data management function must be developed.
     c. Data management will be placed physically at one network location.
  2. Design
     a. All data system functions will have access methods specifically designed for use by data management.
F. Dictionary/directory
  1. Architectural
     a. The dictionary/directory will be active. All changes to the data or its context will update the dictionary/directory automatically.

       b. The contents of the dictionary/directory are considered to be base data.

       c. The dictionary/directory contents may be spread throughout the network.

  2. Design

       a. All data system functions will have access methods specifically designed for use by data management.

G. Data repository

  1. Architectural

       a. Physical data storage will be located as close (shortest network data path) to the highest volume user as possible.

  2. Operational

       a. Base data and transaction data should not be stored in the same physical DBMS.

II. Standards

A. Global

  1. Architectural

       a. All interfaces in the data system will be declared to be enterprise standards and will be defined as such with appropriate documentation and enforcement means.

       b. Data system standards should follow international or other industry standards when possible.

       c. Commercially available products should be used in the data system when possible.

       d. The standard data language will be SQL.

B. Data definition

  1. Architectural

       a. The data design methodology chosen should be used consistently. No deviations from the process should be allowed.

C. Data integrity

  1. Architectural

       a. Enterprise standards will be developed for all data integrity functions.

D. Client access
   1. Architectural
      a. Enterprise standards will be developed for all client access functions.

E. Data management
   1. Architectural
      a. Enterprise standards will be developed for all data management functions.

F. Dictionary/directory
   1. Architectural
      a. The dictionary/directory will have a standard format for all contents. To the extent possible, this format will be self-defining.
      b. The dictionary/directory will use relational technology for storage.

G Data repository
   1. Architectural
      a. Standard data storage procedures will be developed and used by the enterprise.

III. Guidelines
   A. Global
      1. Architectural
         a. Enterprise-defined guidelines should follow accepted industry practices whenever possible.
      2. Design
         a. Data system design should follow good engineering practice.
         b. The data system design methodology should be similar in step structure to the network system design methodology.
   B. Data integrity
      1. Architectural
         a. As many data integrity functions as economically justifiable should be implemented.

   b. Changes to the operational characteristics of the data integrity functions should be minimized.

C. Client access
 1. Architectural
  a. Client access should be able to be transferred easily from one network location to another by the client.
  b. Client access function requests for additional direction should be in natural language form.
 2. Design
  a. The same client access system design should be used for all clients. Individual variations should be accomplished through the use of parameters.
  b. As little client intervention as possible should be required in the view process.

D. Data management
 1. Architectural
  a. Planning for data needs should be done using a five-year horizon.
 2. Operations
  a. A help desk for data-related problems should be established.

E. Data repository
 1. Architectural
  a. Relational technology should be used for storage whenever possible.
 2. Operational
  a. DBMS parameters should be examined continually and tuned as necessary.
  b. The number of different types of DBMS products in the network should be kept as small as possible.

IV. Rules
 A. Global

    1. Architectural
       a. Documentation for the data system will be in machine-readable form and will be available in the dictionary/directory.
       b. A member of the data management organization will attend all application design inspections.
    2. Operational
       a. All changes to official data will be transparent to the clients.

B. Data definition
    1. Architectural
       a. The data design process will use advanced computer aided design (CAD) techniques.
       b. No local changes or additions to the data definition process will be allowed.

C. Data integrity
    1. Architectural
       a. Before an application program from any source may be placed on the network, the application system data verification procedure must be performed.
    2. Design
       a. Client verification will utilize "call-back" techniques when system network access is obtained through a public network.

D. Client access
    1. Operations
       a. Client requests for new access privileges will be processed within one hour.

E. Data management
    1. Architectural
       a. The data management function will be structured such that 95 percent of all problems will be resolved in two hours.

F. Dictionary/directory
    1. Architectural

a. The dictionary/directory will support all data storage facilities on the network.
G. Data repository
  1. Architectural
    a. Every database management system on the network must have the following capabilities:
      • Dynamic transaction backout
      • Backward and forward recovery
      • Checkpoint/restart capability
      • Log generation
      • Kernel security at every data level
  2. Design
    a. No DBMS will be designed internally.
  3. Operations
    a. A software maintenance contract must be maintained on every deployed DBMS.

SUMMARY AND CONCLUSIONS

The data architecture is one of the most complex subarchitectures in the entire system architecture. It must provide an effective framework that allows many complex functions to work together synergistically. If this does not occur, the operation of the entire corporation will be compromised, because the data system, which is at the heart of all corporate activities, will not function properly. In spite of the necessary complexity, the data architecture must be structured in such a way that the maximum amount of information can be gleaned. The complexity must not hinder the use of the architecture in shaping data system development and deployment. It is left to you to decide whether the architecture presented in this chapter has achieved that goal. Suitable changes in the architecture that meet the needs of an enterprise and its personnel more precisely are always acceptable and welcome. You are challenged to "have at it."

The complexity of the data architecture is compounded by the terminology confusion that continues to await a solution.

As revealed in the discussions of the chapter, not even recognition of the problem and explicit attention to avoiding ambiguity can always succeed in eliminating confusion. Overcoming this barrier requires continuous effort. Enterprise-wide standards in this area would certainly help, as long as those involved agree to use and promote them. Standards in this or any other area do more harm than good if they are not used actively.

In my experience, much more attention generally is paid to application system development and network design than is given to the data system. If this chapter has at least drawn some attention to that imbalance, it will have fulfilled a significant part of the total task necessary. Data, information, knowledge, and wisdom are the building blocks of the future. It is time to give them the needed respect.

F I V E

SERVER ARCHITECTURE

INTRODUCTION

The ultimate purpose of the information network is to provide services to the end users. Implementation of these services requires some amount of processing capability, usually in the form of computers. For the purposes of this chapter, the required processing facilities will be provided by network entities called *servers*. Although this notation probably resulted from the concepts of queueing theory, it is appropriate here, because the emphasis will be on providing service and not on supplying raw processing power.

If the selection and deployment of network processing facilities is not done properly, the result can be significant inefficiencies and difficulties in network operation and management. A reduced level of service and higher costs to the service provider and end user may also occur. The purpose of this chapter is to develop the structures and principles necessary for the definition, specification, and deployment of servers in a cost-efficient manner consistent with the needs of the network and all network clients. Because of the multiplicity of servers that is allowed by modern networks, a highly structured approach to this process is required. The server architecture is designed to provide the framework and understanding needed to develop a server design that will meet the needs of the enterprise.

This chapter deals directly with servers required for services that interact with users in the conduct of the business. Servers associated with services that provide system and software implementation functions, including compilers, test facilities, and configuration management needs, are not considered specifically. Also not covered here are those services and associated servers that are concerned with operating the network. These services would include switching, protocol conversion, path establishment, and network-to-network connectivity. Although much of the discussion also applies to these latter two service cases, space does not permit a detailed discussion of their server-related aspects. Some network server needs are discussed in the next chapter on communications but these presentations do not provide the same detail as is given here. Certain aspects of server involvement in the system implementation process are explained in the discussion of application development in chapter 8.

This chapter assumes a commitment to utilizing the network environment to the fullest extent possible through the mechanisms of distributed and cooperative processing. Adherence to the architecture presented in this chapter will usually result in systems that use multiple processors for execution. This is different from the philosophy of using one or at the most two processors (host and workstation) to implement an entire service. This latter type of implementation uses the network only for access and does not allow the capabilities of the network to be utilized to their fullest extent. The commitment to distributed and cooperative processing also allows the full utilization of the deployment infrastructure, and the architecture is also oriented toward that purpose.

Many networks and systems use servers controlled by external information providers. These servers do not necessarily need to conform to the architecture before deployment. However, a set of standards must be established by the enterprise to manage this type of connection. Again, because of space limitations, this aspect of the server deployment process cannot be considered in detail. Although some mention of this is made in the next chapter, most of the necessary discussion must be left to other publications.

The development of the server architecture starts with a short discussion of the purpose of the processing function and the major types which can be used in the network. The philosophy of the architectural approach to the server specification problem is then discussed. Following that presentation, the server architecture structure, along with some of the closely integrated principles, is developed and explained with the use of several examples. The remainder of the architectural principles are then presented. Finally, the major concepts of the chapter are examined and several important conclusions are presented.

Although the server architecture provides the basic constructs, principles, and methods for specifying servers, these elements must be interpreted by a development methodology before they can be useful for implementing usable systems. The methodology must select among alternatives allowed, select when and where the application of the server architecture will occur, and define the relationships with the other subarchitectures. The interrelationship of the server architecture and the communications architecture is especially critical in this respect. The companion book, *Information Networks: A Design and Implementation Methodology*, presents one such methodology.

PROCESSORS AND COMPUTERS

Because servers are defined to be the facilities that provide processing capabilities in the network, a short discussion is needed to define what processing accomplishes and what constitutes processing power. Most people have an innate feeling as to what a computer or processor is. It is wise to provide as rigorous a definition as possible, however, so that there will be no confusion as to how a particular term is used. In their most general definition, processors are entities that transform a set of input quantities into a set of output quantities. This definition would include such entities as prisms, lightbulbs, and food mixers. Clearly a restriction is needed. The most obvious one is to restrict the input and output quantities to those discussed in the previous chapter. Thus, a processor transforms a set of items of intelligence into another set of items of intelligence. As discussed previously, these items will be called *data* to comply with current practice.

No implementation considerations are attached to this definition. The processor could be human, mechanical, electronic, or pneumatic. To remedy this, the next restriction deals with implementation. Processors are limited to those that use a stored program architecture in some form. The processors of interest are defined as follows: Processors utilize a stored program architecture to transform a set of input data into a set of output data.

Although the characteristics of a stored program architecture could be explored, that level of detail is not necessary for the remainder of the discussion. Refer to other publications for additional information, if desired. It should be noted that the generality of the term *stored program* allows a great deal of latitude in the specification of computers and processors. For example, a supercomputer, which has a different architecture than more conventional computers, would certainly be an acceptable choice.

The term *computer* originally referred to the computational aspects of problem-solving. These included the arithmetic and logical operations of mathematics. As an example, analog computers are used to solve differential equations. In adhering to the "stored program" concept as required above, computers were subsets of processors, because they formed one component (the Arithmetic Logic Unit, or ALU) of a processor. In the current context, the definitions have been reversed. The term *computer* has come to mean "computer system," which includes capabilities not provided by processors. In fact, most modern computers contain several processors that are assigned specific tasks. They are connected by specialized networks. These entities are certainly *systems* in every sense of the word, because they consist of a number of asynchronous functions and activities, all of which contribute to the final result. The further use of the word *computer* will be assumed to be in this latter context. Computers are defined to have the same capabilities as defined for processors, with these additional capabilities:

• Nonmemory input/output capabilities
• System software
• Communications
• Maintenance and recovery functions
• Power supplies
• Cabinetry
• Cooling
• Secondary storage

Although these additional capabilities do not affect the basic processing function, they do considerably improve the ease with which processing capability can be deployed and utilized.

This discussion can be summarized by the following statement: Computers are considered to be complete deployable entities, whereas processors must be embedded in other equipment or facilities in order to be used.

For the purpose of the remainder of this chapter, it will not matter whether computers or processors provide the processing capability required by the network. In fact, both will be required, because every entity in the network must have some form of intelligence in order to participate fully in the management and operations aspects of the network. As an example, physical security might require monitoring of the fire or intrusion alarms of a structure housing some network equipment. The intelligence required for this function could be provided by a small processor attached to the network

177

equipment involved. There would be no need for a stand-alone computer.

SERVICE DEFINITION

The business planning and modeling process, as discussed in connection with the data architecture presented in the previous chapter, also plays a fundamental role in determining the services that will be made available on the network. In addition to specifying the data that is fundamental to the business, the model must specify what use will be made of the data in meeting the business objectives of the enterprise. Generally this takes the form of a set of services (or systems) that are required to support the various organizations of the enterprise. These could include:

- Budgeting
- Financial accounting
- Customer service
- Marketing research
- Order processing
- Human resource planning
- Manufacturing scheduling

Services are defined from a business needs perspective. They must be accomplished or the business will fail! However, the means to be utilized in providing these services are not specified. They may be done manually, handled by computer, done in house, contracted out, or any combination of these. This chapter, of course, assumes that these services will be provided through the information network. Because the exact services needed and defined by the enterprise depend on the characteristics of the enterprise, this particular aspect of the process is not discussed in detail. However, it is assumed that the necessary set of services for the enterprise has been defined through use of the business model.

178

SERVICE ABSTRACTION LEVELS

As discussed in the previous section, a service is initially described in general terms. Only enough detail is present to identify its business purpose and possibly its interactions with other services. Additional detail must be added for two purposes:

- To provide the explicit characteristics of the service and determine how it will be utilized in the business
- To provide the operational characteristics that will allow the service to be implemented.

The abstraction levels of a service can be categorized into three groups: business, design, and implementation. The business group consists only of requirements. The specific levels within the business group are defined by a planning model. Depending on the detail wanted, the business group can have several levels. The design levels and implementation levels are defined by a development methodology. The relationships between the levels can be complex, consisting of combinations of all of the detail-adding processes: decomposition, assignment, augmentation, and discovery. For this discussion, it is not necessary to identify explicitly the various types of level relationships or to differentiate between the different types of levels. Thus, to simplify references to these relationships, the term *decomposition* will be used to indicate any type of relationship between the service abstraction levels. This will adequately separate the service-level relationships from the server-level relationships, which will be described using the standard level relationship terms.

The amount and type of detail in a service is an important input to the server assignment process. In order for this information to be used effectively, a gross quantitative measure of the amount of detail in a service description must be available. This section defines such a measure and discusses some of its major characteristics. It is possible to describe the amount of detail in a service by the following quantities:

- Organization level
- Decomposition level
- Processing specificity

Because each of these is independent of the others, the measure must be represented by a triple (OL, DL, PS). This representation format can result in a large set of possible values. This creates no difficulty, however, because the service generalization measure is needed directly only by the assignment rules, and even then only certain values will be referenced. Changing any of the three parameter values will result in a new service abstraction level.

As an example, consider a budgeting service. The most general condition would be a service at the highest corporate level that has not been decomposed into its component functions and that has had no processing needs specified. The measure of abstraction would then be (0, 0, 0), indicating that no detail has been added to any of the quantities. Although the measure is presented here in numerical form for the purpose of illustration, it will not be used in that form in the selection of the servers, for reasons which will become clearer as the discussion proceeds.

The general service can be made more organizationally specific by referring to a given organizational unit such as the Subsidiary A budgeting program, the Subsidiary B budgeting program, etc. Each of these may require different attributes or have different values associated with them. The generalization measure of the resultant level would then be (1, 0, 0), which would indicate that detail about the organization has been added. This process could be carried down to the department or group level, giving a measure of (5, 0, 0), for example. Although the service would then be organizationally specific, little would be known about what the enterprise considers to be in a budgeting program or what specific processing needs are indicated.

In the same way, the two other aspects could be made more

specific. The budgeting service could be projected into its component functions. As examples, some of these could be:

- Capital needs analysis
- Expense needs analysis
- Personnel needs analysis
- Space needs analysis
- Five-year budget projection
- Report distribution

These functions could exist at any organizational level. Other functions may exist only at certain organizational levels. Corporate borrowing needs analysis, for example, would exist only at the corporate organizational level. The projection as listed above would result in a measure of $(N, 1, 0)$, where N indicates the level of organization used.

Processing specificity refers to the amount of knowledge available about the type of processing necessary for the service decomposition and organizational levels. Processing needs include such items as human intervention requirements, throughput, location, etc. These are defined by an attribute set, and the known values indicate the amount of available knowledge concerning the processing needs. The more is known about these requirements, the less general the service becomes.

Some possible processing attributes are presented in the following list:

- Throughput
- Administrator
- Interaction with other services
- Data types required
- Specific data required
- Community of interest
- Complexity
- Usage characteristics
- Media

TABLE 5.1   PROCESSING ATTRIBUTE VALUE EXAMPLE

Usage Characteristics Attribute	Possible Values
Locations	Single, multiple Geographic proximity
Time of day volume profile	By location By day, month, year
Number of users	By location By day, month, year
Type of users	Clerks Knowledge workers Executives Salesmen Managers

- Confidentiality
- Stability

The associated value sets can be quite complex, as illustrated in table 5.1 for the usage characteristics attribute. For this reason, and because the level of the current discussion does not require that amount of detail, a comprehensive set of values has not been developed for all of these attributes. In production use, the architecture would require appropriate value sets to be made available.

Certain attributes and/or values will be valid only for certain levels of service decomposition. Some organizations rigorously define the levels of decomposition as part of the planning model; others do not. If the levels are rigorously defined, a set of processing attributes/values can be explicitly attached to each level. If the levels are flexible, the attribute/value selection must be done on an empirical basis as the design process proceeds. The architecture does not require one method over the other. Either will produce acceptable results. Additional discussion of the decomposition process is provided in chapter 8, which is concerned with application development.

182

Including the processing need attributes might yield a measure of (N, R, 5), which would indicate the following specific knowledge:

- Level N organization usage
- R levels of service decomposition
- 5 processing attribute values known

The design process thus progresses from a general service definition to a specific one along a rather complex three-dimensional path. The measure of the service detail available at each point of the assignment process will be used by the assignment rules to define the type of server needed in each level of abstraction.

SERVER ARCHITECTURE PHILOSOPHY

The ultimate goal of the server architecture is to insure that network services utilize network processing facilities in the most cost-effective manner possible. Philosophically, this is accomplished by assigning each service component at a given level of abstraction to a processing facility which "best" meets the needs of the component. The "best" fit is determined empirically as a part of the assignment process, using the individual service component and processing facility characteristics. This assignment structure is illustrated in figure 5.1. Theoretically, the assignment could be made in one step as shown. In practice, however, the process is too complex to allow that to happen. As is discussed in the next section, the architecture assignment process consists of multiple phases. Each of these phases must be defined and utilized effectively in order for the overall assignment result to be satisfactory.

As was the case with the various forms of data discussed in the previous chapter, servers can be defined on multiple levels of abstraction. For the purposes of this chapter, four such levels are defined: business, logical, physical, and deployed. All but the deployed level may be subdivided into more narrowly defined levels as necessary. The definition of

183

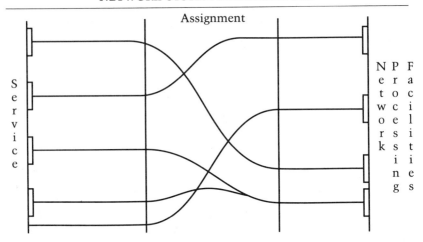

FIGURE 5.1   SERVICE-SERVER ASSIGNMENT

each of the levels is accomplished by means of attributes that determine their resultant characteristics.

The relationship between server levels is usually one of assignment. Each server level is defined independently. Sublevels may also be defined on either an assignment or decomposition basis. The relationship between service levels and server levels is also one of assignment, because the server and service levels are defined independently. A server level can be assigned services specified at different abstraction levels. As is illustrated later, some assignments are better than others.

To understand a server reference, a developer must know the server abstraction level and a measure of the service generalization. Both must be known and characterized before the server can be specified in the required detail. Lack of understanding of this dual need has resulted in a great deal of confusion as to how to characterize a server under a large number of environments and conditions.

The architecture uses the definitions above to help determine the "best" set of deployed servers that can meet the specific service and network design needs and conditions. It is also desirable in many cases to refer to a service or server

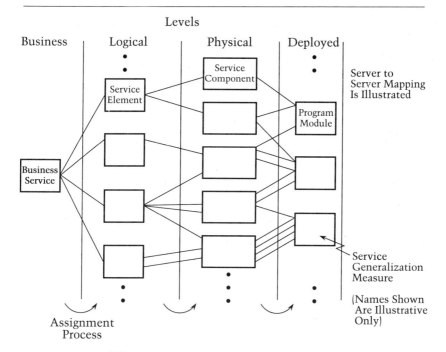

FIGURE 5.2   SERVER SUBARCHITECTURE STRUCTURE

at a relatively high level of generalization or abstraction. The architecture is structured to allow service and/or server access to take place on any of the abstraction levels or generalization conditions. The particular one used in a given design will depend on the specifics of the situation.

SERVER ARCHITECTURE STRUCTURE

The server architecture structure must be designed to guide the assignment process efficiently, as discussed in the previous section. It consists of the four major levels of server abstraction and the assignment rules required to specify the specific servers needed in each level, as shown in figure 5.2. By convention, levels are always drawn so that the information available becomes more specific when going to the right. This is easier to follow than the top-to-bottom orientation of the pyramid structure defined in chapter 1. Also, the lines

185

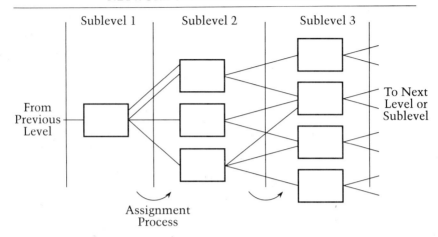

FIGURE 5.3   GENERIC SUBLEVEL STRUCTURE

indicating assignment paths are drawn assuming that the server-to-server assignment process is used. This is defined and justified later in the discussion.

Four levels seems to be the optimum number for the types of systems that use an information network. However, the number of levels is not critical to the assignment process, and a different number could be used if circumstances dictate. Because the assignment rules require that the service generalization measure be known, this aspect is also indicated in the diagram. The exact number of servers at each abstraction level and the location and number of the possible assignments among them are functions of the assignment rules and each individual design decision. This diagram is meant only to communicate the general structure that must emerge from the design process. The determination of the specific servers and assignments is discussed shortly.

Figure 5.3 illustrates the definition of sublevels. The number of sublevels in the structure may range from one to many depending on the needs of the enterprise. More than three or four levels would probably be unwieldy, however. All levels except the deployed level may be divided into additional sublevels if desired or if dictated by the design needs. As before,

TABLE 5.2   REFERENCE CONTEXT VALUES

Value	Abstraction Level
Business service	Business server
Dominant characteristics	Logical server
Product characteristics	Physical server
Deployed characteristics	Deployed server

the lines indicating the assignment process merely identify possibilities. Additional detail concerning sublevels is provided in the detailed discussion of each server level of abstraction.

SERVER ABSTRACTION LEVELS

The four server abstraction levels are defined with a single attribute. This attribute is called the *reference context,* and its values are listed in table 5.2, along with the abstraction levels they define. The attribute is called *reference context* because the abstraction level of a server is dependent on the type of references made to it. Business servers are defined in terms of the service they provide to the enterprise. Logical servers are defined in terms of one or more dominant characteristics, which may be technical, business, or a combination thereof. Physical servers are defined in terms of product characteristics (enterprise standards). Deployed servers are defined in terms of those computers or other processors which actually exist or are scheduled to exist on the network (manufacturer, exact location, size, capacity, etc.).

In the following presentations, attributes and associated value sets are illustrated for each level. Because these attributes and value sets are somewhat lengthy and in a few cases quite complex, their meanings cannot be discussed in detail.

This lack of detail will in no way affect the comprehensibility of the overall presentation.

Business Servers

As stated previously, this chapter assumes that all of the required business services will be provided to the users through the information network. In order for this to occur, the services must utilize network servers to provide the required processing power. The assignment process begins with the business server level.

Because business services are usually specified very generally, the specification of the required servers initially can be on a one-to-one basis. A business server will be assigned to each general business service identified. The differentiation between the service and the server on which it resides in the network is necessary in order to distinguish between the function and the means of providing it. The explicit service definition is also necessary so that a basis can be established on which to begin the assignment process that results in the selection of appropriate servers in different abstraction levels.

In accordance with the above discussion, business servers are defined in terms of the particular service they provide to the business. Examples of these servers might include:

- Financial accounting server
- Budgeting server
- Customer service server
- Marketing research server
- Order processing server
- Human resource planning server
- Manufacturing scheduling server
- Purchasing server
- Planning server

Note that the servers encompass both data and processing functions. They are not applications, however, nor are they

TABLE 5.3 BUSINESS SERVER ATTRIBUTES AND VALUES

Attribute	Allowable Values
Relationship	Connections with other business servers
Ownership	Organization with administrative responsibility
Scope	Client organizations using server
Security	High, medium, low
Cost recovery	Flat fee, no charge, usage sensitive, allocation
Access permission	Application, by user, by terminal
Information	Type and specific items

databases, although both of these, as well as communications facilities, are used in the server(s) to provide the associated service. Individual business servers are defined by a set of attributes whose values determine the characteristics associated with them. The attributes of the business server, along with the applicable value sets, are shown in table 5.3. Remember that these attributes are for the server — *not* the service. The service attributes were presented earlier in the chapter. A business server must be characterized for each business level that will utilize the service.

The characteristics of the business server are derived from the characteristics of the defining service. No attempt is made to define a standard set of business servers with specific characteristics, as will be done later with the remaining levels. Because of the generality of the specification of both service and server at the business level, there is no need to restrict the allowable characteristics.

The business server level may contain multiple sublevels if the original service is decomposed into component services that are still at the business level (that is, if no operational detail has been added). For the budgeting example, the component services might include:

189

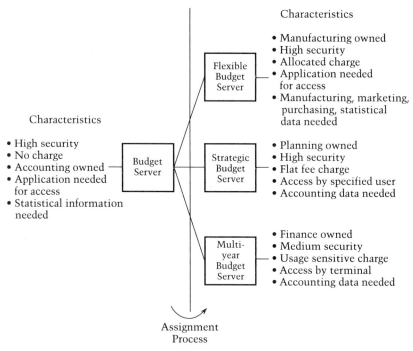

FIGURE 5.4 BUSINESS SUBLEVEL DECOMPOSITION EXAMPLE

- Flexible budgeting
- Strategic budgeting
- Multiyear budgeting

These services are at the business level but are clearly parts of the overall budgeting service. They would thus be placed on a one-to-one basis with a business-level server. Figure 5.4 diagrams the result of this business-level partition. Also indicated are some specific values that could be assigned to each sublevel. These values are taken from those which were shown in table 5.3. As illustrated in the diagram, the assignment at the business level is straightforward, because the service (original and decomposed) and server remain in a one-to-one relationship.

Logical Servers

Logical servers are generally referenced by their dominant characteristic(s). The referencing characteristic may be anything that can be associated with a server, including:

- Network connection
- Type of service contained
- Using organization level
- Using organization
- Major function
- Processing power
- Media processed
- Computer architecture
- Coverage
- Location type

Using this definition, it is easy to understand the reasoning behind some of the popular server reference names shown in the following list:

Simple characterization:

- LAN server
- Database server
- Host server
- Application server
- Department server
- CAD/CAM server
- Videotex server
- Audio server
- Image server
- Personal server
- Knowledge server
- Supercomputer server
- Switch server
- Gateway server

Compound characterization:

- LAN database server
- Engineering CAD server
- Host application server
- Network management knowledge server
- Department word processing server
- Backbone host document server
- Remote access security server

The number of possibilities is extremely large, but the number defined in a particular enterprise should be kept as small as possible. Otherwise, the assignment process will become more complex and difficult than necessary.

Regardless of their reference characteristics, logical servers have a significant number of attributes that are used to determine the type of processing needed and to define specific logical server types that will be used in systems developed by the enterprise. The values of these attributes determine the processing characteristics of the logical server types selected.

The attributes and associated values of the logical servers are shown in table 5.4. Without further restriction and definition, the number of possibilities is too large to be useful. The quantity of logical servers that are available for an enterprise must be held to an acceptable level. An example of a set of logical servers that could be used by the enterprise for all of their systems is presented in table 5.5. These are defined in accordance with overall business needs.

Multiple sublevels can be defined for the logical level if desired. These sublevels would contain servers with different reference generalizations. This concept was originally illustrated by figure 5.3. Figure 5.5 shows the concept specifically for the logical level, including some obvious assignment paths. Multiple logical levels are not used often but can simplify the assignment process when a large number of logical servers must be defined.

In order for the service to be assigned to the best set of logical servers, the service must be decomposed beyond the

TABLE 5.4   LOGICAL SERVER ATTRIBUTES AND
VALUE SETS

Attribute	Value Set
Network connectivity	Backbone
	LAN
	Vendor specific
	Public telephone
	Public packet
	Proprietary
	Bridge
Data type	Primary
	Secondary
	Derived
	Base
Processing type	Batch
	Transaction
	On-line
	Real-time
	Scientific
	Inferencing
Environment	100% availability
	Attended
	Unattended
Resources available	Operating system
	DBMS
	Object-oriented
	Relational
	Network
	Hierarchical
	TP monitor
	Graphics packages
	User interface
Scope (community of interest)	
Media processed	Voice
	Image
	Full motion video
	Compressed video
	Graphics
	Data
Class	Network
	Application

TABLE 5.4 (CONTINUED)

Attribute	Value Set
Range	Universal Multipurpose Specialized Single function
Access (from other servers)	Universal Restricted Single point
Location type	Data center Office Equipment room

strictly business-oriented decomposition discussed in the previous section. The decomposition process must produce component functions that are at a level suitable for determining their operational characteristics. Continuing with the budget service example, assume that some functions that result from the decomposition of the service include the following:

• Inflation analysis
• Graphical results presentation
• Multiple organization integration
• Comparative analysis

These functions are now at the proper level for specifying values at the logical level for the attributes. After this is done, the service components can be used to specify the particular logical servers needed through the application of the assignment rules. This aspect of the assignment process is discussed later.

Physical Servers

Physical servers are generally referenced by a product name. This product could be a computer type, system software,

TABLE 5.5   LOGICAL SERVER DEFINITIONS

Server Type	Definitions
Host server	Backbone connectivity required Not connected to a LAN Not scientific or inferencing processing Attended 80% available Hierarchical database resource TP monitor resource Graphics resource No user interface resource Community of interest enterprise-wide Accessed only from other logical servers
Department server	Backbone connectivity allowed LAN connectivity allowed Attended Database resource available Community of interest less than enterprise-wide No user interface resource
Scientific calculation server	Backbone connectivity not allowed Unattended Scientific or inferencing processing Base data not resident 100% availability
LAN document distribution server	Backbone connectivity not allowed Unattended Single task unit assigned Proprietary network connectivity Batch processing not allowed
Personnel server	Backbone connectivity not allowed Proprietary connectivity not allowed Primary data not allowed 100% availability User interface resource available Individual community of interest

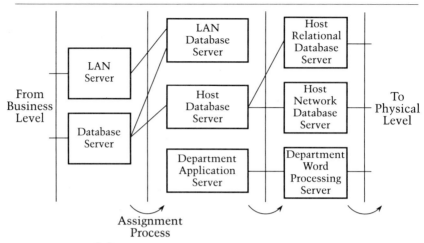

Assignment
Process

FIGURE 5.5   LOGICAL SUBLEVEL STRUCTURE EXAMPLE

major function, or a combination. These references could include the following:

- UNIX-based server
- IBM 3090 computer running MVS and CICS
- DEC VAX running VMS
- PC running DOS
- Intel 80386 processor
- Computer with Oracle DBMS
- PC with Multimate word processor

Although the names reference products, they do not refer to specific deployed entities. They are used only as standards (albeit very specific ones) that can be used in the development of systems. Although systems are developed that use these product standards, considerable latitude is still available in the deployment process, because any installed computer or processor that meets the selected product standards can be used as required. This, of course, includes clones, plug-compatible models, etc.

As examples of the selection and definition of the physical level server, table 5.6 contains selected attributes and associated values. Using these attributes and values, table 5.7

TABLE 5.6   PHYSICAL SERVER ATTRIBUTE VALUES

Attribute	Values
Owner	Network owner External information provider System operator Third-party lessor Other
Physical location	Data center Office Central office
Communication protocols	SNA (LU 2, PU 2) SNA (LU 6.2, PU 2.1) DECNET X.25 Expand Proprietary Async
Power	MIPS Storage capacity
Operating system	UNIX MS-DOS MVS Other
Vendor	IBM Amdahl NAS DEC Other
Class	Supercomputer Mainframe Minicomputer Workstation

shows the definition of a set of physical level servers that will be used by the enterprise. Based on its own unique experience and system development needs, every enterprise must select its own set of physical servers. The relationship of the selected physical servers to computers and processors contained in a standard product list will be discussed later.

TABLE 5.7 STANDARD COMPUTER PRODUCTS

Server	Definition
Mainframe–IBM 3090	Located in data center SNA (PU 4,5) Greater than 10 MIPS Greater than 10 GBYTES primary storage Greater than 400 GBYTES secondary storage MVS operating system DB2 DBMS CICS
MiniSupercomputer–Sequent Balance	TCP/IP communications Office location Oracle DBMS Unix operating system Parallel processors
Minicomputer–VAX 8500	DECNET PU 2.1, LU 6.2 communications Office location Oracle DBMS VMS operating system No operator needed
Minicomputer–Tandem T32	Expand Office location Fault-tolerant architecture
Minicompuer–TI Explorer	KEE Shell Lisp-based DECNET connectivity TCP/IP connectivity Single user
Personal–IBM PC	MS DOS operating system DECNET connectivity ASYNC connectivity TCP/IP connectivity Single user
Personal–IBM PC	UNIX operating system DECNET connectivity ASYNC connectivity TCP/IP connectivity Multiple user

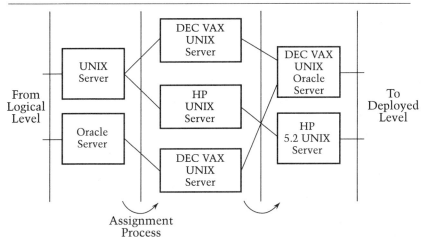

FIGURE 5.6   PHYSICAL SUBLEVEL STRUCTURE EXAMPLE

As with the other abstraction levels, the physical layer may also be divided into sublevels. The servers would become more specific in terms of product as the sublevels progressed from left to right. Figure 5.6 illustrates this concept.

The service must be more completely specified than that needed on the logical level in order to allow a selection of physical level servers. The generalization measure allows this specification to take place in two ways: through additional decomposition levels or by assigning values to additional attributes for each service function. The particular method chosen depends on the specifics of the situation.

Deployed Servers

The final step in server assignment is to determine which existing or planned servers with the proper product characteristics can be used most efficiently for the deployment of the service. After any necessary characteristics of the service have been accommodated, this assignment problem becomes an economic issue having to do with computer and communications capacity. The arrangement that provides the least overall operating and/or capital cost would be utilized. This

199

is a present-worth analysis that may be complex if the number of options is large. However, the amount of money involved in such a deployment situation is generally large enough to make the effort worthwhile.

Such an analysis may also include moving other deployed services from one deployed server to another in order to minimize the cost over all services. This is an extremely difficult problem whose solution can only be approximated.

Some of the communications-oriented aspects of this assignment problem are discussed in the next chapter. Discussion of approaches to the overall minimization problem is beyond the scope of this presentation.

ASSIGNMENT PRINCIPLES

The process of converting a server definition at one level (or sublevel) to those at a lower level is by assignment. Because specific servers, at any level, can be selected only as the result of the needs of a service, assignment depends directly on the service involved. The large number of assignment possibilities and the severe economic penalties that could result from the selection of the wrong set of servers requires that the process be tightly controlled. The architecture provides for this control through a mechanism called *assignment rules*. Although these are the same type of architectural principles that have been developed from the structure definitions, assignment rules are presented somewhat differently. Their close association with the architecture structure requires that they be introduced during the structure discussion. This does not change the basic character of the principles, however.

The philosophy behind the assignment process is to optimally match the service specified by its generalization measure to the servers in each of the levels. This requires that the generalization measure of the service become more specific with each assignment. The matching process is controlled by the rules. If the rules are selected and executed

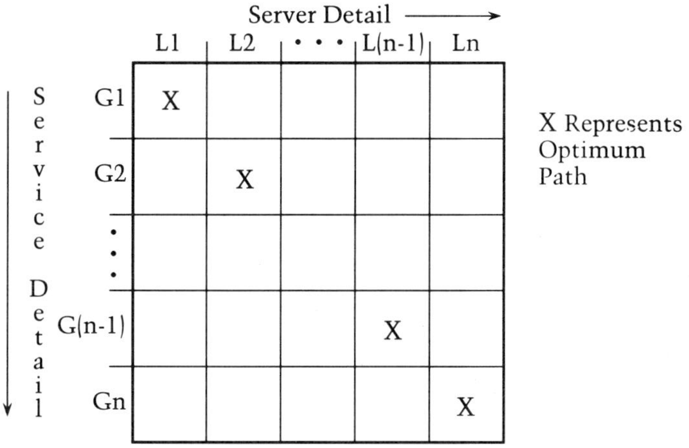

		Server Detail $\longrightarrow$				
		L1	L2	• • •	L(n-1)	Ln
S e r v i c e	G1	X				
	G2		X			
	. . .					
D e t a i l	G(n-1)				X	
	Gn					X

X Represents
Optimum
Path

FIGURE 5.7   SERVICE-SERVER ASSIGNMENT MATRIX

properly, the match will be a good one. If not, the match will be poor. Selection of the rules thus becomes the critical aspect of this section of the architecture. One qualitative metric by which the assignment rules can be evaluated is shown in figure 5.7. An optimum match requires that the server abstraction levels be consistent with the service generalization measure (that is, that the assignment proceed along the diagonal of the matrix). If the rules do not enforce this requirement, the match will be suboptimum.

Unfortunately, in much current practice, the diagonal assignment requirement is violated consistently. This is represented by the diagram in figure 5.8. The upper and right arrows illustrate the case where the servers are assigned without decomposing the service. This can happen for a variety of reasons but usually results because a computer has some spare capacity, and a high service generalization level is mapped to a physical computer without proceeding through the intermediate server levels (for example, the budget server is mapped to a deployed computer on the third floor of the headquarters building). Although this may indeed satisfy the needs of the service, the result may well be unsatisfactory

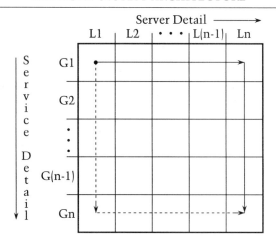

FIGURE 5.8 NONOPTIMUM ASSIGNMENT PATHS

because the needs of the service do not match the character-istics of the computer selected.

The left and lower arrows illustrate the case where the service is decomposed completely without any assignment to servers. This can also occur for a variety of reasons but usually results when it is required by company or client policy. Over-emphasis on extensive documentation or rigorous adherence to many of the current software decomposition techniques can easily produce this type of approach. Under these condi-tions, the decomposition may be such that assignment to a server at any level becomes difficult, because the character-istics of the derived component are not functionally separated enough to allow assignment to a server that closely matches the overall needs.

As an example, a budget system component produced by a decomposition process that does not consider the server as-signment function until the process is complete may require both direct user access and connection to the backbone net-work. From the server definitions utilized in the budget ex-ample, it can be seen that there is no defined server type at any level that will allow a suitable assignment to occur. The

TABLE 5.8   SERVICE GENERALIZATION MEASURE FOR LOGICAL
SERVER ASSIGNMENT

Level	Definition
Organization level	Specification of all organizational levels that will utilize the service
Decomposition level	The service must be decomposed into components in sufficient detail to uniquely assign each component to a logical server
Processing level	Values must be assigned for all of the logical level attributes for each component

above discussion again illustrates the need to traverse the diagonal of the server-service level matrix. This is the only way in which an optimum assignment can be obtained in a consistent and demonstrable manner.

As was discussed previously, the business server level requires only the highest generalization of the service involved. The logical server level requires a service measure that indicates a more specific characterization. The three parts of the measure must be defined to the extent shown in table 5.8 for an optimum logical server assignment to be made. If any or all of the three parts are not known to the level of detail indicated, an assignment may still be made but the fit may not be as good as possible. This reduced detail may be sufficient for initial cost estimates or other planning purposes, however.

Enough background has now been presented so that the assignment process and the associated rules may be defined in detail. Assignment can be accomplished in two fundamental ways. These are illustrated in figures 5.9 and 5.10. Figure 5.9 illustrates the server-to-server assignment method. In this method, a server at one level is mapped to a set of servers at the next level. This is accomplished by the following process.

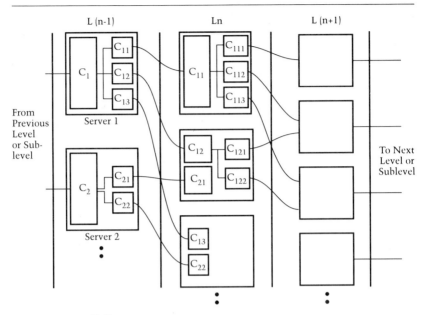

FIGURE 5.9   SERVER-TO-SERVER ASSIGNMENT METHOD

1. Decompose the service assigned to the higher level server.

2. Match the resulting components to find the best fit among lower level servers.

3. Assign the higher level server to the identified lower level servers.

4. Assign the components to the identified lower level servers.

Figure 5.10 illustrates the service-to-server assignment method. In this method, the service is mapped directly to a set of servers at a specific level. This is accomplished by the following process:

1. Decompose the previous service level.

2. Match the resulting components to find the best servers on the level of interest.

3. Assign the components to the identified servers.

204

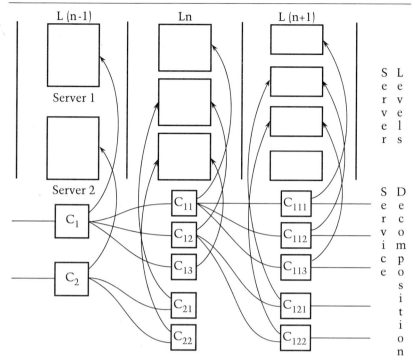

FIGURE 5.10   SERVICE-TO-SERVER ASSIGNMENT METHOD

Either of these methods can be used as a basis for the assignment process. I prefer the former, because there is a closer association between the service level and the server level, which will tend to enforce the diagonal assignment presented previously. In addition, the server-to-server method tends to force a service decomposition better suited to the server-assignment process because of the closer integration. For these reasons, the server-to-server method is used for further discussion of the assignment process.

The following list shows examples of business server to logical server assignment rules:

- A business server containing a service component with any of the following characteristics
  - Size > 1 Meg
  - Throughput > 10 messages/sec

205

- High security
- Data concurrency = 0

and not having the following characteristics

- Scientific or inferencing processing
- Close coupling to central office equipment
- Department or group organizational level

is assigned to a HOST server.

- A business server containing a service component with scientific or inferencing processing is assigned to a SCIENTIFIC CALCULATION server.
- A business server containing a service component with an individual community of interest is assigned to a PERSONAL server.
- A business server containing a service component with a required human intervention characteristic is assigned to a HOST server or a DEPARTMENT server.
- A business server containing a service component with a characteristic requiring it to be close to equipment or an activity center is assigned to a DEPARTMENT server.

Examples of logical server to physical server assignment rules are given in the following list:

- Host server components can be mapped only to mainframe processors.
- Department server components can be mapped to mainframe processors if a business reason exists to do so; otherwise they must be mapped to a minicomputer processor.
- Personal server components can be mapped to PC, minicomputer, or host products, with the preference in the preceding order.
- Preference should be given to products currently deployed by the selecting organization.
- If a PC currently exists, no other PC product can be selected unless the original PC is eliminated from deployment.
- All other assignments are possible.

Notice that all of these rules are in terms of the service generalization measure. The assignment rules can be simple, as illustrated in the examples, or they can be complex, depending on the needs of the enterprise. In general, the more complex the rules, the better the match can become.

The budget service identified previously is used here to provide an example of the architecture's required assignment procedure.

ASSIGNMENT EXAMPLE

To simplify the assignment example, the following assumptions are made:

- Only one organizational level is involved.
- There are no server sublevels.
- A limited number of service functions will be mapped.

These assumptions do not affect the explanation of the process but do shorten the amount of space required.

Initial Assignment

The budget service is assigned to the budget server. The known characteristics of each are shown in table 5.9. There is, by definition, a close match between them.

Level 1 Service Decomposition

The service is then decomposed into a set of components suitable for use in the business to logical server assignment process. The subset identified previously will be used. Characteristics for each of these components are shown in table 5.10. After the decomposition, there is a mismatch between the generalization level of the service and the abstraction level of the server. To get back on the diagonal, the server level that contains the decomposed functions must change.

TABLE 5.9   BUDGET EXAMPLE SERVICE AND SERVER
CHARACTERISTICS (HIGHEST LEVEL)

Attribute	Value
Service Characteristics:	
Administrator	Strategic planning
Interaction with other services	Financial accounting, manufacturing planning
Data types required	Base data
Community of interest	Management through first level
Usage characteristics	Middle of fiscal year
Confidentiality	Highly confidential
Stability	Complete change every cycle
Server Characteristics:	
Relationship	Financial accounting, manufacturing planning
Ownership	Strategic planning
Scope	All management through first level
Security	High
Cost recovery	No charge
Access permission	By application
Information	Previous budget, current operating results, sales projections

Logical Server Assignment

The servers at the new level are found by applying the business to logical server assignment rules previously discussed. This results in the logical assignment shown in table 5.11. Optimally, the assignment should be made by minimizing some metric that quantifies the difference between the service level and the server abstraction level. Currently, no such

208

TABLE 5.10   BUDGET EXAMPLE SERVICE COMPONENT
CHARACTERISTICS (LEVEL 1)

Component	Characteristics
Inflation Analysis	
Throughput	Low
Administrator	Strategic planning
Interaction with other services	All budgeting
Data types required	Base data, outside databases
Community of interest	Strategic planning
Complexity	High
Usage characteristics	One month in the middle of the fiscal year
Confidentiality	Low
Stability	Low
Graphical Results Presentation	
Throughput	Low
Administrator	Office automation
Interaction with other services	All analysis
Data types required	Transaction data
Specific data required	Budget analysis output
Community of interest	All management
Complexity	Medium
Usage characteristics	One month in the middle of the fiscal year
Media	Graphics
Confidentiality	High
Stability	High

TABLE 5.10 (CONTINUED)

Component	Characteristics
Multiple Organization Integration	
Throughput	High
Administrator	Strategic planning
Interaction with other services	All budgeting
Data types required	Transaction data
Specific data required	Department results
Community of interest	Strategic planning
Complexity	Medium
Usage characteristics	One month in the middle of the fiscal year
Confidentiality	High
Stability	High
Comparative Analysis	
Throughput	Medium
Administrator	Strategic planning
Interaction with other services	Results
Data types required	Transaction data
Specific data required	Results
Community of interest	Strategic planning
Complexity	Inferencing
Usage characteristics	One month in the middle of the fiscal year
Confidentiality	High
Stability	Low

TABLE 5.11   BUDGET EXAMPLE LOGICAL SERVER
ASSIGNMENT

Service Component	Server Assigned
Inflation analysis	Host
Graphical results presentation	Personal
Multiple organization integration	Host
Comparative analysis	Scientific calculation

metric has been defined, and the interpretation of the closeness of the fit is an empirical process. The degree of difference
that could result from different people or organizations performing the interpretation is directly dependent on the intelligibility, number, and detail of the assignment rules. For this
reason, a great deal of time and effort should be expended by
the organization in determining the rules that best fit its
needs.

Level 2 Service Decomposition

The level 1 components of the service are then further decomposed into a more detailed set of components suitable for
use in the logical to physical server assignment process. Characteristics for each of these are shown in table 5.12. After the
decomposition, there is again a mismatch between the generalization level of the service and the abstraction level of
the server. To return to the diagonal, the server level that
contains the newly decomposed functions must change.

Physical Server Assignment

The servers at the new level are found by applying the logical
server to physical server assignment rules discussed previously. Taking into account the above discussion on the as-

TABLE 5.12   BUDGET EXAMPLE SERVICE COMPONENT
CHARACTERISTICS (LEVEL 2)

Component	Characteristics
Inflation Analysis	
Throughput	Low
Administrator	Strategic planning
Interaction with other services	All budgeting
Data types required	Base data, outside databases
Specific data required	Financial, marketing, sales, manufacturing, databases
Community of interest	Strategic planning
Complexity	High
Usage characteristics	One month in the middle of the fiscal year
Confidentiality	Low
Stability	Low
Graphical Results Presentation	
Throughput	Low
Administrator	Office automation
Interaction with other services	All analysis
Data types required	Transaction data
Specific data required	Budget analysis output
Community of interest	All management
Complexity	Medium
Usage characteristics	One month in the middle of the fiscal year
Media	Graphics
Confidentiality	High
Stability	High
Multiple Organization Integration	
Throughput	High
Administrator	Strategic planning
Interaction with other services	All budgeting
Data types required	Transaction data
Specific data required	Department results
Community of interest	Strategic planning
Complexity	Medium
Usage characteristics	One month in the middle of the fiscal year
Confidentiality	High
Stability	High
Comparative Analysis	
Throughput	Medium
Administrator	Strategic planning
Interaction with other services	Results
Data types required	Transaction data
Specific data required	Results
Community of interest	Strategic planning
Complexity	Inferencing
Usage characteristics	One month in the middle of the fiscal year
Confidentiality	High
Stability	Low

TABLE 5.13 BUDGET EXAMPLE PHYSICAL SERVER ASSIGNMENT

Service Component	Server Assigned
Inflation analysis	DEC 8600
Graphical results presentation	IBM PC with MS DOS
Multiple organization integration	IBM 3090
Comparative analysis	TI Explorer

signment process, this results in the physical assignment shown in table 5.13.

Although the ideal situation would be for the selected products to also be on the standard product list, this does not necessarily have to be the case. Nonstandard products could be on the selected products list if the rules clearly define when a nonstandard product could be used.

Deployed Server Assignment

This example will not be continued to the deployed server level of abstraction until the next chapter, because the communications aspects must also be considered in that part of the assignment. The capacity of each deployed processor and the capacity of the communications paths that connect them must both be considered in the physical server to deployed server assignment process. As previously mentioned, there are significant economic considerations in this part of the assignment architecture, but because of the amount of detail involved they cannot be considered in depth.

SERVER ARCHITECTURE PRINCIPLES

The following statements are the principles, other than those associated with the assignment process, that are derived from the structures defined for the server architecture. In keeping with the practice established for this section, the principles are grouped according to the components of the architecture.

Although service decomposition is an integral part of this architecture, many of the principles relating to the decomposition process are presented in chapter 8, which deals with application development.

I. Strategies
  A. Global
    1. Architectural
      a. The servers will be selected in accordance with the architecture.
      b. The selection of the servers will occur concurrently with the execution of the development methodology.
      c. Selection of the appropriate network servers for any level will be the responsibility of the network engineering organization.
      d. Servers controlled by external information providers must conform to a specific set of enterprise policies defined for this relationship.
    2. Design
      a. All physical servers and/or integrated products that are identified as candidates for selection must be on the approved product list.
      b. Identification of new physical servers and/or integrated products designed to meet a need that is not served effectively by existing candidates must first be qualified for the approved product list.
      c. A heterogeneous set of servers is desirable and encouraged.
      d. Servers must be synergetic with the communications architecture.
    3. Operational
      a. Before any product server that has no deployed

equivalent can be assigned permanently, an extensive test program must be completed successfully.

B. Levels of Abstraction
  1. Architectural
    a. The fewest number of abstraction levels that still meet the needs of the enterprise should be used. (The four major ones must always be present.)
  2. Design
    a. The number of servers defined for each level should decrease as the amount of detail in the level increases.
    b. All intermediate and final results of the assignment process as it concerns data shall be stored in the dictionary/directory in a self-defining form.
  3. Operational
    a. No server shall be placed on the network unless it results from applying the concepts of the server architecture.

C. Assignment
  1. Architectural
    a. Server-to-server assignment will be used.
    b. Application of the level-to-level assignment rules should be mechanized through the use of artificial intelligence so that there is (1) consistency and (2) a way to manage the complexity.
    c. The level-to-level assignment rules should be as complete as possible even though the complexity becomes great.
  2. Design
    a. The development of server-to-server assignment rules are the responsibility of the network engineering organization.

        b. Server-to-server assignment rules must be approved by the network/system implementation organization and the network management organization.

   D. Service Decomposition
      1. Architectural
         a. Any well-established decomposition technique may be used, but object-oriented techniques are encouraged.

II. Standards
   A. Global
      1. Architectural
         a. All server selection candidates at any abstraction level will be declared to be enterprise standards.
         b. Server standards should follow international or other industry standards when possible.
   B. Levels of Abstraction
      1. Architectural
         a. A standard set of attributes and associated values will be developed for each level.
         b. A standard set of server selection candidates will be developed for each level.
   C. Service Decomposition
      1. Architectural
         a. The decomposition technique should follow an established industry standard.
         b. If desirable, an enterprise-standard decomposition technique may be established that differs from other published procedures.

III. Guidelines
   A. Global
      1. Architectural
         a. Enterprise-defined guidelines should follow accepted industry practices whenever possible.
      2. Design

      a. Server selection candidates for all abstraction levels should follow good engineering practice.

B. Levels of Abstraction
  1. Architectural
     a. Once defined, the levels should not change from system to system.
     b. Server selection candidates should be stable. Changes to the list should be minimized.

C. Assignment
  1. Architectural
     a. Once defined, level-to-level assignment rules should not change from system to system.
     b. Server-to-server assignment rules should be stable. Changes to the rules should be minimized.
  2. Design
     a. Experts in the enterprise, as well as outside consultants, when necessary, should be asked to contribute to the server-to-server assignment rules.
     b. A procedure to verify and validate changes to the server-to-server assignment rules should be developed.

D. Service Decomposition
  1. Architectural
     a. Decomposition should be a joint effort between the network engineering, implementation, and service definition organizations.
     b. Decomposition should always be accomplished using the same procedure. It should not vary from system to system if possible.

IV. Rules
  A. Global
    1. Architectural
       a. Documentation for the entire assignment procedure will be in machine-readable form.

    b. No system will begin the deployment step of the development methodology until the assignment process is completed.

  2. Operational

    a. All changes to the server architecture must be approved by the network engineering, implementation, and technology management organizations.

B. Levels of Abstraction

  1. Architectural

    a. The number of candidate servers in the logical level will be between 10 and 20.

    b. The number of servers in the physical level will be between 5 and 12.

C. Assignment

  1. Architectural

    a. Changes in the server-to-server assignment rules will be approved by the technology management organization.

D. Service Decomposition

  1. Architectural

    a. Changes to the service attributes and associated values must be approved as part of the strategic planning process.

SUMMARY AND CONCLUSIONS

Server selection and deployment is a misunderstood process in most development organizations. This is one of the reasons that distributed and cooperative processing seem so hard to implement and operate. The tendency is to go directly to deployed computers without proceeding through a formal assignment process. The causes of this tendency are many and varied.

First, many software development organizations have not yet emotionally left the world where the users are connected to a mainframe and receive all of their services from that one

218

source. They immediately assume that the closest mainframe is where their software will reside.

Second, the process is complicated and time-consuming and requires considerable resources to do well. A belief exists that the results are not worth the effort.

Third, in order to provide estimates of development cost to the customer before a software development project is started, some organizations select the physical or deployed computer before any decomposition work is started.

Finally, there is a lack of understanding as to what can be done to match the computer to the service. Some organizations are simply not aware of the possibilities in this area.

Although there is a great proliferation of servers in all of the lower three abstraction levels, the selection of those which fit the needs of the organization most closely can be handled efficiently by using an architecture similar to the one presented in this chapter. Without a selection technique, many organizations find themselves in the position of having "one of everything" as servers in their network. This can result in a great deal of inefficiency, with attendant losses in time and money.

If servers are selected in accordance with the architecture, the enabling development methodology, and the needs of the enterprise, the result can be a significant competitive advantage. Network and system development represents large expenditures, and with the growing strategic importance of networks and systems for many firms, saving even a little can return large dividends.

S I X

COMMUNICATIONS ARCHITECTURE

INTRODUCTION

The information network cannot exist without a comprehensive set of communications facilities. *Communications*, in the sense the term is used in this chapter, is the transmission of items of intelligence from one server to another by means of the information network transmission paths. Because items of intelligence and servers are defined on a number of levels of abstraction, the communication facilities must also be defined in a similar manner. This will be accomplished architecturally by establishing abstraction levels using structures similar in nature to those used to establish the abstraction levels of servers. As will be noted, however, there are significant differences in the ways each is defined and used.

The communication attributes include the specification of the familiar layered systems that have been used for a number of years to define data communications. Although layered systems are useful for defining certain aspects of the communication process, they are only a part of the total architecture needed to define the communications aspects of the information network. However, because of their historical importance in communications and their usefulness in other aspects of system design, some discussion of layered systems is provided.

Communications processes cannot be separated from the networks on which they are defined. In fact, communications paths and servers are the base components that form the information network. Because of the amount of material inherent in each of these components, they must be discussed separately. For this reason, the discussion of servers in the previous chapter concentrated on the non-network aspects of the servers. Servers as network elements (in the communications sense) are covered in this chapter as integral parts of the communication system. In order to differentiate between the two uses, the term *node* will be used for the server functions that enable network communications to take place.

The close connection between the communications aspects of networks and the networks themselves makes it difficult, if not impossible, to separate the two. The attributes of communications and the attributes of communication networks cannot be discussed independently of one another. In addition, the term *communications architecture* has become attached to the layered systems mentioned above, and some confusion would result if that term were used to refer to the overall network communications architecture. For these reasons, the term *network communications architecture* or simply *network architecture* will be used to indicate the broader aspects of communications considered in this chapter.

The structures and processes defined as part of this architecture are quite complex and may take considerable study and thought to understand and utilize. This complexity is a direct result of the current chaotic state of communications and networking as applied to information systems. Computer companies, telephone companies, other common carriers, transmission equipment companies, government agencies, the judicial system, large users, and standards bodies are all looking at the problem from their particular vantage point and attempting to define the solution in that narrow context. The result is a variation of the Tower of Babel.

This presentation is an attempt to keep the good and throw away the bad among all of these entities, thus developing an overall framework that can be used to explain the global nature of communications and its interaction with the other aspects of the information network. This must be accomplished without doing violence to the concepts promoted by one or more of the above organizations that have found some acceptance and use.

The main need is for a unifying structure against which various concepts, direction statements, technologies, costs, etc. can be measured to generate a comparative analysis that has some quantitative content. Although the architecture specified in this chapter is certainly one way to provide this type of guidance, other approaches probably could be used as well.

Before the architecture structure and principles can be defined, a number of general concepts need to be defined. As with previous chapters, this chapter relies heavily on the concepts of pyramid structures discussed in chapter 1. If necessary, review the information in that presentation before proceeding.

UNIVERSAL CONNECTIVITY

It has been observed that in modern communications, "everything is a network." This is true in the sense that most telecommunications facilities are tied together in some fashion. Actions that would seem to affect only one set of facilities frequently have undesirable side effects in areas that are not supposed to be directly associated. As an example, consider the tragedy that affected a telephone switching office. In 1988, a fire destroyed the Illinois Bell Central office in Hinsdale, Illinois. The public telephone service for the surrounding area was disrupted, as would be expected. In addition to this problem, however, a large number of *private networks* were also compromised. This was a totally unexpected result for a large number of organizations that thought designing and implementing their own networks would protect them from adverse events such as fire or storms.

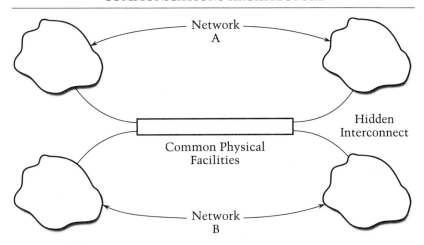

FIGURE 6.1   UNINTENDED GEOGRAPHICAL INTERCONNECTION

Even though their networks were not electrically or optically connected to the public telephone network, they were geographically connected in the sense that they utilized the same cables and terminating facilities, as illustrated in figure 6.1. This type of geographical connection is likely to increase as transmission equipment with higher and higher capacities is deployed. The higher capacity can be utilized economically only by combining traffic from a large number of users. Few organizations have the financial depth and traffic needs required to build their network from facilities that are completely separate from those utilized in other networks. In fact, the deployment of the Integrated Services Digital Network (ISDN) by telephone companies throughout the world will accelerate this sharing process. Further enhancement of the shared facility concept will result from the development of "intelligent networks" that provide extensive user services and control over the communication process. Using this type of system, it is possible to create a logical private network from public facilities. The geographical connection remains, however.

In many cases, proprietary networks are being connected deliberately to gain efficiency in transferring information be-

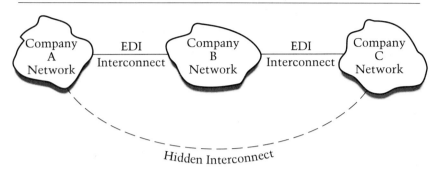

FIGURE 6.2   UNINTENDED NETWORK INTERCONNECTION

tween organizations that have a business relationship. One result of this need is reflected in the increased use of Electronic Data Interchange (EDI) systems to transmit commercial documents between suppliers, customers, and internal departments of an organization. The following scenario, illustrated in figure 6.2, shows how this can result in unknown and perhaps unwanted interconnections.

> Assume that Company A and Company B decide to connect their proprietary networks together in order to make the transfer of orders and invoices easier and faster. Now suppose that Company B and Company C also agree to interconnect their networks for the same purpose and that neither Company A nor Company C is aware of the existence of the other's relationship to Company B. In a real sense, the networks of Company A and Company C have now been connected, although neither of them is aware of that fact.

What, if any, problems can result from explicit interconnections of multiple EDI networks? Consider the next scenario:

> Company A orders 10,000 widgets from Company B through the network. Company B has an inventory program that takes an incoming order, calculates the amount of raw material involved, and automatically places orders

224

for the material from its suppliers (for example, Company C). Those suppliers, in turn, perform the same process. Orders begin flying throughout the network.

Result 1:

Everything works as planned. Company A gets its widgets and all of the suppliers in the chain replenish their raw materials and begin manufacturing replacement items. Everyone is happy!

Result 2:

The same raw material is used by several suppliers to Company B. Only Company Z supplies that material. Orders flood Company Z, which does not have enough material to replenish all of its customers. The loser, Company T (by a split microsecond), gets nothing. Company T loses a contract to Company V because Company V is the only one with enough raw material to produce the needed good. Company T is dissatisfied and begins searching for an alternate supplier to Company Z.

Result 3:

Company A made a mistake. Only 100 pieces were supposed to be ordered. By the time Company A discovers its mistake, 89 associated orders for replacement material have been sent and partially filled. If held to the order, Company A will go bankrupt. Call the nearest law firm!

The problem (or feature) causing the imperfect results is the near instantaneous processing of each step in the chain. There is none of the delay which was present in the manual and non network automation of the process. In addition, because all of the connections are autonomous, there is no overall plan for the behavior of the service system. Without sufficient delay and with the presence of feedback loops, control theory predicts that the system can go unstable, which leads to:

Result 4:

> Company B cannot fill the order of Company A until it makes more widgets and quickly sends out the appropriate orders for materials. Company Q, somewhere in the procurement chain, needs material from Company A, which cannot supply it until it receives all of its order from Company B. Messages begin flowing over the network, ordering, back-ordering, looking for alternate sources, until the service network becomes totally clogged or reaches a deadlock. Everyone reaches for the aspirin.

One solution is to design the service and its protocols in such a way that any configuration will result in a stable network. If this is impossible, the next approach is to allow network management to control the service network in the same way it controls the physical network. This is discussed in the next chapter.

Without knowing the exact circumstances, it is impossible to predict what other events may occur. However, this type of situation does reinforce the premise of this discussion; that most communications networks are becoming interrelated. If they are not connected in some fashion now, they will be in the near future.

Universal interconnection has perceived advantages and disadvantages. In the global economy, it is necessary for an organization to exchange information with large numbers of other entities, both public and private, if it is to survive. For this purpose, the existence of the facilities to accomplish that interchange is an asset rather than a liability. The control of such networks, however, is a difficult task, and the resources required could be considered to be a serious disadvantage. As indicated, some of the control issues are explored in the next chapter and an architecture is proposed that can help minimize the cost involved.

In addition, universal interconnection has perceived disadvantages that result from the moral issues associated with having large amounts of information instantly available. Although this is certainly a valid area of enquiry, it is not possible to treat it in this discussion. Refer to other publications dealing specifically with this type of issue.

LAYERED COMMUNICATIONS SYSTEMS

This subject is touched on briefly as background material for the discussion of this chapter. The discussion includes some of the historical perspective necessary to place these systems in their correct context. The detailed theory of layered systems is not covered; neither are specific implementations. Ample literature is available on these subjects.

The original communications networks were the telegraph systems put in place to provide communications throughout the expanding United States continent, and then a little later, the telephone network that replaced the telegraph systems. Although the telephone network has grown to be an extremely sophisticated communications vehicle, voice communications alone did not contain the complexity that would require the development of layered systems. This was true for three main reasons.

First, voice communication generally involves at least one human being. Humans bring a great deal of intelligence and understanding to the communications process. Second, voice is a very redundant signal. Unless the communications link is almost inoperable, it is possible to understand what information the voice signal is trying to convey. Third, data communications between telephone central offices during the path set-up phase of a call is rather primitive, and the amount of data involved is small. This has resulted from historical limitations. Early technology could support only small amounts of data transmission.

Data communications does not have the advantages of voice as denoted above. Initiating, maintaining, and terminating a data conversation is much more complex than doing the same for an equivalent voice conversation. For this reason, a great number of formalisms and associated theory have been applied to data communications. The most well-known aspect of this theory is the development and utilization of layered communications systems.

Layered systems partition the communication process into segments (layers), each of which is designed to handle a specific part of the communications process. By this method, data communications standards can more easily be specified and the actual implementation of a data communications system can be greatly simplified. The disadvantage to such systems is the increase in processing overhead required to pass data between all of the layers. This is generally considered to be a small penalty, however, for the enormous benefits that result from such systems. It should be noted that voice (and image) communications can also be partitioned into these layers. This is possible because of the universal foundations on which all communications rest, regardless of media.

Developing layered protocols for voice and image has not been accomplished in any formal way, because of the reasons discussed above. However, with the intermingling of all forms of communications into digital integrated application systems, layer theory is currently being applied to all media types, and preliminary standards have been developed by Bellcore, among others, for this purpose. Eventually, layered models for all types of communications media will become prevalent and accepted.

Many different layered data communications systems have been developed and deployed. The early ones were the products of computer vendors who were trying to simplify the development and deployment of communications systems for their own products. The most widely deployed of these is the System Network Architecture (SNA) developed by the International Business Machines (IBM) Corporation in the early 1970s. It utilized seven layers and became the model for later efforts.

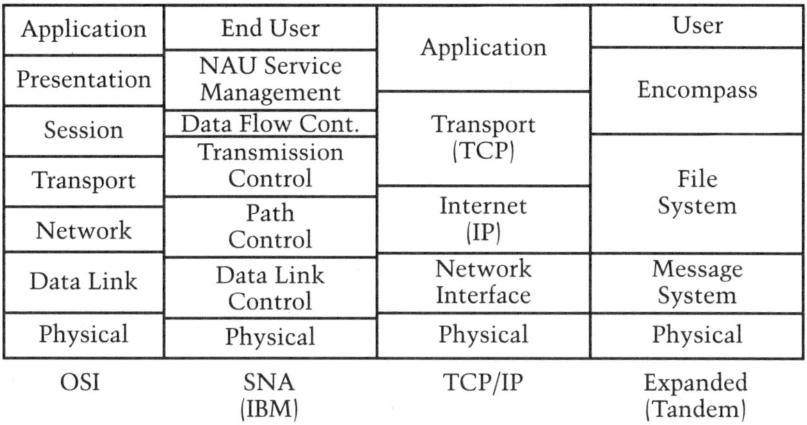

Application	End User	Application	User
Presentation	NAU Service Management		Encompass
Session	Data Flow Cont.	Transport (TCP)	
Transport	Transmission Control		File System
Network	Path Control	Internet (IP)	
Data Link	Data Link Control	Network Interface	Message System
Physical	Physical	Physical	Physical
OSI	SNA (IBM)	TCP/IP	Expanded (Tandem)

FIGURE 6.3 REFERENCE MODEL COMPARISONS (APPROXIMATE)

Other vendors developed layered systems for their own communications systems. Among these were DECNET, developed by the Digital Equipment Corporation (DEC), and EXPAND, developed by the Tandem Corporation. Another widely used protocol is the Transmission Control Protocol/Internet Protocol (TCP/IP), which was developed for ARPANET. A general comparison of a few of these layered systems is presented in figure 6.3. Notice that all of the same functions are required. The only difference is how they are distributed among the layers. Most of the early layered systems are in the process of being broadened in scope and changed to accommodate a wider range of products, including those from different manufacturers. A few, such as DECNET, are being changed to be compatible with OSI.

Originally, network servers that used a specific proprietary layered system could communicate only with other servers that used the same system. When the advantages of using layers to facilitate the communication process became widely known and understood, there was a widespread search for a standard that could be used so that all vendors' products could communicate with one another. For a further discussion of the standards process, refer to chapter 1 of the companion volume, *Information Systems and Business Dynamics*. The dominant standard that has emerged is the Open Systems Interconnect (OSI) system, which was produced by the International Standards Organization (ISO). This standard is also shown for comparison purposes in figure 6.3.

Layered systems consist of three basic components: the reference model, the architecture, and the implementation. The reference model determines the number of layers and the actions that will be performed by each layer. The architecture determines the definition of the allowable protocols and the interfaces between the layers. The implementation generates the actual embodiment (code) of the architecture. The implementation need not follow any particular structure as long as it presents the proper protocols to a communicating entity.

Layered systems have definite limitations when the overall communications problem is considered. They inherently do not consider network management, network topology, or network interoperability. These must be specified separately; except for network management, which is discussed in the next chapter, these issues are the focus of the architecture discussed in this chapter. Unfortunately, communications architecture has come to mean the architecture portion of a layered system. Thus, as discussed early in the chapter, the term *network (communications) architecture* is utilized to mean all of the architecture needs of the communications process. This, of course, includes the parts of the process addressed by layered systems as well as the expanded requirements needing additional constructs.

THE THEORY OF OVERLAYS

In order to define an architecture for a communications network in a well-ordered fashion, a number of properties of these networks have to be defined so that they can be used to establish the philosophy that will be followed. The approach taken in this section allows a robust communications network architecture to be established. It also overcomes many of the problems and confusion that have resulted from efforts to unify the many aspects and viewpoints of communications that must be considered in the implementation of modern networks. This discussion assumes that you are familiar with the basic theory of networks.

Assume a communications network has the following two fundamental properties:

- A network can be partitioned into component networks (subnetworks).
- A network can be defined with different levels of abstraction.

Based on these properties, the following definitions can be made.

- *Overlay* — A set of component networks that forms a larger network. A given network may have many overlays, depending on how the subnetworks are defined.
- *Gateway* — A connection point between two or more networks. The gateway is considered to be a node that is a member of all networks to which it is connected.
- *Network abstraction level* — A set of characteristics as determined through an attribute set applied to a network. These characteristics indicate the amount of detail present in the network definition.

Based on the above properties and definitions, the following statements concerning overlays are postulated to be true, and these form the basis of the overlay concept of network architecture.

- Subnetworks in the same overlay must be mutually exclusive.
- Subnetworks in an overlay must exactly form the larger network.

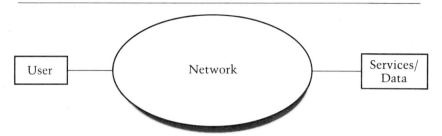

FIGURE 6.4   TARGET COMMUNICATIONS NETWORK

- Subnetworks in the same overlay may have different levels of abstraction.
- A network may have multiple overlays.
- Different overlays of the same network may be either consistent or inconsistent.
- Consistent overlays consist of subnetworks that have the following characteristic: If A and B are consistent overlays, then every subnetwork of A (1) has an overlay that consists of subnetworks of B or (2) is part of an overlay of a subnetwork of B.
- If a set of overlays is not consistent, it is said to be inconsistent.
- The relationship between inconsistent overlays is assignment.
- The relationship between consistent overlays is decomposition.
- Every subnetwork of an overlay must have at least one gateway.
- Different gateway patterns do not change the overlay. The same overlay can have many different interconnection definitions.

As an illustration of these concepts, assume that a communications network (the target network) exists, as shown in figure 6.4. One overlay of that network that consists of four subnetworks is shown in figure 6.5. The set of subnetworks shown in figure 6.6 does not form an overlay of the target network, because in (a) the subnetworks overlap, in (b) they

232

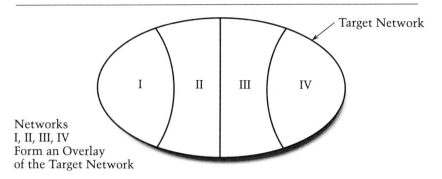

Networks
I, II, III, IV
Form an Overlay
of the Target Network

Target Network

FIGURE 6.5   TARGET NETWORK OVERLAY

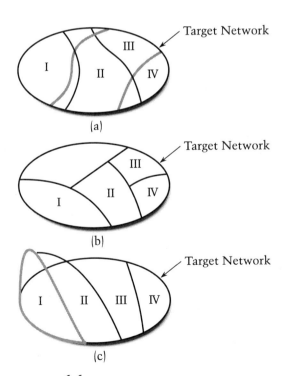

FIGURE 6.6   NONOVERLAY SUBNETWORKS

233

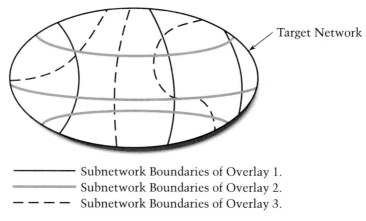

Subnetwork Boundaries of Overlay 1.
Subnetwork Boundaries of Overlay 2.
Subnetwork Boundaries of Overlay 3.

FIGURE 6.7   INCONSISTENT OVERLAYS

do not form the entire network, and in (c) they form a network larger than the target network. A set of inconsistent overlays for the network is shown in figure 6.7, and a set of consistent overlays is shown in figure 6.8. In general, overlays that are consistent with a given overlay are those that contain a decomposition of the given overlay or, conversely, a consolidation of the subnetworks of the given overlay.

The logical and/or physical meaning of each of these concepts is considered in the following sections, as the results of

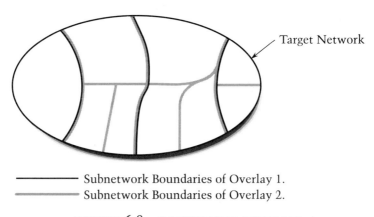

Subnetwork Boundaries of Overlay 1.
Subnetwork Boundaries of Overlay 2.

FIGURE 6.8   CONSISTENT OVERLAYS

overlay theory are applied to a number of communication network concepts and requirements.

LEVELS OF ABSTRACTION

Network communications must serve two basic purposes: one is business-related and the other is technical in nature. The business requirements are to ensure that the data flow between entities of the business meets the needs of the enterprise and follows appropriate business practices and policies, that all services can be obtained and/or provided in an efficient and cost-effective manner, and that responses to changes in the business environment can be accommodated easily. The technical requirement is to move data (items of intelligence) from one server to another in the most efficient and effective manner possible. These two needs give rise to the different levels of abstraction in the communications network. In general, the business requirements drive the higher levels and the technical needs form the lower levels, although each level contains some of each view.

Levels of abstraction are a convenient way to:

- Determine the requirements for the deployed network
- Verify that it will meet the needs of the business
- Provide for the effective use of technology

In this sense, they are used in much the same fashion as abstraction levels described in previous chapters. However, the separation between the different network abstraction levels is much more pronounced than that between data and servers, and network abstraction levels have a dual set of relationships, which increases the complexity considerably.

Using a procedure similar to that presented in the previous chapter, five major levels of abstraction have been identified. Each of these may have sublevels as necessary. The major levels are as follows:

235

- Business
- Service
- Logical
- Physical
- Deployed

Most of these names are similar to those used for the server abstraction levels. However, though a close relationship exists between server and communications levels, there are significant differences between them. For example, by selecting the proper values for the server attributes, logical servers can be assigned to a physical network. This aspect will be reconsidered in a later section.

Two relationships exist between the levels. The first is an assignment relationship between generic overlays at different levels. Generic overlays form the templates for the detailed specification of the network at each abstraction level. The second relationship is one of decomposition between the detailed overlays. The detailed overlays at a given level are constructed using the requirements generated by the needs of the generic and detailed overlays of the adjacent higher level. These concepts are illustrated by the diagram in figure 6.9. The specification of the generic overlays is considered during the definition of each abstraction level. The construction of the detailed overlays is covered later.

Assigning a given network to a specific abstraction level is a difficult task, because the level definitions by necessity must allow for a wide variety of cases; the process also tends to be somewhat subjective, because intent is an important part of the classification process. The characteristics defined in table 6.1 should aid in the process, however.

The business level defines the business communications needs and describes allowable connections between business-oriented entities. The service level defines the means for obtaining the set of services that will meet the needs of the business. The logical network defines the network topology

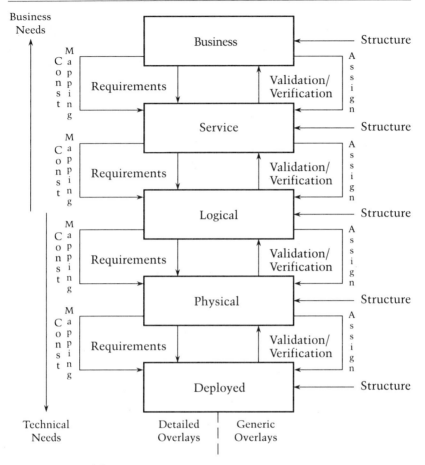

FIGURE 6.9   INTERRELATIONSHIP OF NETWORK LAYERS
OF ABSTRACTION

from a general or specific point of view. The physical network
is the logical network with specific products identified on
which the deployed network will be based. The deployed
network represents the actual embodiment of the network
whether currently in existence or in the preconstruction planning stages. This also applies to additions to the deployed
network.

TABLE 6.1   NETWORK ABSTRACTION LEVEL CHARACTERISTICS

	Usual Values				
Attribute	*Business*	*Service*	*Logical*	*Physical*	*Deployed*
Subnetworks in overlay	1	Many	Many	Many	Many
Explicit gateways	No	Yes	Yes	Yes	No
Products specifiable	No	No	No	Yes	Yes
Business orientation	High	Medium	Low	None	None
Overlay set	Small	Small	Large	Medium	Small
Level use	Communications plan	Service delivery structure	Network topology specification	Product assignment	Operational network

Abstraction Level Definitions

Detailed definitions of each of the major abstraction levels are discussed in the following sections, using the overlay concept as the basic analysis tool. The purpose of this discussion is to allow you to obtain an intuitive feel for the contents of each of these levels and their use in the definition process. A generic overlay set is developed for each level as part of the definition process. As is discussed later, the construction of the detailed overlays adds considerable information to that contained in the generic overlay definition.

Business Abstraction Level   The business network results from an *operations plan* that describes how communications will take place within the enterprise. This plan must describe the use of communications in meeting the goals of the enterprise. As an example of part of this type of operations plan, consider the following:

238

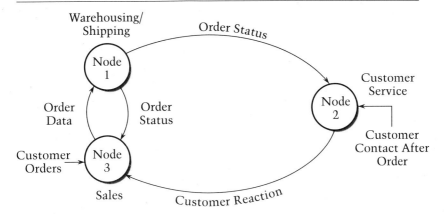

FIGURE 6.10   BUSINESS NETWORK EXAMPLE

An enterprise has three operational departments, sales, warehousing/shipping, and customer service. In order to control the inventory, which is an expensive, easy-to-conceal commodity, the enterprise has instituted strict internal controls. As one aspect of these controls, there is an extensive audit trail on all communications involving orders. In addition, the chain of communication is strictly regulated.

All orders must be taken by the sales department. These orders can be communicated only to the customer service department. Customer service sends the order to the warehousing/shipping department. Warehousing/shipping sends the status of each order to both the sales and the customer service departments. Customers communicate with the customer service department only after an order has been placed. If sales needs to know the customer's reaction to an order, they must make the inquiry to the customer service department. This process is shown in figure 6.10.

From the figure, it is easily seen that a communications network has been created. The nodes are the operational departments and the connections are the allowed communications paths. This is an example of the highest abstraction level of the network. Like the same level for the servers, this level is entirely business-driven. Note that only the communication aspects of the business are considered here. The functions that must be performed by each entity are a part of the server definition and as such were treated in the previous chapter.

This network has one overlay, the network itself. It would be difficult to partition this network into subnetworks of the same or lower levels of abstraction. The network performs one service required by the business. For the purpose of using this example in the remaining discussion, this service will be called the *order service*. Another enterprise might create a different network, in a topology sense, to perform this function, but the service would still be available.

A number of other services may be defined, and these may or may not need to send information to one another. If they do, these *business networks* would have to be interconnected via gateways and would, in turn, become component networks in a larger network. This type of network, called a *service network*, is discussed in the next section. Business networks typically have only one generic overlay that cannot be decomposed. It thus forms the starting point for both the assignment process and the construction process introduced above.

The requirements imposed on the next lower abstraction level (service) are derived from the specific characteristics of the business network (overlay) and its implementation needs. For the example given above, these requirements could be those in the following list:

- Users in each of the functional departments must utilize a security function that controls access to the service.
- The security function will enforce the communications needs and restrictions through use of menu selections.
- All transactions will be saved and used to monitor the propriety of the information transmitted.
- The order network must be isolated functionally from all other functions.

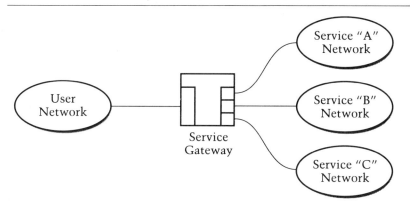

FIGURE 6.11   SERVICE NETWORK OVERLAY EXAMPLE

- The accounting network must have access to the results of each transaction that will produce changes to the enterprise accounting records.
- Summaries of each day's transactions will be made and presented to senior management.

Other requirements could be added, or the ones provided could be changed if additional information becomes available about the business network. Of necessity, the requirements may also involve the servers that ultimately will provide the functionality required by the business. This is the result of the close interdependence of the server and communications components of the network.

In general, few requirements are imposed on the next abstraction level. Only enough direction is needed to ensure that the service network structure can include the needs of the business network.

Service Abstraction Level   A service network overlay is illustrated by the diagram in figure 6.11. For clarity, this type of overlay diagram is used in the remainder of the chapter. Of course, all of the properties of overlays still apply. A service level overlay has as subnetworks the services that the enterprise requires. It may also have other subnetworks that facil-

241

itate the communication process, such as the user network shown in figure 6.11. This user network provides a means to give multiple users access to the services as well as to one another; it also may provide user-oriented services (such as display customization).

Services may be comprised of, or may include, other services. This is a design detail that need not be considered at this level. Interactions of this nature, which can become quite involved, may be considered at the logical level as a part of the assignment process.

The subnetworks at the service level are interconnected via *service gateways*, which provide and administer the access to the service. Service gateways can use a multiplicity of media, including data, voice, video, and graphics formats, as required by the service they access. Some of the functions performed by these gateways are listed below:

• Security
• Billing
• Usage statistics
• Service selection
• Service harmonization
• Service integration

Service gateways are mentioned in this discussion because of their importance in providing services to end users. However, service gateways are only one type of gateway. Because of the importance of gateways in all aspects of the communications process, a more comprehensive discussion of gateways is given later.

A service network for the above example would include the service defined in the previous section as one of the service offerings, as well as including any interconnections required. Note that a user network has also been defined. This network could be a requirement of the enterprise for any network that it uses or produces. The example network overlay illustrated in figure 6.12 consists of five subnetworks, all of which are interconnected via a common gateway. Al-

242

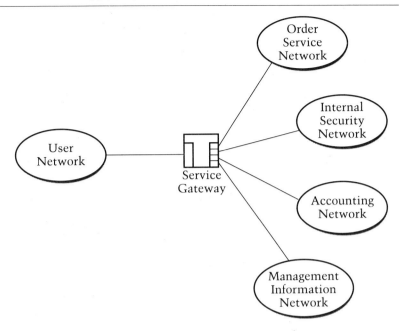

FIGURE 6.12   SERVICE NETWORK OVERLAY (CONTAINING
EXAMPLE SERVICE)

ternative overlays could have been used depending on the
architecture principles that are used to guide service network
design. In addition, multiple gateways could have been
utilized.

The service network shown in figure 6.12 must be examined to determine if it meets the requirements that were set
forth earlier. If the access control functions are assigned to
the gateway and the transaction monitoring functions are
assigned to the internal security network, it should be easily
seen that all requirements are accommodated by the illustrated network. The functions that comprise the services
must be designed and assigned to servers in accordance with
the architecture illustrated in the previous chapter.

Service networks can be combined with other independently specified service networks to form larger service networks. This process can be carried out as many times as
necessary or desired. By the way service networks were de-

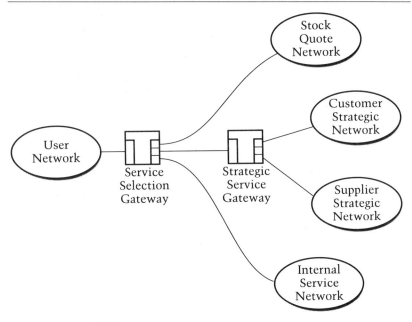

FIGURE 6.13   EXTENDED SERVICE NETWORK OVERLAY

fined, a linear system has in effect been created. This makes it easy for networks at this level to be combined and split into component services. The individual services can then be changed, added, or deleted without affecting others.

Another example of a service network is shown in figure 6.13, which shows the integration of internal business services, such as that discussed above, external services, such as stock quotes or database lookup, and strategic services that connect to other businesses. Although this type of diagram is still predominantly business-oriented, some technical constructs involving the way in which the subnetworks are interconnected (specific overlay format) is included. In this case, two levels of gateways have been used to interconnect the overlay subnetworks. Although both gateways are "service gateways," they have been distinguished by their dominant function. Changing the way in which the service networks are interconnected will not result in a different overlay. Refer to the overlay discussion presented earlier in the chapter for confirmation of this principle.

External service networks will usually remain at the service level of abstraction for the user, because the external network provider may not wish to reveal internal design details of the network and the provider has already performed the hard work of implementing the network. In this case, the service gateway becomes of prime importance in ensuring that all of the enterprise requirements are met.

As in the case of the business network, no philosophical approach exists for decomposing this service network structure into lower levels of abstraction by adding more detail. The network defined at the logical abstraction level must provide support for the services and interconnections defined in the example as well as for all other service networks that will utilize the network. However, the structure of the logical network generic overlays must be arrived at independently according to good engineering design. The approach necessary for the next, more technically oriented, lower levels is discussed next.

The requirements that the service network level may impose on the logical network level are illustrated in the following list:

- The order network must serve users throughout the United States.
- The order network must run on a "real-time" basis and remain available 24 hours per day.
- Order network access must be password-protected, with call-back for access through any public network facility.
- The user network may be decomposed into individual networks as needed.
- All networks other than the order and user networks may by used on a "store-and-forward" basis.
- Users shall have access to a service facility that will resolve any problems with network usage.

245

In actual practice, these would have to be defined by examining all of the service networks that have been defined. As before, the requirements tend to be few in number and are designed only to ensure that the needs of the services network are allowed by the logical network.

Logical Abstraction Level   This is the first level for which technical considerations play a predominant role. The architecture of this level must provide connectivity between all nodes on the network when and where needed. It is recognized that communications requires more than connectivity. The data must be meaningful to each of the communicating entities. Some of the means for providing this type of communication were discussed in chapter 3 on system software, and they need not be repeated here. Instead, the emphasis is on providing the underlying connectivity in a manner that is efficient, effective, and easy to manage. Management of the network is covered in the next chapter.

Logical networks can be approached from a variety of directions, each of which is valid in meeting some set of needs. As an example, consider the generic overlay of the logical network shown in figure 6.14. This overlay consists of subnetworks that provide a hierarchical approach to node interconnectivity. The hierarchy in this example is geographically oriented. Each of these subnetworks can be further subdivided into networks that remain at the same level of abstraction. This is discussed in greater depth in the section on construction. An example effect of this partitioning process on the geographical overlay is shown in figure 6.15. A new detailed overlay has been defined that is consistent with the previous overlay. The gateway symbols have been omitted for clarity. Because interconnections do not affect the overlay, a different interconnection pattern among the subnetworks could be defined as desired (for example, LAN 5 could be attached to MAN 2 instead of MAN 1).

Contrast this set of overlays with the logical generic overlay of the same network that is shown in figure 6.16. The sub-

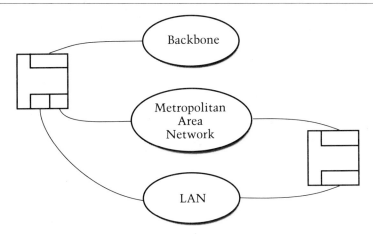

FIGURE 6.14   LOGICAL NETWORK LEVEL — GENERIC
GEOGRAPHICAL OVERLAY

networks in this overlay are oriented toward the facilities provider aspects of the network. These generic logical overlays are inconsistent, but each is valuable in defining the needs the network must meet. Other generic logical overlays oriented toward different needs could also be defined. As with the overlays illustrated, consistency would not be required.

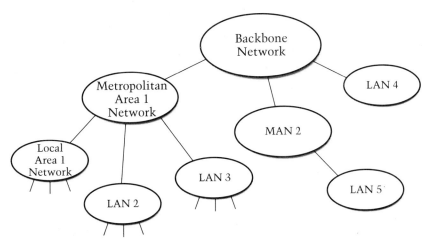

FIGURE 6.15   LOGICAL NETWORK LEVEL — DETAILED
GEOGRAPHICAL OVERLAY

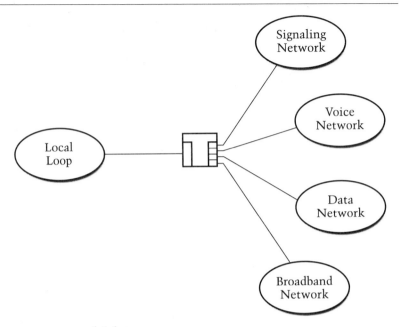

FIGURE 6.16   LOGICAL NETWORK LEVEL NETWORK
PROVIDER GENERIC OVERLAY

The test of the validity of any of these logical overlays is whether the logical overlay (generic or detailed) supports the requirements of the service level overlays. Can the required services be obtained in the manner indicated through the use of the logical overlays? If the answer is yes, the logical overlays are useful. If not, the logical overlays must be modified until they do meet the requirements.

In the case of the example, examining the list of requirements presented previously reveals that the requirements are satisfied by using both the geographic and provider generic logical overlays. One of these, by itself, would not be enough to meet the imposed requirements. If additional requirements were imposed at the service level that were not satisfied by either of these overlays, additional overlays might have to be defined. For example, an additional requirement could deal with the type of transmission media needed for the services. The need to control delay or noise could cause this type of

248

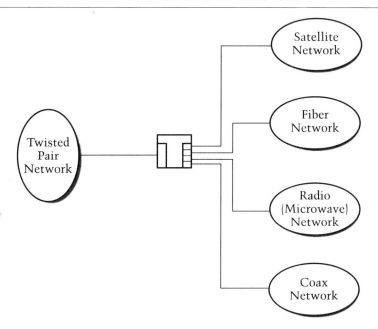

FIGURE 6.17   LOGICAL NETWORK LEVEL
TRANSMISSION MEDIA GENERIC OVERLAY

network partition to be needed. An overlay such as the one illustrated in figure 6.17 would then satisfy this need. As anticipated, this overlay is inconsistent with the previous two.

The key to utilizing inconsistent overlays is to realize that no direct mapping between them is possible. Each can be used only within its specific context. Each imposes requirements on the next lower level (physical), and the network defined at this level must meet all of those requirements. Although it might be possible to force consistency in defining the logical overlays representing different views, the result would probably be a contorted complex set of overlays that would be difficult to apply in any practical design situation. In addition, forcing consistency does not seem to have any particular advantage to the specification of the required network except, perhaps, to discover hidden relationships among the views that could be exploited in some fashion.

TABLE 6.2   EXAMPLE LOGICAL NETWORK REQUIREMENTS
IMPOSED ON PHYSICAL ABSTRACTION LEVEL

Overlay	*Requirements*
Geographic	The backbone network must have the capacity to carry the 100 megabytes of video. LAN networks must support up to 50 users. If more users are located in a single geographical area, multiple LANs will be utilized. Metropolitan area networks will be used if more than four LANs are located in a single metropolitan area. Otherwise, the LANs can be tied directly into the backbone. Metropolitan area networks may be either public or private networks.
Provider	The broadband network must have the capacity to carry 10 channels of NTSC video. The signaling network will serve the voice, packet, and broadband networks. If the packet network becomes congested, overflow traffic will be sent over the voice or broadband networks.
Transmission Media	All types of transmission media shown must be available and selectable by the user if desired.

Some possible requirements imposed by each of the two logical overlays on the physical level are shown in table 6.2. Although this possibility is not illustrated in this table, conflicting or inconsistent requirements may be generated as a result of this process. These would have to be resolved by examining the reasons for the problem's occurrence. One or more of the logical overlays may need to be changed to resolve the problem. Because of the many possibilities that can occur, it is not possible to treat the resolution of this problem in this discussion.

Physical Abstraction Level   The physical abstraction level requires the subnetworks to contain specific characteristics that would allow them to be implemented. The exact manner

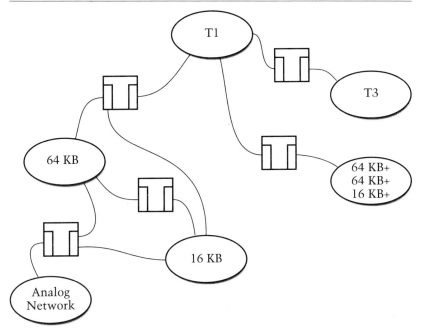

FIGURE 6.18   PHYSICAL NETWORK LEVEL CAPACITY
GENERIC OVERLAY

of implementation does not have to be specified, but enough information to select product types or perform development must be available. If this level of information is not available, the subnetwork reverts to logical status.

As with the other abstraction levels, multiple physical network generic overlays may be defined that are inconsistent with one another and with those of the logical level. Two overlays on the physical level are shown in figures 6.18 and 6.19. The first is oriented toward networks of different capacity, and the second is oriented toward the selection of protocols. There is enough information in each to be implemented and deployed.

Performing the deployment in the abstract, based only on the information in the physical level, will probably not do much good, however. This is another example in which decomposition will not work. Because the assumption is that

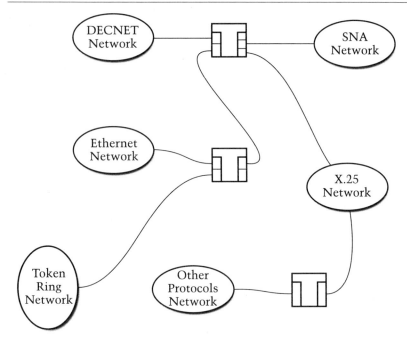

FIGURE 6.19   PHYSICAL NETWORK LEVEL PROTOCOL
GENERIC OVERLAY

there will be only one deployed network, this network must meet the requirements of both physical overlays.

It is up to you to verify that the physical network will meet the needs of the overlays defined at the logical level. The verification process is the same as that utilized in previous verifications. Unfortunately, all of the verification steps must be predominately qualitative in nature. Quantitative verification is a theorem-proving problem similar to that required to prove software correct. The state of the art must advance considerably before that type of approach can be used.

Only one requirement is imposed on the deployed level by the physical level for the physical overlays presented: the facilities and protocols contained in these diagrams must be part of the deployed network. Other requirements could also be inferred if they have been determined to be necessary by the enterprise. The assignment process will determine how each of the physical networks becomes assigned to deployed facilities.

Deployed Abstraction Level   The deployed abstraction level is the actual implementation of the network. It too must support the needs of all of the physical level overlays and must provide the indicated facilities and capabilities. If some of these are lacking, they must be added to the existing network. The manner in which the deployed network supports the requirements of the physical network can vary. The design of the deployed network is usually determined by a large number of forces that are out of the direct control of the network user. These forces include tariffs, government regulations, specific economics, and traffic projections that exist at the time the network is being designed or changed. This situation again indicates the need to design each level of the network independently of the others, utilizing the set of principles that provides the "best" result consistent with the needs of the other levels.

Mixed Overlays

Mixed overlays are overlays that contain subnetworks of different levels of abstraction. These arise naturally for a variety of reasons. As an example, consider the following scenario:

An enterprise decides to provide a service to other businesses. This service is a complex database offering that will make it more cost-effective for businesses to perform a competitive analysis. Because of strong cost factors, the enterprise decides to use as many existing communication facilities as possible while maintaining the integrity of the service. In addition, the use of a LAN to connect multiple users from the same company is recommended as a cost-saving measure.

The resulting initial network proposal might contain an overlay similar to the one presented in the diagram of figure

253

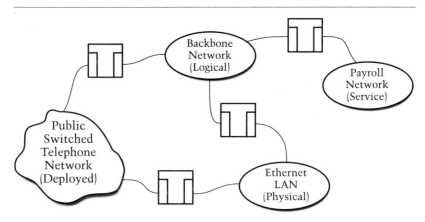

FIGURE 6.20   MIXED ABSTRACTION LEVEL OVERLAY

6.20, which consists of service, logical, and deployed subnetworks. This type of situation arises quite often, and there is no need to discourage it. However, the mixed case does imply that abstraction levels should be treated subnetwork by subnetwork until all overlays are at the same abstraction level. This process is illustrated schematically in figure 6.21.

Server Assignments

At some point, the servers must be assigned to a specific subnetwork. This is usually a function of the attributes of the server. As indicated previously, servers of any abstraction level may be assigned to a subnetwork with any abstraction level (below the business level), as long as the assignment makes sense. As an example, consider a LAN server that is specified at a logical level. If a deployed LAN already exists, the server could be assigned to that deployed network.

Alternatively, a deployed server could be reassigned to a new backbone network that has just been defined. Because network levels of abstraction are defined separately and do not result from a decomposition of a previous level, this type of cross-level interaction is allowable. As indicated in the previous chapter, the final network containing deployed serv-

254

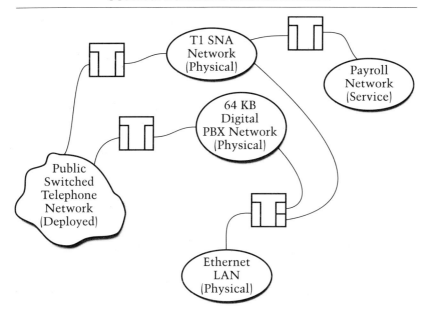

FIGURE 6.21   MIXED OVERLAY REDUCTION EXAMPLE

ers and deployed networks must be tuned so that the capacity of the servers and networks meets the needs of the services and users.

Construction

The overlay specification process results in a set of generic overlays for each level. These overlays reflect the general needs of each level and have been determined to support the requirements of the next higher level. At this point, however, the overlays are broad and do not provide enough information to be utilized as design guides. To remedy this situation, a construction process is used. This process partitions (decomposes) the overlays at each level into a new set of overlays, each of which is consistent with its associated unpartitioned overlay. The partitioning is accomplished by using the requirements of a given level to force a specific set of generic overlay partitions of the next lowest level. This process starts

255

with the business level and proceeds to the deployed level. In effect, the overlays at each level then contain all of the known topological information through that level.

When a new business network is defined, the construction process must be performed for that network. This will result in additional information added at each abstraction level. Although it was not identified as such, the service overlay of figure 6.12 (shown earlier) is the result of such a construction process. The internal service network was partitioned to reflect the different services needed.

In some cases, the construction cannot be performed because the generic overlays at some level do not have the required functionality to allow the initial assignment. When this occurs, the generic overlays must be altered to add the needed functionality. Previous assignments need not be redone unless it is clear that significant savings will result.

Assignment rules for overlays are in some ways similar to the server assignment rules, because they govern a process that eventually assigns business requirements to deployed facilities. They are different in the sense that the conditions that they govern are a great deal more fluid and arbitrary than those encountered by the server assignment rules. Associated construction rules must also be defined.

As an added complication, the assignment rules may change while the network is in operation because of changes in government regulations, tariffs, etc. For this reason, no specific set of rules is defined here. If desired, you may derive some of the more obvious rules the example below, which illustrates the assignment and construction process.

As an example of the assignment/construction process, the business network diagrammed in figure 6.22 is used. The result of the process is shown by a set of detailed overlays for each abstraction level; these overlays (figures 6.23–6.25) are based on the generic overlays and level requirements examples discussed previously. The associated generic overlays were shown in figures 6.11, 6.14, 6.16, and 6.19. For reasons

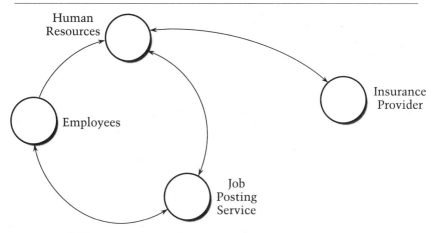

FIGURE 6.22   ASSIGNMENT EXAMPLE BUSINESS NETWORK NEED

discussed earlier, the example will be carried only through the physical level.

In practice, the complexity of the levels and number of overlays would be quite high, and trying to utilize such a real example would interfere with the purpose of this section. Thus, the example and diagrams have been deliberately simplified. Other than this example, the details of the assignment/construction process will not be investigated further.

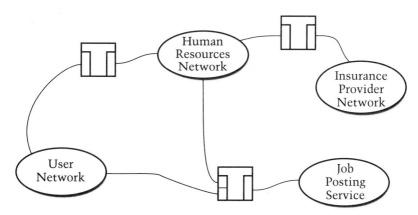

FIGURE 6.23   ASSIGNMENT EXAMPLE DETAILED SERVICE LEVEL OVERLAY

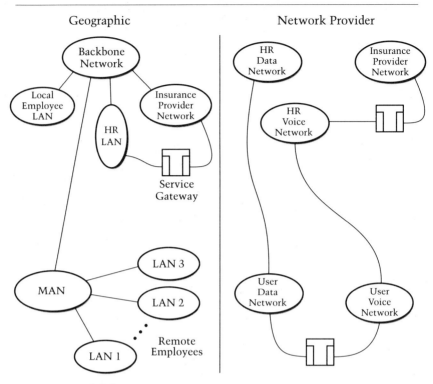

FIGURE 6.24   ASSIGNMENT EXAMPLE DETAILED LOGICAL
LEVEL OVERLAYS

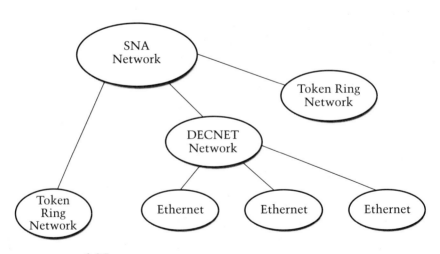

FIGURE 6.25   ASSIGNMENT EXAMPLE DETAILED PHYSICAL
LEVEL PROTOCOL OVERLAY

The complexity of the process must relegate this discussion to other publications.

Mapping

Up to this point, the focus on transitions between abstraction levels has concentrated on the assignment process, which utilizes independently developed generic overlays at each level. As mentioned previously, it is also possible to map between levels if there is a consistent set of generic overlays at each level. Mapping implies a well-ordered relationship between the entities being mapped. Because of the difficulty in defining consistent overlays, this method is used only in those limited circumstances in which consistent overlays occur somewhat naturally.

Mapping is most often used in making the transition from the logical level to the physical level when the logical overlay contains subnetworks that can be directly translated into product classes. The LAN network type is one of these. Given the requirement for a logical LAN level network and some of the necessary characteristics that have to be met, the transition to the physical level is relatively straightforward. This direct mapping will result in a consistent overlay at the physical level.

In fact, the mapping process can be considered to be a design device whereby the physical level is derived from the logical level. This is a somewhat different approach from that used for servers. Although theoretically, mapping is possible between any set of levels, in practice, it is preferable in few circumstances.

SUBNETWORKS

As described in the previous sections, overlays of subnetworks form the basis for specifying the contents of each abstraction level. This section presents a classification and short discussion of several of the more popular subnetworks used

259

TABLE 6.3   POPULAR SUBNETWORK TYPES

Level	Subnetworks
Service	Internal business service
	Proprietary service
	Customer service
	Electronic data interchange (EDI)
	Electronic mail
	Strategic service
	Network management
	Credit card authorization
	"800" number translation
Logical	Backbone network
	Local area network (LAN)
	Metropolitan area network (MAN)
	Wide area network (WAN)
	Broadband network
	Land-based network
	VSAT network
	Control network
	Signaling network
	Data network
Physical	Dial network
	Private network
	Packet network
	Circuit switched network
	Protocol-specific network
	Vendor-specific network
Deployed	Actual network topology
	Products utilized

in the specification of networks at various abstraction levels. This is not meant to be all-inclusive but only to touch on those subnetworks that are used to design the vast majority of the current information networks.

Examples of subnetwork types that can be defined in the information network are listed in table 6.3. Many of these networks will form overlays that are inconsistent with overlays formed from other subnetworks, so the list must be used with some discretion. Any enterprise is, of course, free to define and utilize overlays and subnetworks of its own design. This aspect is considered more fully in the section on architecture philosophy later in the chapter.

The following sections define example major subnetwork types from the list in table 6.3. These types are singled out because of the frequency of their use or because a specific point needs to be made concerning the definition or characteristics of the network.

Backbone Network

The major subnetwork in the information network is called the *backbone network*. Only one subnetwork of this type exists in any overlay, although it may in turn be subdivided into smaller components (such as regional backbone networks). The backbone network is the foundation of a hierarchical network design. It is not necessary to have a backbone network if another design philosophy is used.

The backbone network usually is the main transport mechanism in the information network and as such should be designed to carry data, text, voice, image, and graphic information. It is also usually the network to which the large-capacity servers are assigned. As such, it should be able to carry relatively high data rates. The backbone network is designed to be a resource shareable by the entire enterprise and/or its customers/suppliers. Individual users are not generally attached directly to the backbone network but access it through a smaller connecting network.

Local Area Networks (LANs)

LANs are networks designed to serve a limited geographical area (for example, within a building or a campus). They are used to facilitate communications among a cohesive group of users as well as to provide an efficient means of sharing services through an internal or external gateway function.

Services that are of interest mainly to the users on the LAN are usually designed to be resident on the LAN.

Metropolitan Area Networks (MANs)

These networks are similar in nature to the LANs discussed above, but the area served is enlarged considerably. This category of network is relatively new, and as a result, the uses and characteristics of such networks have to be further defined.

Wide Area Networks (WANs)

WANs are networks that encompass a large territory; they may serve the entire country or even the world. These networks may be public or private and are usually used to implement backbone networks, as described previously. The most widely used WANs are those supplied by common carriers such as ATT and Telenet.

Circuit-switched Networks

Circuit-switched or dial networks are used to interconnect geographically isolated equipment or users requiring low-volume asynchronous or synchronous traffic where direct access to a packet network is not available. These networks may be private or they may utilize the common carrier telephone system. Other than low bandwidth, the disadvantages of these networks are that establishing a connection generally takes a long time and that they provide low inherent security.

With the advent of the Integrated Services Digital Network (ISDN), which is in the process of being defined for both international and United States usage, the services and functions available via the switched public network will increase dramatically and many of the disadvantages will be reduced.

262

Full-time Networks

Circuit-switched networks are generally not considered to be full-time networks, because the facilities utilized are shared by other nonrelated users. Full-time networks are those dedicated to a particular user or related set of users. Private networks are usually put in place to provide full-time access because the expense involved is necessary to overcome the deficiencies of public networks. When shared networks can provide a rapid set-up time and the required facilities can always be obtained when required, shared facilities may replace many of the current dedicated networks, because using shared facilities has an inherent economic advantage.

Packet Networks

Packet networks are used to interconnect geographically widespread equipment requiring a low to moderate volume of asynchronous or synchronous data traffic. Such networks currently are unacceptable for real-time voice and video transmission, although some schemes are being proposed that will allow packet transmission of voice. These "fast packet" proposals are based on a combination of time-slicing and standard packet transmission.

Packet networks may be public or private and are popular as WANs or MANs for data-only transmission.

Protocol-specific Networks

Various equipment manufacturers have defined proprietary networks that are specifically designed to interconnect their processors. Some of these proprietary networks are SNA (International Business Machines), Wangnet (Wang Laboratories), DECNET (Digital Equipment Corporation), Expand (Tandem Corporation), and Distributed Systems Network (HP Corporation). All of these have obtained a considerable following, although as mentioned previously, SNA has reached the status of an de facto standard because of its widespread use.

Use of this type of network is not desirable because of the basic incompatibility between the networks of different vendors and the lack of information and documentation as to the architecture of the networks. As a practical matter, however, until all suppliers conform to the OSI standard, subnetworks of this type will exist in the information network, and provision must be made for them. These subnetworks will usually be requested when a significant number of a single-vendor processors exist within an organizational entity or within a limited geographical area.

A network of this type must have appropriate gateways defined and implemented to allow it to be connected to a subnetwork with a standard protocol set, such as SNA or OSI, when its usage becomes more widespread. In addition, a minimal set of functions must be available to allow the network to interact, where necessary, with the standard features defined on the network (for example, electronic mail).

Other Networks

Other subnetwork types in addition to those that were listed in table 6.3 may be defined at any abstraction level and with any set of characteristics that may be necessary. The principles detailing the use of these networks also must be defined.

GATEWAYS

As was indicated previously, a gateway is the connection between two or more subnetworks of a larger network. This is illustrated in figure 6.26. The icon used to represent a gateway shows that a gateway both connects subnetworks and performs some intermediate processing as a part of the coupling process.

Originally, gateways were defined to connect two networks that had differing layered communications architectures.

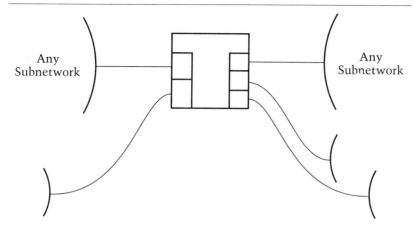

FIGURE 6.26   GENERIC GATEWAY CONCEPT

These gateways existed only to perform protocol conversion. In this definition, gateways could exist at any layer of the reference model, depending on where the differences existed. This is shown in figure 6.27. If layers 7 through 4 were the same but layers 1 through 3 differed, the two networks could be connected using a layer 4 gateway. A gateway at this level is a common occurrence, because many transport mechanisms may exist throughout a large network (Ethernet, X.25,

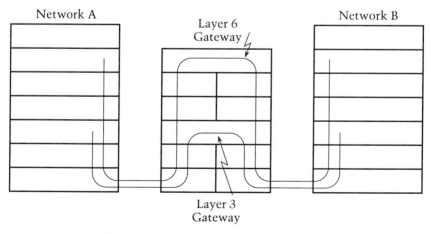

FIGURE 6.27   GATEWAY DEFINITION IN A LAYERED
COMMUNICATIONS MODEL

265

SNA, etc.) while the protocols at the higher layers remain constant. Another common gateway is defined at layer 6. This allows different transport and session mechanisms between networks but keeps the application-oriented data the same. A special type of gateway, called a *bridge*, was also defined for cases in which two networks had the same layered architecture but, for administrative or other reasons, it was undesirable to combine them into a larger network.

In the discussion of this chapter, the definition of *gateway* has been expanded to include a connection between any two networks. This allows the definition of gateways that

- Exist on different levels of abstraction
- Connect networks of different levels of abstraction
- Perform functions other than or in addition to protocol conversion
- Allow subnetworks to be defined in terms other than their layered architecture

This expansion of the role of a gateway was exploited earlier in the chapter in the discussion of service gateways. Some of the functions that have been proposed for gateways are presented in the following list:

- Security
- Billing
- Usage statistics
- Service selection
- Service harmonization
- Service integration
- Protocol conversion
- Store and forward
- Media conversion
- User isolation
- Network management

Not every gateway will have every function, and the use of a gateway may be tailored to a particular need by selecting the proper set of functions.

NETWORK COMMUNICATIONS SUBARCHITECTURE PHILOSOPHY

The philosophy of the network communications architecture leans heavily on the concepts discussed earlier in the chapter. It requires the development of an approach to specifying in parallel the structure and principles for all of the network levels of abstraction. The particular structure and principles chosen would reflect the needs of the enterprise and/or its clients by optimizing one or more metrics at each level. Once the generic structures have been defined, an assignment/construction process can be used to provide a set of robust overlays at each level; these overlays are used as design guides.

The structure for each level is specified in terms of allowable generic overlays and gateway locations. A base set of requirements for each level is generated as a part of the architecture. Additional requirements could, of course, be generated during the design process. These would have to be validated by examining the proper level as a part of the service/system design process, but by themselves, they would not be able to change the overlay structure required by the architecture.

Because the assignment/construction process has been discussed previously in sufficient detail to allow you to understand its role in the architecture, this process is not considered explicitly in this section. The generic overlays specified in this section are considered to be the base architectural specification. You are invited to perform the assignment process using the information generated in this section. The process should result in a set of overlays similar to the ones developed in the previous example.

NETWORK COMMUNICATIONS SUBARCHITECTURE STRUCTURE

This architecture is mainly concerned with the topology, or fabric, of the network. It determines how nodes are interconnected from a variety of viewpoints related to the levels of abstraction defined earlier. The overall architecture structure

267

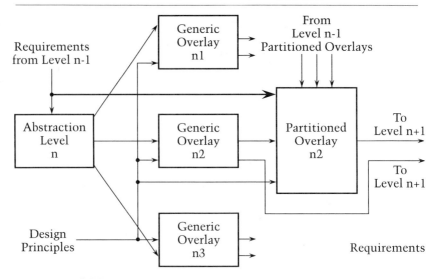

FIGURE 6.28   NETWORK COMMUNICATIONS ARCHITECTURE
STRUCTURE

is shown in figure 6.28 at a general abstraction level. This structure consists of the individual structures (overlays) defined for each of the five levels of abstraction, along with the functions that are necessary to define and use the information at these levels. The remainder of this section is devoted to examining the allowable overlays at each of these levels.

An adequate discussion of the requirements imposed by each level on the next has already been provided. There is no need to repeat this process as a part of this discussion. However, a full architecture structure description would also contain a set of requirements imposed on the next lower level.

Business Network Structure

The business network requires that nodes be business entities — either organizations or functions. Interconnections between the nodes represent actual communication needs between these nodes. The structure of the service needed by each entity or the type of communication is not important

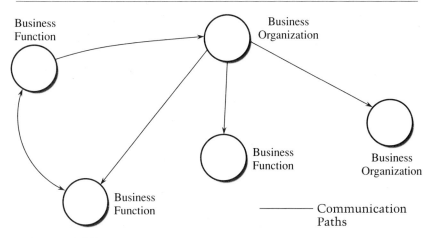

FIGURE 6.29   ARCHITECTURE BUSINESS NETWORK STRUCTURE

for the design of the business network. These elements may be used in developing the requirements that must be satisfied by the service network structure. The structure of the business network level is represented by the diagram in figure 6.29.

Server Network Structure

The server network structure is shown in figure 6.30. Note that only one overlay exists at this level, and it requires two networks in addition to those which reflect the particular services being defined. The user network is required for three reasons:

• The trend toward sophisticated workstations
• The need to accommodate the special needs of groups of related users
• The need for an efficient way to couple the user to the network and its services

In the telephone industry, this network is known as the *local loop*. In data communications, a LAN serves this function.

269

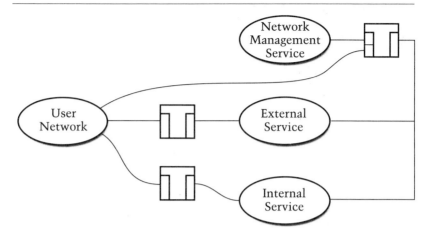

FIGURE 6.30   ARCHITECTURE SERVICE NETWORK STRUCTURE

Cable television and other specialized networks have their versions of the same function.

The second required network is the network management network, which is required to ensure that the needs of network management are considered from the beginning. It is also required so that the services themselves reflect the need to be coupled directly into the network management process. This is also indicated by the gateway structure of this overlay, which gives network management its own interconnection into each service.

Logical Network Structure

The logical network structure consists of three inconsistent overlays, each of which addresses a specific need of the network. This structure is diagrammed in figure 6.31. The orientations of these overlays are as follows:

- Network management
- Network geography/routing
- Network capabilities

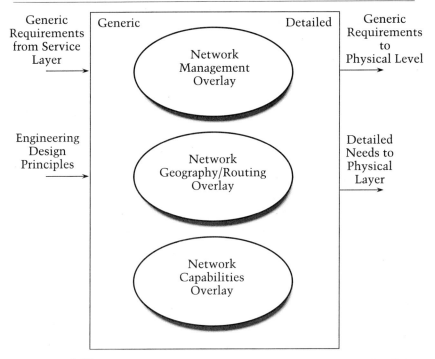

FIGURE 6.31   ARCHITECTURE LOGICAL NETWORK STRUCTURE

The structure of the network management overlay is shown in figure 6.32. The required subnetworks in this overlay are those for transmission, administration, operation, and signaling. Transmission represents all of the network used for normal traffic. Administration represents the part of the network dedicated to providing the users with the facilities and capabilities needed. Operation represents that part of the network used to keep the network running and the users happy. Signaling represents that part of the network used by internally generated traffic needed to keep the network operating at peak efficiency. Additional discussion of this overlay and further details of network management are presented in the next chapter.

The network geography/routing overlay describes the basic network transmission topology and locations. The required subnetworks will depend on the particular approach used.

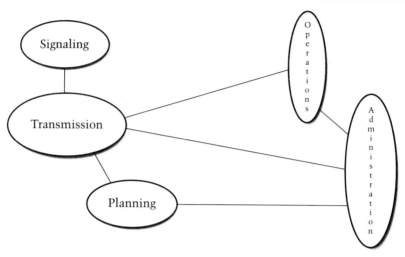

FIGURE 6.32   ARCHITECTURE LOGICAL NETWORK STRUCTURE
NETWORK MANAGEMENT GENERIC OVERLAY

Some of the more common are hierarchical, flat, and a combination of hierarchical and flat. All of these have merit; to
minimize complexity and yet allow a great deal of flexibility,
a combination of hierarchical and flat is used as an example.
Following this approach, a basic three-level hierarchy is defined. Three is a good working number. In practice, more or
fewer levels could be used if desired. However, all users/
services on the same LAN will be allowed to communicate
directly, as are users/services on any network that have an
affinity for one another and can benefit from direct communications. An example of this structure is shown in figure
6.33. The three network types are LANs, MANs, and the
backbone.

The network capability overlay is designed to indicate the
type of transmission facilities available and the interrelationships among them. An example overlay of this type is shown
in figure 6.34. The only required subnetwork is the access
network. This network provides the means to utilize the most
effective combination of facilities. The other subnetworks

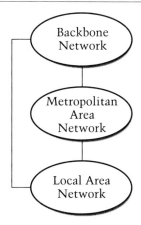

FIGURE 6.33 ARCHITECTURE LOGICAL NETWORK
STRUCTURE GEOGRAPHY/ROUTING
GENERIC OVERLAY

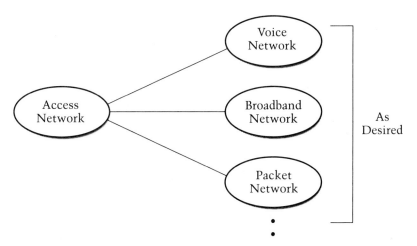

FIGURE 6.34 ARCHITECTURE LOGICAL NETWORK
STRUCTURE CAPABILITY GENERIC OVERLAY

273

represent the type of transmission available, and they exist only if the particular transmission type exists.

Physical Network Structure

The architectural requirements for the physical network are best described by the principles because of the wide range of possibilities and the resultant complexity. A great deal of effort must be invested in determining a physical structure that will meet the requirements of all of the logical overlays.

Deployed Network Structure

The architecture of the deployed structure is determined by a large number of factors, as was discussed previously. As in the previous section, the architecture requirements are best left to the principles.

NETWORK COMMUNICATIONS PRINCIPLES

The following statements are the principles that are derived from the structures defined for the network communications architecture. In keeping with the practice established for this section, these principles are grouped according to the components of the architecture, which in this case are the generic overlays at each of the five levels of abstraction.

   I. Strategies
      A. Global
         1. Architectural
            a. The overlays will be selected in accordance with the architecture.
            b. Selection of the appropriate network overlays for any level will be the responsibility of the network engineering organization.
            c. Networks controlled by external information

        providers must conform to a specific set of enterprise policies defined for this relationship.

2. Design
   a. All physical network overlays should use products that are on the approved product list.
   b. New physical level products designed to meet a need that is not served effectively by existing candidates must first be qualified for the approved product list.
   c. A heterogeneous set of network products is desirable and encouraged.
   d. Networks products must be synergistic with the server architecture.

3. Operational
   a. Before any physical overlay product that has no deployed equivalent can be used permanently, an extensive test program must be completed successfully.

B. Levels of abstraction — general
   1. Architectural
      a. The fewest number of abstraction levels that still meet the needs of the enterprise should be used. (The five major ones must always be present.)
   2. Design
      a. The number of overlays defined for each level should be kept to a minimum while still meeting the anticipated design needs.

C. Levels of abstraction — business
   1. Architectural
      a. Any defined business system or application shall have the communications aspects defined as an integral part of the service definition.

D. Levels of abstraction — service
   1. Architectural

275

       a. The basic service level generic overlay shall have the following subnetworks.
- User
- Network management

Others may be added as necessary.

   E. Levels of abstraction — logical
     1. Architectural
       a. The basic logical level generic overlays shall consist of the following:
- Network management
- Network geography/routing
- Network capabilities

   F. Levels of abstraction — physical
     1. Architectural
       a. The basic service-level generic overlays shall consist of the following:
- Protocol
- Capacity

       b. Peer-to-peer protocols shall be used whenever possible.

II. Standards
  A. Global
    1. Architectural
      a. All generic overlays at any abstraction level will be declared to be enterprise standards.
      b. Overlay standards should follow international or other industry standards when possible.

  B. Levels of abstraction — physical
    1. Architectural
      a. Recognized layered communication architecture standards shall be used.
      b. The number of layered communications architectures used should be kept to a minimum.

III. Guidelines
  A. Global

      1. Architectural
        a. Enterprise-defined guidelines should follow accepted industry practices whenever possible.
      2. Design
        a. Assignment should follow good engineering practice.
        b. Digital networks should be used whenever possible.
  B. Levels of abstraction — physical
      1. Architectural
        a. The number of layered communications architectures used should be kept to a minimum.
  C. Levels of abstraction — deployed
      1. Design
        a. Artificial intelligence should be used as part of the network design process.
        b. The network design should not be based totally on a tariff that is subject to unilateral change.
        c. Geographically diverse facilities should be used for multiple access to any node.
  D. Assignment
      1. Architectural
        a. Assignment should be a joint effort among the network engineering, implementation, and service definition organizations.

IV. Rules
  A. Global
      1. Architectural
        a. Documentation for the entire assignment procedure will be in machine-readable form.
        b. No system will begin the deployment step of the development methodology until the assignment process is completed.
      2. Operational
        a. All changes to the communications archi-

tecture must be approved by the network engineering, implementation, and technology management organizations.

B. Levels of abstraction — general
1. Architectural
a. No more than 6 generic overlays will be defined for any abstraction level.

SUMMARY AND CONCLUSIONS

Communications and the network fabric that supports it are at the heart of the information network. The architecture that encompasses these entities must allow for the wide variety of possibilities needed to meet complex and often-changing circumstances. It must also allow the specification of suitable constraints that will make the design process as efficient and cost-effective as possible. The result should be a structure that can effectively guide the translation of business communication needs into a deployed network that takes advantage of the most effective technologies.

Most networks are currently designed by "seat-of-the-pants" techniques instead of state-of-the-art techniques. Although many of these ad hoc methods seem to work as intended, there are few ways of determining whether the result is as cost-effective as possible and takes advantage of the proper technology. As complexities grow and the interrelationships between public and private networks blur, this informal approach will not be sufficient, even to "get something up and running."

This chapter has presented a framework for network specification and design that eliminates much of the confusion inherent in reconciling conflicting viewpoints, abstraction levels, and business/technical orientations. This approach applies some degree of formalism to the network communications architecture specification process and will help to ensure that the deployed network will indeed meet the needs of the business as expressed by its differing participants and users.

The degree of linkage between the communications architecture and the server architecture is high. Both the physical server needs and the physical network needs must be known to determine the propriety of using deployed entities to perform the indicated functions. This again emphasizes the interrelationships among the major subarchitectures and the need to consider all their aspects during the design and implementation process.

SEVEN

NETWORK MANAGEMENT ARCHITECTURE

INTRODUCTION

Heterogeneous networks that incorporate products from a multitude of vendors and manufacturers will eventually form the vast majority of communication networks. No one supplier will be able to provide the vast array of products on which business will come to depend. These networks will integrate voice, data, text, image, and graphics information and will allow significant user control of network facilities. Both the network users and the network providers will be competing for control during day-to-day operation as well as under fault conditions. The users will have an obligation to protect their individual interests, and the common carriers or other network facilities suppliers will have an obligation to protect their network. The complexity that results from these multiple needs requires a sophisticated network management structure that will be capable of addressing the concerns of all participants.

For the purposes of this discussion, Network Management can be defined to be the art and science of provisioning a network and providing access to its services in a manner that meets the needs of the user.

All functions that are needed to accomplish the above activities can be considered to be part of network management.

Because of the broad definition, a large number of functions comprise network management and must be considered as part of the architecture.

Until recently, network management has been an "add-on" that was considered after most other details of the network were decided. This is not sufficient for the complex communication networks that are currently being put in place and that will be necessary in the future. In fact, the importance of the network management process and the need to integrate it with the other aspects of network design and implementation is the fundamental reason that network management was defined as one of the major (level 1) sub-architectures.

Network management schemes abound — every major vendor of computers and communications equipment seems to have at least one. Like many of the communications models and protocols, these network management approaches are incompatible. Although some claim to be able to incorporate a wide variety of equipment, most do not. One of the major purposes of the network management architecture is to create order from chaos and provide a structure that can be utilized to design, select, and deploy the most advantageous management systems, procedures, and tools. As with the other sub-architectures, this will be accomplished with considerable attention to the philosophy and theories underlying the approach selected. In fact, most of the chapter is spent defining and justifying a number of basic concepts. Once this has been accomplished, the actual specification of the architecture structure in terms of these fundamentals is quite simple.

SCOPE

Network management in an information network is concerned with providing and maintaining efficient and cost effective end-to-end communications. Network management must insure that any user on the network, whether a person or a program, can access any other user or program on the network, within the limits of their privilege and security classifications. This access must meet the needs of both the user and the application and, in addition, should minimize the costs to all parties of the transaction.

The end-to-end communications focus requires that communications be maintained on all layers of all reference models that are used as a part of the communications path. Thus, not only physical end-to-end connectivity but also application connectivity must be available between the two communicating ends. This is an especially difficult requirement when considering large networks with many subnetworks containing equipment developed by a multitude of vendors. The reference models, architectures, and implementation of these subnetworks may be completely different from one another, and yet they must communicate on an end-to-end basis as described above.

As discussed in the previous chapter, network management may also be utilized to keep entire services stable. This requires that network management be considered in the initial design of services as well as in the physical network. The network management architecture specifically makes provisions for this use.

The systems software must provide a number of functions that allow higher layer communications to take place, as described in chapter 3, and network management must insure that the process is functioning properly. As might be expected, a close relationship exists between many of the requirements of the system software architecture and the network management architecture.

Participation of network management in maintaining the higher layers of communication also places requirements on the application developers. Functions that allow the applications to participate in the network management process must be included as an integral part of the application. If this is not done and the application system malfunctions, the entire network could be adversely affected. This is especially true if many users are trying to utilize the application.

Traditional network management techniques have evolved from those utilized by telephone networks and "terminal-to-mainframe" computing networks. These are not adequate for the modern information network. This is true for several reasons that will become clear as the discussion progresses. Most importantly, current network management techniques are concerned only with the bottom layers of the reference models. This insures physical connectivity but does not insure that the proper sessions are maintained or that the applications are able to talk to each other on the application layer. This particular aspect will be addressed through a layered approach similar to that used in the communications model.

WHO'S IN CHARGE HERE?

Network management has traditionally been the responsibility of the network provider (such as the telephone company). If more than one network was involved in a given connection (switched telephone network and a public packet carrier), separate network management responsibilities and activities existed. If the user had difficulty communicating, finger-pointing between network management organizations was (and is) common.

With the advent of large-scale private networks, network management became the responsibility of the user organization that owned the network. Because few private network owners also own all of their own facilities, the facilities providers still retained the responsibility of managing their own equipment and transmission facilities. The potential for conflict was starting to exist.

As illustrated in the previous chapter, the question of control grows more complex: individual private networks are being interconnected; private networks are being implemented using a variety of public facilities, giving rise to multiple managers; geographical interconnections abound. Who controls (or wants to control, or tries to control) the network?

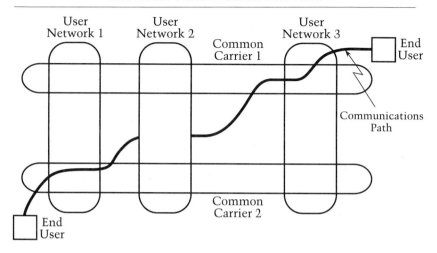

FIGURE 7.1   NETWORK CONTROL CONFLICTS

The answer is *everyone:* the user, the network operator/owner, the facilities supplier, and, unfortunately, unknown persons and organizations who are linked by circumstance.

One common occurrence of this multiple responsibility is illustrated in figure 7.1. An end-to-end connection between two users may use individual private networks (LANs, MANs, Satellite) and multiple public networks (local exchange and interexchange telephone, packet). If a problem exists, how is it to be identified and repaired? Who is going to try to circumvent the difficulty until it is eliminated? Who will be responsible for any additional expense caused by the problem? Any network management authority that can influence the result will certainly try to resolve it to the advantage of their own organization. Because these individual efforts may conflict, the end result may not be satisfactory to anyone and could eventually bring down some part of the network. Situations of this nature invite bad feelings and eventually lawsuits. This problem must be approached in a structured fashion that will produce results satisfactory to all participants.

One solution that can be eliminated immediately is a single gigantic network management system that has the responsibility of total control over everything. This is obviously not feasible for any but the smallest networks, but some of the proposals that have been advanced in this area by some suppliers seem to be espousing this approach. Even if it were possible, the complexity of the task would almost certainly force poor solutions to be utilized.

The key to success is in allowing individual network management processes and functions to communicate with one another using some form of gateway. Artificial intelligence will probably be needed as a major part of this type of process to provide the necessary response time, consistency, and level of expertise. Unfortunately, the state of the art is not yet at a point where this distributed AI-based network management function can be widely implemented. It will be necessary to achieve rapid advances in this technology area so that the complex networks planned for the future can be successfully deployed.

The architecture developed in this chapter is intended, among other purposes, to be a first step in providing a framework suitable for cooperating network management systems. This framework must be independent of any product or specific implementation so that it can be used to evaluate both. It must also be consistent with the other major subarchitectures and must act as an integral part of the networking process — not just as an add-on.

NETWORK MANAGEMENT ACTIVITIES

Network management is an umbrella term for a wide variety of activities that must take place in order to maintain continuous end-to-end communication among the users. For purposes of discussion, these activities can be divided into three types: administration, which is concerned with routine activities; planning which is concerned with future network utilization; and operations, which is concerned with current or real-time activities. This separation is made only for convenience; it must be understood that the activities of all three types are dependent on the same base data and that a signif-

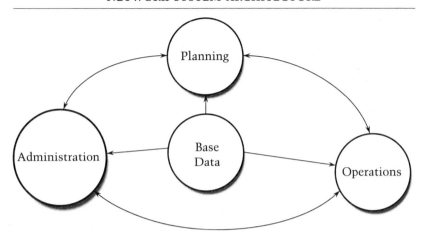

FIGURE 7.2   NETWORK MANAGEMENT FUNCTION INTERACTION

icant amount of sharing of derived information between the activities is necessary. This interdependence is illustrated in figure 7.2.

There is a tendency to equate network management only with its operation aspects. This occurs because operations is the most visible and exciting aspect of the function. Without a significant amount of attention to the other two parts of the management process, however, the operations activities will be ineffective. Operations cannot make up for poor design, inadequate funding, poor user service, and the lack of planning. Although many of the examples in this chapter are drawn from operations activities because of the familiarity of these activities and the number of illustrative possibilities available, it is important to remember that network management requires robust administrative and planning activities as well as operations.

Specific activities that are included in each of the three classifications are shown in table 7.1. Although this list is not exhaustive, it is representative of the many functions and features that a comprehensive network management architecture must consider. Because the purpose and function of most of these activities are relatively self-evident, only two

TABLE 7.1   NETWORK MANAGEMENT ACTIVITIES

Category	Activities
Administration — routine activities	Location changes User profiles Security Billing Training and education New users, services, and facilities Provisioning

Planning — future activities	Needs forecasting
	Modeling
	Design
	Usage analysis
	   Clients
	   Equipment
	   Transmission facilities
	Benefit analysis
	Disaster planning
	Change scheduling

Operations — real-time activities	User interaction for problem resolution
	Exception reports
	On-line data gathering
	Availability maintenance
	   Fault handling
	   Alarming
	   Performance analysis
	   Status and configuration
	   Congestion control
	Network control center

of the operations activities, which have significant architectural requirements of their own, are discussed individually. However, overall characteristics of each of the groups are discussed briefly to place their needs and characteristics in the proper perspective.

Administrative Activities

Administrative activities are not considered glamorous or technically challenging. In many cases, they are relegated to

287

an almost invisible status or become a burdensome bureaucracy. As long as these activities are based on human-to-human interaction, this will probably always remain a problem. Requests always seem to come in groups, associated with events such as:

- The end of the fiscal year
- The start (end) of a new project
- A major upgrade in facilities
- Personnel reorganization

Because of this peak loading characteristic, the response of many administrative organizations is not sufficient to meet the needs of the users.

If the administrative activities are assigned to a specific subnetwork of the network management overlay, most of the administrative functions can be made automatically, using artificial intelligence along with appropriate database techniques. Requests to change assigned services, billing inquiries, name and location changes, etc. are natural candidates for automation. To some extent, education and training can also be provided through the network using audio- and image-based mechanisms. Because network administration is essentially a service required by a specific group of clients, the service scenario presented in chapter 4 of the companion volume, *Information Systems and Business Strategies*, describes many of the benefits provided by an automated service approach for both client and enterprise.

Although the above reasons are certainly of significant value, one of the major reasons for utilizing automated administration is the ability to transfer information automatically from the operations and planning activities to the administration functions. For example, this would allow user profiles to be updated automatically to reflect equipment and facilities changes. The reverse information flow is also of considerable value. If a large number of users suddenly request access to a specific service, planning and operations could profitably use this data in their activities.

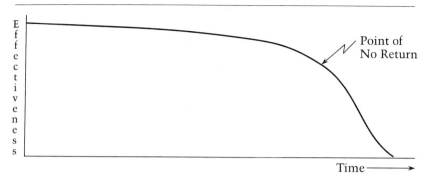

FIGURE 7.3   RESULT OF INADEQUATE NETWORK PLANNING

Although these information transfers can be accomplished with a manual system, it is certainly not efficient, and a great deal of the usefulness of the interaction is lost.

Planning Activities

Planning activities are designed to ensure that appropriate network changes are made as the requirements of the users and the enterprise change. Because these activities are oriented toward the future, they seem to be the most expendable and often are the first to be reduced or eliminated during a budget or other resource problem. Although the decline in planning may not be immediately evident, at some point, the usability of the network will suffer greatly, as shown in figure 7.3. Enough forces of change exist in the network so that the decrease in effectiveness tends to be quite sharp when all of these forces are felt to their fullest extent.

After the decrease in network performance has caused it to drop below the knee of the curve, it is difficult to restore, even with a significant increase in the resources applied. Even then, the technical restoration is easy compared with the restoration of confidence in the clients who use the network. This is extremely difficult at best and impossible at worst.

The best approach is to treat the planning activities with the same degree of concern and involvement as the operations activities. As a part of this, planning activities must be continuous, and the best information which can be obtained must be used in the process. Although this can be a significant undertaking, the network will not remain viable for long if these activities are neglected.

Network design has been defined as a planning activity. This includes initial design as well as changes that become necessary. This is an interface point with the communications architecture, where the structures and principles that determine network design reside.

Operations Activities

Of these categories, operations activities have had the most attention, and the greatest array of products and services exist for these activities. The excitement of responding in real time to the needs of the users in maintaining network viability and seeing the instantaneous effect of actions is a powerful attraction for work in this area. It is in many ways like the emergency room of a hospital. Although there is sometimes great danger, there is usually a great deal of action, and the potential to be a hero is always present.

However, in a sense, when events reach the point where operations activities must be utilized, especially those initiated for an emergency action, some other part of the network management process has failed. As an example, suitable applications should be in place to detect, isolate, and repair a facility or other problem before it becomes apparent to the end user, who then utilizes an operations activity to request assistance. Administration or planning activities should anticipate possible problems and develop procedures and processes to neutralize them. The place to deal with known or anticipated events is not operations, although with the current emphasis on those activities, operations usually ends up with most of the responsibility for controlling all problems. Operations should deal directly only with random acts of nature for which an *a priori* defense is not possible.

290

Most network management activities are extensive and complex enough that they require subarchitectures of their own. As one example, a subarchitecture for the user interaction function will be developed in the next section. Unfortunately, space does not allow subarchitectures to be developed for all of the activities that need them.

The user interaction, or *support activity* as it is commonly known, must be responsive to the needs of the end user, providing information not only to this user but also to organizations that are responsible for correcting problems that might arise in the network. This activity is commonly performed manually, but it can be automated using the same techniques as those previously discussed for the administration activities. The discussion in this section is oriented toward the current manual methods, but most of the approach could also be used in an automated system.

Because of the complexity of most information networks, if User A cannot reach Application B, no practical way exists for the end user to resolve the problem. One method for alleviating this problem is through the use of a *resolution structure*, as depicted in figure 7.4. This "hourglass" structure is designed to allow individual networks to retain their own management features and functions, provide for efficient end-to-end management, and require the end user to interact with only a single contact.

The hourglass structure of the problem-resolution process is designed to allow the scope of the search to be expanded only when necessary, and to separate the "help" function functionally from network and data center control. The function of the top half of the structure is to provide levels of problem resolution from operators of help facilities (usually called *help desks*). The lower half consists of network control centers that have jurisdiction over a specific subnetwork or group of subnetworks.

The scope of control increases toward the center of the hourglass. The sections at either end of the structure represent local help and control over a single or limited number

291

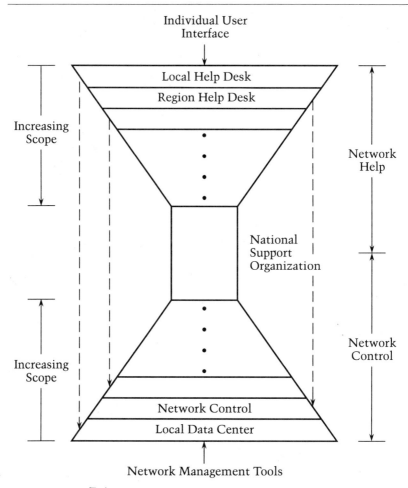

FIGURE 7.4 USER PROBLEM-RESOLUTION STRUCTURE

of locations or subnetworks. The middle section represents help and control over the entire network. Those sections between the ends and the middle represent help and control over a specific set of subnetworks and/or locations, such as a region. Although any number of levels could be utilized, three are used in the example: local, regional, and network-wide. This number will usually match the number of subnetworks in the generic geographical overlay for a hierarchical topology, as discussed in the previous chapter. If a flat network topology

292

is utilized, other means of determining separate management areas could be utilized, such as the organizational lines of the enterprise.

The following is an example of how the structure is used to solve network-related problems.

If an end user discovers that a certain application cannot be accessed from his/her workstation, the end user would call the local help desk (represented schematically by the upper section of the hourglass). This help desk would attempt to locate the problem within its limited area (probably only within the specific location concerned).

After ruling out user error or workstation malfunction, this local help desk might go to the local network control, such as for a LAN, to try to determine if the problem resides there. This local network control is represented in schematic form by the bottom section of the hourglass structure. The vertical line connecting the top and bottom sections represents this local scope.

If the problem cannot be determined by the local help desk, it is sent to a help desk with a broader scope (such as a regional help desk). This is represented by the second section of the hourglass. This help desk might have jurisdiction over all of the locations and subnetworks in an entire region. It would have the ability to discover if the problem resides anywhere within the region through interaction with the network control center for the region. If the problem is not found, responsibility transfers down to the next section, if any, until the center of the hourglass is reached. It is at this location that a view of the entire network, from both a help and a control point of view, is available. If it could not be handled elsewhere, the problem would finally be resolved here.

The data that each help desk draws upon will be acquired in the same way. The only difference is in the scope of the network being investigated. The integration layer of the reference model, described in the next section, is central to the implementation of this type of responsibility sharing. Without it, there is no assurance that the data that each level is

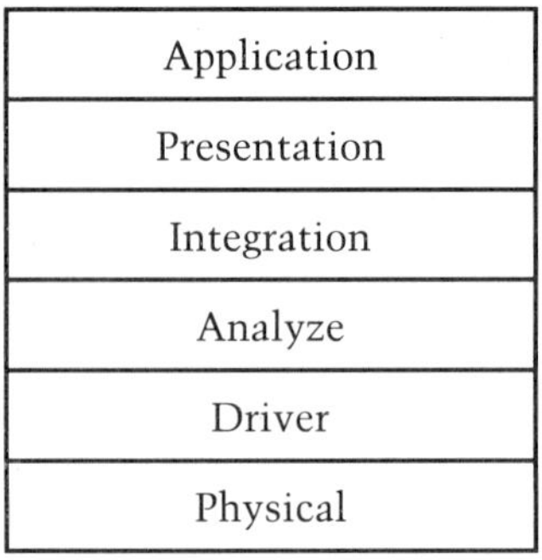

Application
Presentation
Integration
Analyze
Driver
Physical

FIGURE 7.5   NETWORK MANAGEMENT REFERENCE MODEL

using for resolution is the same or even consistent. It would be entirely possible for different help desks to draw different conclusions as to what constitutes the problem.

NETWORK MANAGEMENT REFERENCE MODEL

The distributed nature of the network management function and its close association with communications indicates that a layered approach may be useful in describing the fundamental concepts of various architectural components, in addition to serving as a basis for defining the more detailed architectural needs. Toward this end, a reference model for the network management architecture has been defined. This reference model utilizes six layers, and the names of the layers, along with their relationships are shown in figure 7.5. A short description of the functions of each layer is presented in table 7.2 for comparison purposes. The layers are described in somewhat greater detail in the following sections.

The layers in the network management architecture reference model should not be confused with the layers of the communications reference model. Although they are necessarily interrelated, the functions of each layer are completely different, even though the names of the layers may be the same (such as the physical layer). The relationship between the two reference models is described in a later section.

294

TABLE 7.2   NETWORK MANAGEMENT REFERENCE MODEL
LAYER FUNCTIONS

Layer	Functions
Application layer	Functions that combine elements of all partitions, that cannot be assigned individually to any one partition, or that involve the transfer of data from one partition to another. Also: • Ad hoc queries • Management reports • Historical analysis • Statistical analysis • Data transfer between network management systems
Presentation layer	Functions that are specific to the administrative, planning, or operations activities and that utilize data organized for one of these partitions. Also: • Data formatting • Display techniques
Integration layer	Functions that integrate, store, and organize the data received from and sent to the network entities. Also: • Data reduction • Data audits • Pattern analysis • Network-wide activity coordination
Analyze layer	Functions that must be carried out immediately, such as emergency alarm handling. Also: • Active feedback • Unit coordination • Polling
Driver layer	Functions that involve interaction with the transducers. Also: • Logical to physical translation • Error detection/correction • Condition setting/matching
Physical layer	Functions that involve direct interaction with the network entities to be monitored and controlled. This layer generally consists of the transducers that are placed into a network entity for monitor and control purposes.

In a layered system or reference model approach, the next step after the definition of the layers of the model is the formal definition of the protocols and interfaces of each layer. These protocols and interfaces are sometimes referred to as the *architecture* of the layered system, as was discussed in the previous chapter. Defining this architecture is a complex and involved task that can consume a significant amount of resources. Because of the complexity and attendant effort involved, it is not possible to develop these definitions in this book. This discussion must be postponed to a later publication.

The lack of specification of formal protocols and interfaces will not interfere with the use of the reference model in defining other aspects of the network management architecture. As discussed previously, the layered system architecture is only one component in the overall architecture of the process using it. An enterprise that is establishing an architectural approach to network management should develop simple protocols and interfaces as initial enterprise standards. These can be changed and expanded as the technology matures. Establishing these initial standards makes it possible to develop a formal approach to the specification of network management gateways and attendant protocol conversion needs.

As is the case with the communications reference model, each network management layer has its own view of the universe (span of knowledge). These views are indicated during the discussion of the individual levels.

Physical Layer

The physical layer of the network management reference model contains the transducers that couple the network management system to the operational network entities. The word *transducer* is used here to indicate either a sensor or an actuator, depending on whether a monitor or control function is indicated. The scope of this layer is a single transducer. It does not contain the knowledge necessary to coordinate or understand interactions between multiple transducers.

If the operation of a piece of hardware is to be monitored/controlled, the transducers will be a combination of hardware and software that provides the interface. The hardware (such as a transmission line) must have the proper design and "hooks" that will allow it to be utilized with the network management transducer. Most equipment intended for network use now contains the necessary functions for network management interfacing.

If the operation of a piece of software is to be monitored/controlled, the transducers usually will be implemented in software and imbedded in the software to be coupled. Interaction is usually through tables of various sorts, which are read and written by both the function software and the network management software. The operating system must play an important role in this type of interaction, and the architecture developed in chapter 3 is designed to support that function. As with the hardware entities, the functional software (such as a business application) must have the proper design and "hooks" that will allow it to be utilized with the network management transducer. Although some software does have some type of interface that can be used for network management purposes (usually system or support software), all software must eventually contain provisions for a network management interface.

The current lack of software product interfaces to a network management function results partially from the low priority given to network management as a whole and particularly for the higher layers of the communications reference model. Although an understanding of the need for broad based network management systems is growing, there will be a continuing lack of such facilities until some widely accepted standards are developed for the transducers and their functions. Table 7.3 provides a list of some of the more obvious functions that a software transducer should be able to perform. The format of the data will be highly dependent on the

297

TABLE 7.3 SOFTWARE SYSTEM TRANSDUCER NEEDS

Monitoring Functions	Controlling Functions
Sanity check	Initialize
Error counts	Slow down
Response time	Stop
Traffic volume	Test execution
Test results	Condition setting
Condition occurrence	Report state
Indicate inconsistent request	

functional software. In addition, it must be remembered that this is just raw data. The interpretation of the data must be left to higher layers in the network management reference model.

Driver Layer

The driver layer contains the functions necessary to accept information in a standard form from the analyze layer and provide the information to the physical layer in a form suitable for the particular transducer being accessed. The reverse transformation is, of course, also a function of this layer. This logical-to-physical function mapping enables a wide variety of transducers to be used for both hardware and software while maintaining higher-level functional equivalence.

This layer also provides a fundamental link in the real-time monitor and controller structure. It is used to set a condition in the entity being managed and to determine when that condition has been met. The conditions may be quite complex, involving multiple transducers in the same entity. Managing conditions across entities is the function of the analyze layer.

The driver layer also determines whether the interaction between the transducer and the entity being managed is performing correctly. This is one aspect of the error detection/correction function that is assigned to this layer. This function is concerned only with the proper coupling of the network entity and the network management system. It is not concerned with the proper functioning of the network entity. This is left to higher layers.

The scope of this layer is the network functional entity. Because a single entity may have multiple transducers, this layer needs to be able to coordinate among all of the transducers in an entity.

Analyze Layer

The analyze layer performs a number of processing functions, including data integration or separation, so that a number of network entities can be controlled or monitored as a coordinated unit. In addition, the first level of data reduction takes place in this layer, although the bulk of the reduction is left to the integration layer. The analyze layer also performs alarm processing based on the condition occurrence information from the driver layer. It also provides the means by which active feedback is accomplished for real-time control and measurement. This latter function includes any timing and selection of specific network entities to be monitored and/or controlled for the function under test.

In order to understand this active feedback activity, it is necessary to categorize monitor and control operations into two types, passive and active. Passive operations are concerned with non real-time measurement and parameter-setting activities. Passive monitoring would include activities that measure the amount of traffic on a particular link by time of day, measure the response time of a particular application or piece of physical hardware, and count the number of retries for a particular communications link. Passive control would include such activities as setting the permissible number of retries on a communications link and updating a table containing specific routing information.

Active operations, on the other hand, require coordination between monitor and control operations. As an example: In order to determine the response time for a particular piece of equipment, dummy operations may have to be utilized. The operations would be formulated by an appropriate activity and entered into the system by a control operation. The results would be detected by a monitor operation, and the resultant information would be interpreted through the use of an appropriate function.

In order to insure that the correct entities are being observed, close coordination would have to be maintained, and this coordination is the function of the analyze layer. It is necessary to perform the active feedback at this layer because it is close enough to the physical entities to ensure that timing requirements are met and yet has the necessary span of control to utilize effectively the relatively high-level commands indicating the type of operations needed.

The analyze layer scope is that of a group of network entities that form some sort of a logical unit. The definition of this unit is a function of the higher layers. The definition is dynamic and may change slowly or rapidly depending on the specific need being addressed.

Integration Layer

The integration layer is the first layer with a scope that includes the whole network. It has two basic responsibilities: It is responsible for all of the data in the network management system, and it is responsible for coordination activities that involve multiple units (as defined in the analyze layer).

As a part of its data responsibility, this layer collects all raw and processed data from the other layers and integrates and organizes it along functional lines. Developing new forms of the data through statistical analysis and other reduction techniques is also performed at this layer. This layer is also responsible for the security and validity of the data and contains functions such as database audits that aid in this area.

300

As part of the integration layer's coordination function, it performs the initial pattern analysis required to determine whether specific network-wide events are occurring. It is also responsible for setting the conditions that define those events.

Presentation Layer

The presentation layer contains those functions which are specific to the administration, planning, or operations partition of network management. Each of these classifications, in general, has specific needs in the way data is stored, presented, and manipulated, and this layer contains functions that are unique to one of these classes. In addition, specific applications written for the various functions contained in these classes also reside in this layer. Because these different classes utilize different types of user interface equipment and software, these functions are also considered to be a part of this layer. Most of the activities that were listed in table 7.3 would be resident in this layer.

Although the scope of the presentation layer is network-wide, it is limited to the activities in one partition. Cross-partition functions are the responsibility of the application layer.

Application Layer

The application layer contains functions that span multiple partitions of the network management activities. One of the major classes of functions in this layer consists of functions that transfer information from one partition to the next. As an example, consider the case where operations determines that a given transmission link continuously overloads to the point that it must be taken out of service. This information should be sent to the planning partition, along with a recommendation for the proper sizing of the link. The function that does this analysis and notification would reside in the application layer.

301

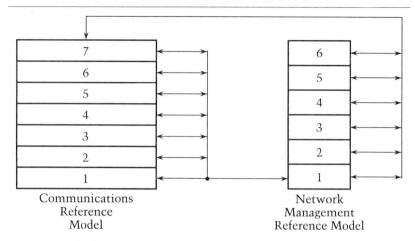

FIGURE 7.6   NETWORK MANAGEMENT REFERENCE MODEL
INTERACTION WITH COMMUNICATIONS REFERENCE MODEL

The scope of the application layer is all aspects of the entire network. It is the only layer with this broad range, and any functions that require processing or data across this spectrum must belong to this layer.

Reference Model Interaction

Figure 7.6 shows the interaction between the network management and communications reference models. In order to provide the network management system with the information it needs, each of the layers in the communications reference model must have imbedded in it the appropriate transducers, be they hardware or software, in order to detect and store that information. As an example, layer 1 might contain a hardware sensor to determine whether the timing on a particular link function is correct, layer 7 might contain an application program with network management software, as discussed previously, designed to detect whether the application is running and whether it is being accessed properly by other entities in the network.

The output from these transducers, no matter which layer

of the communications reference model they belong to, becomes part of layer 1 (the physical layer) of the network management reference model. In order to send this information through the various layers of the network management reference model, the constructs defined by the communications subarchitecture have to be used if the network management layers are on different nodes. Thus, the information garnered from an appropriate layer in the communications reference model and fed to layer 1 of the network management reference model would then be sent to layer 2 of the network management model. This would be done by taking the output from layer 1, treating it as application data, utilizing the communications subarchitecture to send it to the node at which layer 2 resides, and then taking that information again on the application layer and putting it back into the network management reference model at layer 2. This process would continue throughout all the layers of the network management reference model.

From a communications point of view, all of the information contained in the network management subarchitecture is treated as application data when it is sent to a node or from layer to layer throughout the network. Data in the communications reference model that is utilized by network management is treated as if it were physical data. Utilizing this type of interconnectivity gives network management a powerful yet flexible means of insuring end-to-end connectivity at all of the communication layers.

If the network management system is performing a control function rather than a monitoring function, the directions of the arrows between the network management model and the communications model would, of course, be reversed.

NETWORK MANAGEMENT ARCHITECTURE STRUCTURE

The architecture consists of two major parts: the reference model and associated architecture, which were discussed in a previous section, and the structures necessary for the utilization of the model in a network environment. To help explain the structures needed for network use of the model, some aspects of the required migration from current network management structures to those defined by the architecture of this chapter are discussed in the following sections.

Distribution Model

In the communications reference model, all of the layers must be co-resident on a participating network node. The number of layers needed depends on the function of the node: gateway, end user, switch, etc. This puts the emphasis on the protocols of the model, because these are the units being transferred across the network. In the network management reference model, each of the layers can reside on different servers/nodes and geographic locations within the network. This puts the emphasis on the interfaces between layers, because these now become the unit of network transfer. Some protocols are still of interest, because cross-layer communication (such as active feedback) still occurs.

The distributed nature of the network management reference model is shown in figure 7.7. The term *server/node* is used in the context of this discussion because of the interface of network management with both the communications architecture (node) and the various architectures defined for network application systems (server). Obviously, both utilize processing power and are kept with separate identities only to ensure that the proper context is being used.

To determine what servers/nodes the different layers of the network management system are assigned, a process similar to the one described in the server architecture discussion of chapter 5 is utilized. In this context, network management behaves similarly to a complex network application. In utilizing this type of approach, it must be kept in mind that the attributes and values of the "network management application" and the servers/nodes to which it will be assigned are somewhat different than described in the server discussion.

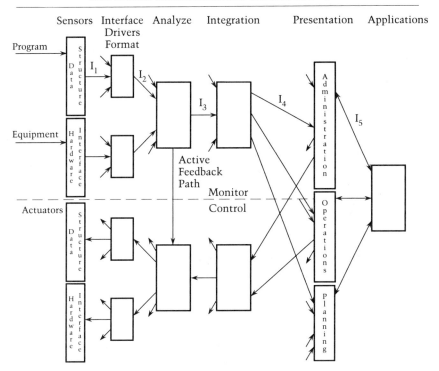

FIGURE 7.7   NETWORK MANAGEMENT DISTRIBUTION MODEL

Because of space limitations, the assignment process as modified for network management is not presented here. You should have enough knowledge at this point, however, to be able to define a simple set of suitable modifications.

Individual functions of each layer may also be assigned to different nodes/servers as appropriate (for example, a layer may itself be distributed). Although this capability is not shown in the diagram, it is only a minor extension of the concept to allow this type of sublayer partitioning and distribution.

In essence, each layer (or groups of layers) could also be considered a subnetwork of the network needed to support the network management system. This would form an overlay as defined in the network communications architecture described in the previous chapter. In that discussion, a net-

305

work management overlay of four subnetworks was defined for illustrative purposes. The correspondence between that overlay and the layers could be as follows:

Overlay	*Layers*
Signaling network	Transducer, driver layers
Transmission network	Analyze, integration, presentation (planning), application layers
Administration network	Presentation (administration) layer
Operations network	Presentation (operations)

This assumes that most network management traffic is sent over the same facilities or uses the same communication model and architecture as that of the application traffic. If this is not the situation, a different correspondence would have to be made. Most of the network management layer communication would transfer from the transmission network to the signaling network. The split between the two is, of course, an engineering issue.

This area is another interface between the communications architecture and the network management architecture. In any of these interface points, satisfying the requirements of both architectures usually requires an iterative approach. This results from the necessity to verify changes made to meet the requirements of one architecture with the interfacing architecture(s).

Migration Issues

Current network management architectures (when they exist at all) are, for the most part, structured according to the diagram shown in figure 7.8. Essentially, layer 3 (analyze), layer 4 (integration), and layer 6 (application) of the reference model are null or at best all combined with the presentation layer. The most significant drawback of this approach is that

306

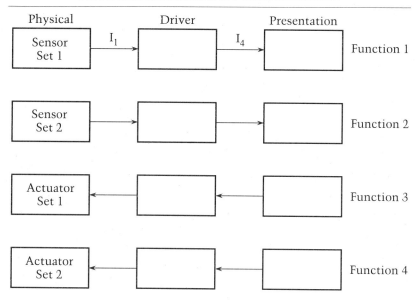

FIGURE 7.8   CURRENT NETWORK MANAGEMENT
IMPLEMENTATION

a functionally separate system is utilized for every network management function or requirement. This also implies that there is no need to standardize any of the interfaces and protocols, because every application can develop its own. This common assumption also partially explains the present chaos in network management approaches, structure, and standards.

A human being is usually the coupling between presentation functions when necessary. The actions of the human become the application. This is especially true in going from monitor functions to control functions. True coupling between operations, planning, and administration presentations does not occur, because human intervention is required and the available resources in this area are generally not sufficient to allow this interaction.

In addition, without any integration facilities, real-time control facilities, and cross presentation functions, it is difficult to treat a large network as an entity, and the network management problem has to be broken up into a series of small management functions and areas. This does not meet the end-to-end criteria that has been observed to be one of the fundamental objectives of network management in information networks.

In order to migrate from this kind of structure based on small functions to one based on integrated network management, it is necessary to define and implement the missing layers. The order in which this is accomplished should be from lower to higher layers. An analyze function should be implemented first, then a integration function, and finally an application function. This assumes that elements of the other layers exist and can be suitably modified without an inordinate amount of resources. If this is not the case, a migration may not be the answer, and an entirely new system may have to be implemented and deployed. This would have to be performed in a fashion that does not interfere with the use of the network — not a small task. The alternative, however, is not acceptable in technical or economic terms.

ARCHITECTURE PRINCIPLES

The following statements are the principles that are derived from the structures defined for the network management architecture. In keeping with the practice established for this section, these principles are grouped according to the components of the architecture, which in this case are the layers of the reference model and their associated functions.

I. Strategies
  A. Global
    1. Architectural
      a. A specific procedure will be developed for assigning the network management layers and functions to the nodes/servers on the network.

    b. Individual architectures for complex functions will be developed.

    c. Every network deployed or used by the enterprise will have an explicit network management system that is consistent with the architecture.

    d. Users will be provided end-to-end network management services.

    e. There will be a single point of contact for the end user in requesting information about the network.

2. Design

    a. All network management systems will employ products that are on the approved product list.

    b. New products designed to meet a need that is not served effectively by existing candidates must first be qualified for the approved product list.

    c. A heterogeneous set of network management products is desirable and encouraged.

3. Operational

    a. Before any network management product that has no deployed equivalent can be used permanently, an extensive test program must be completed successfully.

    b. The responsibility for network management will be placed in a network management organization that has no other operational function.

    c. The network management system will be continuously available. No function will be designed such that it requires the network management system to be stopped for any reason.

    d. The same organization will be responsible for the administration, planning, and operations aspects of network management.

B. Reference model — general
  1. Architectural
     a. A set of principles shall be developed to guide the definition of enterprise protocols and layer interfaces.
     b. Sublayers of any layer may be defined as needed to keep the functions simple and easily implementable.
     c. Interfaces between sublayers shall have the same structure and characteristics as those between major layers.
     d. Only one network management reference model and associated architecture should be used in the network, regardless of the number of communication models and architectures employed.
C. Reference model — physical
  1. Architectural
     a. All network entities defined by a communications model layer shall have the means to embed transducers (sensor and actuator).
     b. All transducers should have a core set of capabilities even though their interface characteristics may vary.
     c. The smallest possible number of different transducer types should be used.
D. Reference model — driver
  1. Architectural
     a. There will be one driver function per network entity.
E. Reference model — analyze
  1. Design
     a. Active feedback transactions will not consist of more than .1 percent of maximum traffic or more than 5 percent of current traffic on any involved link.

F. Reference model — integration
   1. Architectural
      a. Database management systems used by the integration layer shall be either relational or object-oriented in design.
      b. The use of DBMSs shall follow all of the architectural tenets of the data architecture.
G. Reference model — presentation layer
   1. Architectural
      a. Presentation layer functions are not required to interface with users. For example, monitor-control pairs may be automated.

II. Standards
   A. Global
      1. Architecture
         a. Enterprise standards will be developed for all network management model interfaces and protocols used in the network.
         b. No interface or protocol will be implemented and/or deployed unless it has been identified as an enterprise standard.
         c. Industry standards or those developed by recognized standards bodies will be used whenever possible.
         d. De facto standards set by a competing vendor will not be adapted unless it is required for competitive purposes. Such standards will be in addition to the one adapted by the enterprise.
   B. Reference model — general
      1. Architectural
         a. A single reference model and architecture shall be defined and used in all networks used and/or deployed by the enterprise.
         b. Approval of the reference model and architec-

ture shall be required by the network management, software engineering, technology management, and implementation organizations.

C. Reference model — presentation layer
    1. Architectural
        a. Presentation layer functions that interface with humans shall be standardized by the enterprise.

D. Reference model — application layer
    1. Architectural
        a. Enterprise standards for network management applications shall be developed.

III. Guidelines
  A. Global
    1. Architectural
        a. Enterprise-defined guidelines should follow accepted industry practices whenever possible.
    2. Design
        a. Interface and protocol design should follow good engineering practice.
        b. Object-oriented techniques should be used whenever possible.

  B. Reference model — physical layer
    1. Architectural
        a. Software transducers should be developed by the vendor of the software being affected whenever possible.
        b. Software transducers should be proved correct using a theorem-proving technique.

  C. Reference model — analyze layer
    1. Design
        a. Active feedback should be used sparingly.
        b. The entities contained in a network group should have some synergy with one another.
        c. Assignment should be a joint effort between

the network engineering, implementation, and service definition organizations.

D. Reference model — presentation layer
1. Design
   a. Artificial intelligence should be used extensively in the network control center to keep human intervention to a minimum.
   b. Artificial intelligence should be used extensively for network design.
   c. Artificial intelligence should be used extensively in automating the administration functions.

IV. Rules
A. Global
1. Architectural
   a. Documentation for all the network management functions will be in machine-readable form.
   b. No system will begin the implementation steps of the development methodology unless the network management interfaces are specified.
2. Operational
   a. Manual overrides to all automatic operation partition actions shall be provided. These overrides shall have appropriate levels of security provided.
B. Reference model — physical layer
1. Architectural
   a. All transmission lines, modems, multiplexers, switches, session control software, application programs shall have transducers embedded in them.
   b. The state of all transducers shall be made available on command.

c. The number of separate transducers in any one network entity will be three or less.

SUMMARY AND CONCLUSIONS

Network management is an evolving function that is trying to leave the limited needs of yesterday to provide for the growing needs of today, while eventually arriving at the unknown but complex needs of tomorrow. A flood of products that promise to be the ultimate in network management has been unleashed by vendors who want to achieve significant market share before anyone realizes the considerable limitations of these products. The products come from established computer vendors, network facilities providers, and start-up companies in backyard garages. They range from very specific niche offerings to those intended to be all things to all people. Some of the latter offerings are touted to be based on comprehensive architectures, when in reality the architecture is the product. This latter result is a generic problem that seems to occur more often as the need for comprehensive architectures becomes increasingly evident.

Almost all of these efforts will fail because of the lack of a suitable architecture that takes into account all of the aspects of network management that must be addressed. This includes a heterogeneous set of facilities; integrated voice, data, image, and graphics; shared control; combinations of public and private facilities; and economic considerations that will become predominant. Business needs will rapidly outstrip any product-based approach and render it useless. In addition, a rapidly changing technology base will make many of these products obsolete before they even hit the street.

The architecture presented in this chapter is an attempt to consider all of the relevant issues and provide a foundation on which to base the overall approach to network management independent of any product or supplier. As such, it can be used for the evaluation of any network management product or set of products as well as to influence the vendors

314

toward producing offerings that meet the needs of the network owner, operator, and — above all — the user.

As an architecture that is intended to bridge to the future, it is a stretch architecture. Functions have been defined that are at the leading edge of the technology — or over it. This is as it should be and continues the tradition of the architecture — understand the past, allow for the present, and provide for the future.

E I G H T

APPLICATION DEVELOPMENT ARCHITECTURE

INTRODUCTION

The application development architecture contains the domain knowledge needed to guide the effective and efficient implementation of network systems. It must provide the structures and principles that can serve four basic needs:

- Focus the other level 1 architectures on the implementation process and system needs (insure that the philosophies, constructs, and principles of the other architectures are followed)
- Specify the characteristics needed in the development methodology (although the development methodology will be selected according to a complex set of needs, it must retain certain characteristics to be compatible with the overall development process)
- Specify the characteristics of the resultant system structures (although many system designs can meet the requirements and specifications, the one chosen must meet specified business and technology needs)
- Specify the operational characteristics of the deployed systems (ensure that the deployed systems behave in accordance with business policies and organization needs)

316

Although all of these needs are interconnected, for simplicity, they will be discussed independently.

Even though the application development subarchitecture is central to the entire architecture structure, it is not a large or complex structure, and the number of principles needed is quite small. It contains relatively few components and functions compared with those needed by some of the other subarchitectures described in previous chapters. Much of the presentation refers to the chapters on the other subarchitectures or the development methodology for further explanations of the technology or principle involved.

ARCHITECTURE FOCUS

Architectural focus can be provided in two ways. The first is by requiring that the appropriate entries be inserted into the system specifications. Each system would define its own services, even in areas that must appear to be the same for all systems. Although the assets necessary to construct these services would be defined and available, this is a relatively inefficient means of providing focus. It is, however, the most widely used approach.

A more efficient process would be to define and implement these services as part of the deployment infrastructure and require that each system provide the proper interface. This would also result in more uniformity and fewer problems than the former method. The application development architecture therefore requires that four systems be developed as part of the deployment infrastructure. Each application system is required to provide the proper facilities to interact with them. The systems to be provided through the infrastructure are:

- Network system software
- Network management
- Data services
- End user services

The characteristics of each of these systems are defined by its associated architecture. Other requirements will be necessary, and these will be defined through the normal system definition process.

The architecture requires that no application system be allowed to redefine or bypass these services. If a required function is not available in the infrastructure system, the system must be changed to accommodate the need. Interaction with the server and communications architectures will be through the specification process.

DEVELOPMENT METHODOLOGY CHARACTERISTICS

A detailed presentation of methodologies in general and development methodologies in particular is presented in the companion volume, *Information Networks: A Design and Implementation Methodology*. In selecting the specific characteristics of a given methodology, however, guidance must be drawn from the architecture. This section addresses the determination of the architectural needs.

A number of philosophical issues must be considered before the characteristics of a development methodology(s) can be determined and a specific methodology that meets the criteria can be defined and documented. These issues generally fall into these classes:

• Intended users
• Verification methods
• Development (historical) generation
• Life cycle range
• Development environment
• Deployment environment
• System (design) structure
• System purpose
• System size

The general philosophical directions set by each of these issues will be discussed along with some other directly associated issues. Keep in mind that it is not the intent of this architecture to define the methodology, only to provide a set of criteria that must be met by the particular methodology eventually selected.

Although certain methodologies may accommodate diverse sets of characteristics, most are directed toward meeting specific conditions. This is one of the reasons that many development methodologies are in current use.

The philosophy directions that are used in determining the characteristics of a methodology specifically suited for the implementation of network systems are indicated in the sections that follow.

Intended Users

A methodology is usually oriented toward a specific set of users. There are many possible ways of defining these sets depending on the particular affinity being addressed. For the purposes of this discussion, the following partitioning is useful:

- Professional personnel with the assigned task of developing permanent systems that will be used by large numbers of operators
- Professional personnel with the assigned task of developing temporary systems that will be used by a small set of people
- End users with a need for simple applications that will be used by others
- End users with a need for simple applications that will not be used by others

The affinity metric is the degree to which one's job is directly dependent on the development process. All of these developers and their organizations can benefit from the use of a methodology tailored to their needs. The most critical requirement, however, is a methodology oriented toward the first group. This methodology will also be the most complex

319

and the most demanding in terms of its formalisms and capabilities.

Validation Methods

The product that results from the application of any methodology must be verified to ensure its usefulness in meeting the need addressed. The two aspects of this need are the method of verification and the timing of the verification. This verification can be accomplished using a number of methods, some of which are listed here:

- User validation
- Formal acceptance criteria
- Industry/government certification process
- Standard specification
- Marketing agreement
- Developer agreement

Some of these are mandated by customers or follow standard industry practice. Others are chosen for arbitrary reasons and may or may not be useful under the circumstances. Unfortunately, one of the most often utilized methods is the developer agreement method. With this method, the developers decide if the product meets the intended need. This certainly puts little pressure on the methodology used. It also does not do a good job of performing its intended function. The other methods do have a considerable influence on the type and characteristics of the methodology needed.

Because the area of concentration is on information networks whose main purpose is to serve the end user, the verification method chosen for the methodology is that of user verification. The individuals who are to use (own, operate, etc.) the system are the ones who should determine if the system meets the intended needs. The methodology includes this user interaction as an integral part of its design.

The second issue is the timing of the verification. Should there be one or many verifications? When in the development cycle should they come? The answers to these questions have a wide range. To some extent, they depend on the verification methods. In fact, different verification methods can be used at different times in the development cycle. The methodology must support whatever decisions are made in this area. Because of the generally high cost of information network systems, a verification process will be conducted during each major step of the implementation methodology. This is specified in an attempt to limit the financial exposure of the development. Changes need to be initiated as soon as the need for them can be determined. In extreme cases, this may even mean canceling the project. The sooner this decision can be reached, the more cost-effective the result will be.

Combining the two needs presented in the above discussion results in the following methodology requirement. User verification will be performed in all of the methodology steps. This has the advantage of consistency and the psychological advantage of continuous user involvement in the development. The penalty is increased demand for management resources and the inefficiencies inherent in the process.

Development Generation (Historical)

The historical development generation that the methodology is designed to support also has considerable influence on the methodology design. Because the development process assumed in this book is that required to support fourth- and fifth-generation development, other generations are not considered in this discussion. The major issue in this area then becomes one of emphasis. Is the fourth or fifth generation emphasized, or is the achievement of a equal balance indicated?

This determination rests on two considerations: the state of the relevant technologies and the type of products being developed. Although the fifth-generation technology is currently lagging behind the fourth, there is an extensive need to use fifth-generation techniques in the design and development of information systems. A balance between the two is therefore indicated. This balance should be reflected in the methodology design. Because of the developing and rapidly changing characteristics of the fifth generation, the methodology must also be designed to effectively accommodate this type of change.

Because fourth-generation technology is used as one of the fundamental design approaches of the methodology, the methodology must be based on the use of assets for providing system components whenever possible and the use of prototypes that contain the embodiment of the system design and/ or implementation knowledge at each phase of the methodology. Because user verification has been selected as the system validation method, the prototypes naturally become the physical vehicle by which this verification will be accomplished.

The fourth and fifth generations define and use common services. This fact was utilized in the earlier discussion on maintaining architectural focus. Effectively utilizing the deployment infrastructure to the maximum extent possible is an associated requirement. This must be supported by the development methodology. Other relevant issues to consider relative to generations as they apply to the development process are migration needs, organization capabilities, and technology availability. These must all be considered and accommodated by the design of the methodology.

Life Cycle Range

The view of the development organization as to the life cycle of the product also has a considerable influence on the methodology. Some of the issues that are related closely to this are discussed in the system structure section later in this chapter (that is, the optimization metric). The main focus of this issue, however, is on when the development can be considered to begin and end. As an example, assume that an organization (internal or external) contracts to design and implement a product.

Scenario 1:

The responsibility of this organization is to take already developed requirements and specifications, implement a product based solely on that input, and deliver that product to the customer with no further involvement. The life cycle of that product as seen by the development organization is quite limited. The methodology need not include any function outside that limited domain.

Scenario 2:

The responsibility of this organization includes the determination or validation of the requirements and specifications as well as responsibility for changes and associated development after the product is delivered and deployed. In this situation, the life cycle of the product is quite broad, and not only must the methodology include those additional functions but the design and implementation functions may also have to change considerably to make the others more efficient or effective.

The methodology presented here is developed using the extended life cycle definition. In most information system developments, one organization has the responsibility from definition to retirement.

Implementation Environment

The implementation environment is a complex entity, as was discussed in the introduction. Many issues, both business and technical, are associated with this environment and must be considered in determining the structure of the methodology. Some of these issues were touched on earlier (for example, tools). For the purposes of this section, however, only one of these issues need be covered. That issue concerns the source of the knowledge that will be used in the development process. That knowledge can come from a wide variety of sources, including knowledgeable individuals, previous developments, customer requirements, etc.

Previous discussions reached the conclusion that, for the purposes of this book, an architecture would be used to provide this domain knowledge. This requires that the methodology be capable of assimilating and using the information contained in the architecture. If this coupling is not a fundamental part of the methodology structure, the methodology will fail. The methodology will be required to have a structure which provides for close architectural interaction.

Deployment Environment

The deployment environment also has a considerable influence on the methodology structure. A large installed base or significant deployed infrastructure elements will place a considerable constraint on the characteristics of the deployed products. The methodology must ensure that that these constraints are recognized and met as required. The constructs of the methodology assume that significant constraints of this nature do exist. It is the rare information system that does not have to fit into an already existing environment that imposes considerable constraints on new arrivals.

The infrastructure can be defined to be a set of capabilities that are external to the application system being developed but that are necessary for its proper functioning. Examples of the infrastructure would be the processors on which the applications execute, the network facilities, interfacing functions, etc. The infrastructure does not include components that will become part of the system itself (assets).

The philosophy governing the development and utilization of infrastructure capabilities must be determined and utilized by the architecture in developing guidance for the methodology structure. There are three approaches to the use of the infrastructure:

- Use the infrastructure whenever possible, even if the system design must be changed slightly to fit.
- Use the infrastructure if it fits the system need exactly.
- Do not use it if at all possible. Control all factors associated with the system.

An associated philosophical direction must be addressed here. If an infrastructure function is needed but does not exist (at least in its proper form), should the capability be developed as part of a separate infrastructure development? Or should the capability be developed as an integral part of the system?

If the infrastructure is used rarely, and needed functions are developed as part of the system, the infrastructure has little or no effect on the methodology. This also seems to be the most often chosen infrastructure utilization philosophy. The result of this is duplication of facilities, higher cost and complexity, as well as substandard facilities.

Using the infrastructure whenever possible will lead to the most efficient development and utilization of resources, although it also places constraints on the system and methodology design. The architecture assumes that this is the philosophy to be followed, and the methodology must contain constructs that allow it to identify and interface systems under development to the infrastructure. It must also contain mechanisms that identify needed infrastructure capabilities and transmit those to the organizations responsible for providing the infrastructure.

System Structure Characteristics

Many attributes are concerned with system structure. Some of the major ones are listed here:

- Module (component) size
- Implementation language (single/multiple)
- Centralized/distributed
- Design methodology (organization)

325

    Structured decomposition
    Data flow
    Decision tables
    Finite state machine
    Object-oriented
    Building elements/scripts
- Size
- Optimization metric

As with the other issues, the methodology must be capable of supporting any relevant value set for these attributes. In many instances, the tools (manual or automated) that will be used in the development process will make assumptions concerning these values. If this is the case, the characteristics and orientation of the tools must be understood and considered in the development of the methodology.

In some respects, a chicken and egg situation exists between the methodology and the tools that are used in its implementation. It is difficult to define a methodology and then find a set of tools that will support it effectively. Likewise, because of the vast array of tools available, it is difficult to settle on a set of tools without having defined the methodology. Obviously, an iterative approach is indicated, so that the two will function in a synergistic mode. The starting point should be the methodology, however. It is far better for the methodology to play the dominant role in the selection of the tools than for the tools to play the dominant role in the selection of the methodology.

Module size and implementation languages are mostly a function of the skill set and specific tools used by the enterprise. I prefer to utilize methodologies that allow a great deal of flexibility in this area. Fortunately, most methodologies can support a wide range of module sizes and implementation languages.

The centralized/distributed decision is much more fundamental to the structure of the methodology. Most current design methodologies emphasize the centralized approach and cannot do an adequate job of producing distributed and cooperative systems. The emphasis of this book has been on the development of network systems, and these require a distributed structure. It is therefore assumed that all systems developed for the network environment will be distributed, and the design methodology must inherently be able to define cooperative and distributive systems in accordance with the architecture directions.

The selection of one or more design methodologies can be accomplished once the distributed/centralized selection has been made. A centralized approach can utilize any of the methodologies listed (with other system structure attributes) at the beginning of this section. The tendency is to utilize them in the order shown to take maximum advantage of proven technology. A distributed approach is probably limited to the last three methodologies listed (the finite state machine approach, the object-oriented approach, and the building elements approach). The others could be used, but a significant amount of additional work would have to be performed in order to produce effective results.

The most proven of the methodologies suited to distributed design is the finite state machine approach. It is also, unfortunately, the weakest of the methodologies. Because of the relatively immature object-oriented and building-element technologies, however, the development methodology must accommodate the finite state machine approach, at least in the short run. To prepare for the future, the development methodology presented here is also required to support the object-oriented and building-element approaches.

An object-oriented approach has much to recommend it in a network environment, because it is an inherently message-based structure. In order for its capabilities to be exploited fully, a number of open issues must be addressed, including the need for explicit state information.

327

Object-oriented methods will certainly be the approach of choice in the near future as current implementation problems become resolved. Whenever possible, they should be used even if the technology is being stretched slightly.

Building-block design methods are an extension of the object-oriented approach. They require a robust library of building elements that can be controlled through the use of scripts. These building elements must be available as part of the deployment infrastructure of the network or as part of a general system design infrastructure. The system software aspects of building elements and scripts were discussed in chapter 3.

Use of the building-element approach for the design of complex systems is in its infancy, although for specific applications, such as those discussed in chapter 3, it is the method of choice. The use of building blocks for the design of business-oriented systems requires further technological developments, although some of these systems have already been constructed using building blocks. Ultimately, however, this extension to the object-oriented methods is expected to find wide application in the design of all types of systems, for the reason illustrated in figure 8.1. Partitioning the application system into control and reusable functionality should increase the productivity of software development dramatically. In preparation for this type of software development, the development methodology is required to be able to accommodate the building-element approach. The building-element design method can then be used for the development of those systems where it is currently feasible. The methodology will also be positioned to allow the building-element method to be used for other systems as the technology matures.

As shown in figure 8.2, it is desirable to use the building block approach for all development because of the close interaction that can be achieved between system application functions and network functions.

328

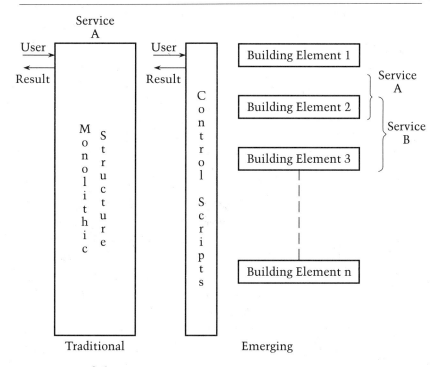

FIGURE 8.1   SOFTWARE DEVELOPMENT IMPLICATIONS OF
BUILDING ELEMENTS

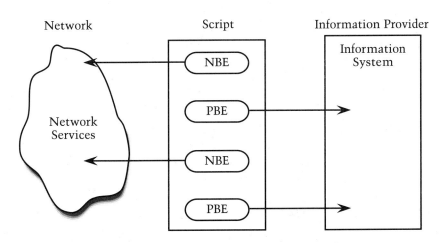

FIGURE 8.2   TYPES OF BUILDING ELEMENTS

System Size

Size is important in determining the resultant system structure. Small sizes can use more monolithic structures, and they can be more centralized than larger ones. The most important influence of size, however, is in determining the fundamental characteristics of the methodology. Large systems require many programmers and engineers, who must operate in a cohesive and coordinated fashion in order to produce an acceptable product. Small systems can use fewer developers and thus use approaches that do not require significant coordination and organization.

The former approach is called "programming in the large," and the latter is known as "programming in the small." The methodology utilized to support large system development is inherently more complex and must contain structures that support the necessary interaction and coordination. Using a methodology designed for one type of development to handle the other type of development will be disastrous. Information systems generally tend to be large developments; for this reason, the methodology assumes programming in the large.

One of the least-understood decisions that must be made in determining system structure is the optimization metric that is being used. Different structures will support different optimization criteria. Some of the optimization views are shown in the following list:

- Maximize execution efficiency
- Minimize network traffic throughput
- Maximize system change efficiency
- Minimize development time/cost
- Maximize fault tolerance
- Maximize ease of use
- Maximize/minimize use of new technology

The development methodology must provide the facilities to support the particular metric(s) chosen. This is an area that may change from product to product depending on the spe-

330

cific environmental conditions involved. For this reason, a methodology that can accommodate a variety of metrics is preferred. If an emphasis must be placed on one of these metrics, however, maximization of change efficiency would be first. Because of the long life cycle of most information systems and the need for frequent change, optimizing against this metric in many cases tends to provide the lowest overall cost to the enterprise.

Product Purpose

The intended purpose of the system under development has a large influence on the required development methodology characteristics and, consequently, on the structure of the methodology itself. Information system methodologies differ significantly from those used to develop system software and real-time systems, for example. This is one reason why organizations tend to specialize in the development of one type of system. When they attempt to change, the methodology (among a large number of other considerations) is not suitable. As before, the methodology structure presented here is designed for the development, in a network environment, of information systems that are oriented toward providing services to the end user. Although real-time systems, embedded systems, and batch-oriented systems could be implemented using a methodology with the characteristics needed by an information system methodology, the results would probably be far from optimum.

SOFTWARE ENGINEERING

The software engineering principles that are to be used in the application development are also important in determining the final characteristics of the deployed product. Although most software engineering principles that are employed in the implementation are the result of good engineering practice, some directions can and should be determined by the

331

needs of the organization. An example of two such directions follows. The first principle is concerned with the size of the system implementation, and the second is concerned with the location of user functionality.

There are no hard and fast rules in these areas. The most that can be accomplished is the setting of guidelines. As a principle, developments should be made as small as possible. If it is possible to replace a single large development with two or more smaller ones, that should be done as long as the requirements or the constraints of the architecture are not compromised in any material sense and the needs of the business can still be met. The second principle is that user functionality should be located as close to the user as possible. "Close" in this sense may mean minimizing geographical distance or the number of gateways between user and function. Keeping functionality close helps insure that the specific needs of the user are met.

Other software engineering principles used in the development of network systems should accommodate the requirements of the architecture and the needs of the specific design methodology chosen through the use of good engineering practice. If there are conflicts between the two, good engineering practice should prevail unless there is an overriding economic reason to reverse the priority. The architecture and/or methodology should then be changed to eliminate the conflict.

NEW TECHNOLOGY INTRODUCTION

As a general philosophical direction, a technical organization will develop and utilize new technologies in their products and development methods as soon as feasible. An organization that merely utilizes another's technology might take the opposite approach. Neither of the approaches is right or wrong in itself.

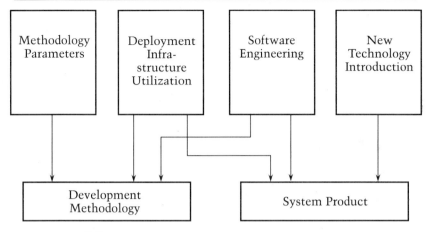

FIGURE 8.3 APPLICATION DEVELOPMENT ARCHITECTURE
STRUCTURE

The approach to technology utilization does have a considerable influence on the methodology as well as on the construction of the final product. It should therefore be made an explicit part of the application development architecture. The architecture presented here assumes that a technology-oriented organization is involved; therefore, it requires that the methodology and product structures be able to take advantage of new technology in a timely fashion. This might take the form of an enhanced asset development and utilization capability or a comprehensive R&D prototyping facility to make new technologies available quickly. The architecture does not specify the specific mechanism(s) to be used — only that one or more be made available to the development process.

ARCHITECTURE STRUCTURE

The architecture structure is illustrated in figure 8.3. As shown, there are four direct architectural influences on the application system development process:

- Methodology parameters
- Infrastructure utilization
- Software engineering
- New technology introduction

Although these are core requirements for the architecture, other components may be defined as necessary depending on the importance attached to them by the enterprise. As was indicated in the beginning of the chapter, the structure of this architecture is simple. However, the application of the architecture principles to the selection of a development methodology and the system design and implementation characteristics is not simple. As discussed throughout the chapter, a great many engineering judgments must be made. If any of these are inappropriate, the resulting systems may not be effective from either an economic or a technical point of view.

ARCHITECTURE PRINCIPLES

The following statements are the principles that are derived from the structures defined for the application development architecture. In keeping with the practice established for this section, these principles are grouped according to the components of the architecture, which in this case are the components defining the areas of direction for the methodology and the information system product structure.

I. Strategies
   A. Global
      1. Architectural
         a. Application systems will be specified such that they use a common implementation of end user services, system software, data services, and network management.
         b. The end user services, system software, data

services, and network management systems will be implemented as part of the deployment infrastructure.

c. Development will be performed in accordance with good engineering practice.

d. All methodologies will have documentation indicating their compliance with the architecture.

e. All finished information systems will have documentation indicating their compliance with the architecture.

f. Methodologies should be developed by the enterprise in accordance with its architecture. Methodologies should not be obtained from the outside.

g. The responsibility for methodology design will be placed in the development organization. Approval must be obtained from the technology management, architecture, and network management organizations.

B. Methodology parameters
  1. Architectural
     a. One methodology shall be oriented toward professional developers of large-scale systems. (LS methodology).

     b. A methodology shall be developed to serve any other significant user classes.

     c. The LS methodology will cover the entire life cycle of a product, from conception to retirement.

     d. The methodology will utilize user validation for all of its functional verification needs.

     e. The methodology will utilize prototypes as the vehicle for interacting with the users for validation purposes.

   f. The methodology will have a balance between the needs of the fourth- and fifth-generation development requirements.

 C. Infrastructure utilization

  1. Architectural

   a. Products will use as much of the in-place infrastructure as possible even if small changes must be made in the system design.

   b. No functionality that should be part of the infrastructure will be put in the application system.

   c. Nonavailable infrastructure needs will be transmitted to the appropriate enterprise organization.

 D. Software engineering

  1. Architectural

   a. Small developments are preferred over large developments.

   b. Functionality will be placed as close to the user as possible, either in a geographical sense or in a network location sense.

 E. New technology introduction

  1. Architectural

   a. New technology should be introduced into products as soon as feasible.

II. Standards

 A. Global

  1. Architecture

   a. Each defined methodology will be designated an enterprise standard and treated as such.

   b. No methodology will be used for application system development or design unless it has been identified as an enterprise standard.

III. Guidelines
   A. Global
      1. Architectural
         a. Enterprise-defined guidelines should follow accepted industry practices whenever possible.
      2. Design
         a. Application development should follow good engineering practice.
         b. Object-oriented techniques should be used for design whenever possible.
         c. Finite state machine approaches should be used for design when object-oriented techniques cannot be used.
   B. Methodology parameters
      1. Architectural
         a. The methodology should allow multiple module sizes depending on need.
         b. The methodology should allow multiple languages to be used for final implementation.
         c. The methodology should allow non-object-oriented techniques to be used in both the design and implementation phases.
         d. The methodology should provide a product structure optimized toward efficient change.
         e. The LS methodology should be oriented toward the development of information systems.
         f. The methodology should be able to utilize the architecture structure and principles effectively.
      2. Design
         a. When object-oriented design techniques are used, an explicit control overlay should be utilized.
         b. The non-object-oriented design technique of choice is the finite state machine process.
         c. Other allowable but not recommended tech-

niques are Data Structured Systems Development (DSSD), Jackson Systems Development Method (JSD), Dataflow Diagram Method (DFD), and the System Analysis and Design Technique (SADT).

C. Software engineering
   1. Design
      a. Functions should be located close to their intended user community. Closeness may be defined on either a network or a geographical basis.
      b. Large developments should be partitioned into multiple smaller developments whenever this can be accomplished without affecting requirements or other architectural principles.

IV. Rules
  A. Global
   1. Architectural
      a. No network system will provide services available in end user services, system software, data services, and network management infrastructure systems.
      b. No network system will redefine or bypass services available in end user services, system software, data services, and network management infrastructure systems.
      c. All methodology documentation will be in machine-readable form.
   2. Operational
      a. Exceptions to any methodology architectural requirements must be approved formally by the architectural organization and senior enterprise management.
  B. Methodology parameters
   1. Architectural
      a. The methodology will provide for all product

development in a distributed/cooperative processing structure.

b. The LS methodology will provide for development in the large.

SUMMARY AND CONCLUSIONS

Because the architecture represents the domain knowledge needed by the application implementation process, the structure and principles of the architecture must provide a foundation for the implementation environment and all of the implementation activities as well as the final structure of the product. The application development architecture specified in this chapter has the most direct relationship with the development methodology as well as the responsibility for unifying all of the Level 1 subarchitectures.

Although development methodologies can be complex, their use and specification can be made easier through the understanding and use of an architectural approach. Relevant issues can be defined and, based on input from the enterprise organizations that have an interest in the methodology, a set of suitable characteristics can be derived. This makes the justification of changes and the determination of their probable effect considerably easier than if no architecture were employed.

An architectural approach has been used in this chapter as possible characteristics and approaches to the implementation process and the structure of the information system products was discussed and specific directions were chosen for the methodology.

APPENDIX

COMPOSITE LISTING OF ARCHITECTURE PRINCIPLES

I. Strategies
   A. Architectural
   1. All end user interfaces will be based on intelligent workstations containing at least one user-accessible processor.
   2. Only one physical workstation will be provided per end user. All necessary functions must be available on that workstation.
   3. All networks will have an explicit distributed NOS.
   4. Only one directory structure will be used in a network. All services and functions will utilize that structure.
   5. All system software should support unattended operation with full recovery and power restore capability.
   6. All networks will have an explicit distributed NOS.
   7. Only one directory structure will be used in a network. All services and functions will utilize that structure.
   8. All system software should support unattended operation with full recovery and power restore capability.
   9. The responsibility for the data will rest in an

organization solely charged with that responsibility. The executive in charge of that organization will be given the title of Chief Information Officer (CIO).

10. Data will be treated as a corporate asset and the effectiveness of the management of the data will be audited periodically.

11. All base data will be owned by the Chief Information Officer.

12. All transaction data will be owned by the Chief Information Officer unless there are compelling reasons to assign that responsibility elsewhere.

13. The servers will be selected in accordance with the architecture.

14. The selection of the servers will occur concurrently with the exccution of the development methodology.

15. Selection of the appropriate network servers for any level will be the responsibility of the network engineering organization.

16. Servers controlled by external information providers must conform to a specific set of enterprise policies defined for this relationship.

17. The overlays will be selected in accordance with the architecture.

18. Selection of the appropriate network overlays for any level will be the responsibility of the network engineering organization.

19. Networks controlled by external information providers must conform to a specific set of enterprise policies defined for this relationship.

20. A specific procedure will be developed for the assignment of the network management layers and functions to the nodes/servers on the network.

21. Individual architectures for complex functions will be developed.

22. Every network deployed or used by the enterprise will have an explicit network management system that is consistent with the architecture.
23. Users will be provided end-to-end network management services.
24. There will be a single point of contact for the end user in requesting information about the network.
25. Documentation for all network management functions will be in machine-readable form.
26. No system will begin the implementation steps of the development methodology unless the network management interfaces are specified.
27. Development will be performed in accordance with good engineering practice.
28. All methodologies will have documentation indicating their compliance with the architecture.
29. All finished information systems will have documentation indicating their compliance with the architecture.
30. Methodologies should be developed by the enterprise in accordance with its architecture. Methodologies should not be obtained from the outside.
31. The responsibility for methodology design will be placed in the development organization. Approval must be obtained from the technology management, architecture, and network management organizations.
32. Each workstation will be able to support text, voice, graphics, and image interfaces through appropriate coupling devices.
33. Enterprise-standard interfaces for all coupling devices will be defined and implemented.
34. Multiple skill levels will be supported.

35. Default user profile, directory, and function set-up data will be provided automatically by the network functions. No end user intervention will be required. The end user will have the ability to alter this information if desired.

36. Each workstation will have a control function that maintains the state of all other functions in process and coordinates their execution.

37. Network function access permission will be obtained automatically through the network administration function.

38. Queries may be made using any of the supported media forms (such as text, voice, image, etc.).

39. All network functions should be made available to every end user unless there is a specific reason to deny access. Users may be required to explicitly subscribe to a function in order to utilize it.

40. The NOS should support simultaneous use of the network for transaction, batch, real-time, and interactive services.

41. The NOS should support distributed and cooperative processing.

42. All OSs should support simultaneous use of the network for transaction, batch, real-time, and interactive services.

43. All OSs should support distributed and cooperative processing.

44. All processors used for the same network server class should use the same OS. Server classes are discussed in chapter 5.

45. All services will use an associated service access function.

46. Service access interfaces will be programmable by the client.

47. All enterprise data shall be defined through the data modeling process.

48. Subject databases will be used as the conceptual layer definition model.

49. Normalized attribute groups will be used as the logical layer definition model.

50. The storage plan will utilize database management systems only for official data unless the life of the data is less than one day.

51. Unofficial data may use file structures for storage if desired.

52. All transaction data shall be verified before becoming official.

53. All network systems will be verified for data before being allowed on the network.

54. The CIO will specify the client verification conditions for all official data. The owner will specify the client verification conditions for all unofficial data.

55. Some form of operation audit trail will be implemented.

56. Explicit data maintenance and recovery procedures will be developed and implemented in the data system.

57. At a minimum, view processing must be able to identify the network location of requested data.

58. Enough usage information must be made available for the DBA to tune the data system effectively.

59. Data access conditions should be independent of network location.

60. The data system must provide the statistics and other information necessary to allow the planning, administrative, and operations functions to be performed effectively.

61. Internal controls for the data management function must be developed.
62. Data management will be placed physically at one network location.
63. The dictionary/directory will be active. All changes to the data or its context will update the dictionary/directory automatically.
64. The contents of the dictionary/directory are considered to be base data.
65. The dictionary/directory contents may be spread throughout the network.
66. Physical data storage will be located as close (on the shortest network data path) to the highest volume user as possible.
67. The smallest number of abstraction levels that still meet the needs of the enterprise should be used. (The four major ones must always be present.)
68. Server-to-server assignment will be used.
69. Application of the level-to-level assignment rules should be mechanized through the use of artificial intelligence so that there is consistency and a way to manage the complexity.
70. The level-to-level assignment rules should be as complete as possible even though the complexity becomes great.
71. Any well-established decomposition technique may be used, but object-oriented techniques are encouraged.
72. The smallest number of abstraction levels that still meet the needs of the enterprise should be used. (The five major ones must always be present.)
73. Any defined business system or application shall have the communications aspects defined as an integral part of the service definition.

74. The basic service level generic overlay shall have the following subnetworks:
    • User
    • Network management
    Others may be added as necessary.

75. The basic logical level generic overlays shall consist of the following:
    • Network management
    • Network geography/routing
    • Network capabilities

76. The basic physical level generic overlays shall consist of the following:
    • Protocol
    • Capacity

77. Peer-to-peer protocols shall be used whenever possible.

78. A set of principles shall be developed to guide the definition of enterprise protocols and layer interfaces.

79. Sublayers of any layer may be defined as needed to keep the functions simple and easily implementable.

80. Interfaces between sublayers shall have the same structure and characteristics as those between major layers.

81. Only one network management reference model and associated architecture should be used in the network, regardless of the number of communication models and architectures employed.

82. All network entities defined by a communications model layer shall have the means to embed transducers (sensor and actuator).

83. All transducers should have a core set of capabilities, even though their interface characteristics may vary.

84. The fewest possible different transducer types should be used.

85. One driver function will exist per network entity.

86. Database management systems used by the integration layer shall be either relational or object-oriented in design.

87. The use of DBMSs shall follow all of the architectural tenets of the data architecture.

88. Presentation layer functions are not required to interface with users. For example, monitor-control pairs may be automated.

89. One methodology shall be oriented toward professional developers of large-scale systems (LS methodology).

90. A methodology shall be developed to serve any other significant user classes.

91. The LS methodology will cover the entire life cycle of a product, from conception to retirement.

92. The methodology will utilize user validation for all of its functional verification needs.

93. The methodology will use prototypes as the vehicle for interacting with the users for validation purposes.

94. The methodology will have a balance between the needs of the fourth- and fifth-generation development requirements.

95. Products will use as much of the in-place infrastructure as possible, even if small changes must be made in the system design.

96. No functionality that should be part of the infrastructure will be put in the application system.

97. Nonavailable infrastructure needs will be transmitted to the appropriate enterprise organization.

98. Small developments are preferred over large developments.
99. Technology should be introduced into products as soon as feasible.
100. Deployment infrastructure systems for end user services, system software, data services, and network management will be specified and implemented.
101. Application systems will be specified such that they use a common implementation of end user services, system software, data services, and network management.
102. No application system will provide end user services, system software, data services, or network management as part of the system.

B. Design
1. Access routines should be used for all network services. A network service that allows new views to be added to access routines must be available.
2. Source code for all operating software must be available.
3. All node system software and the network operating system must be designed such that they interact efficiently.
4. A single end user system will be designed and used for all network functions. Changes to the end user system may be made as required for new systems.
5. The "look and feel" of all functions should be identical.
6. Access routines should be used for all network services. A network service that allows new views to be added to access routines must be available.

7. Source code for all operating software must be available.

8. No one person should be able to alter substantial amounts of data. Approval for such changes must be built into the data system.

9. At least two copies of all data must be located in geographically dispersed areas.

10. Heterogeneous environments for all aspects of the data system must be assumed.

11. Data modeling is a continuous process, and the results should always reflect the current status of the enterprise.

12. All entities should have a global attribute that contains the proper intelligence layer of the entity.

13. All physical servers and/or integrated products that are identified as candidates for selection must be on the approved product list.

14. Identification of new physical servers and/or integrated products designed to meet a need that is not served effectively by existing candidates must first be qualified for the approved product list.

15. A heterogeneous set of servers is desirable and encouraged.

16. Servers must be synergetic with the communications architecture.

17. All physical network overlays should use products that are on the approved product list.

18. Identification of new physical-level products designed to meet a need that is not served effectively by existing candidates must first be qualified for the approved product list.

19. A heterogeneous set of network products is desirable and encouraged.

20. Networks products must be synergetic with the server architecture.

21. All network management systems will employ products that are on the approved product list.

22. Identification of new products designed to meet a need that is not served effectively by existing candidates must first be qualified for the approved product list.

23. A heterogeneous set of network management products is desirable and encouraged.

24. The workstation control function will be designed as an integral part of the network operating system.

25. The NOS should be based on object-oriented principles.

26. Scripts should be used for NOS control and service definition.

27. Messages between NOS sections should utilize the same network as the data. A separate control network should not be established.

28. A robust selection of building elements should be developed and made available.

29. Every OS should be multitasking.

30. Every OS should support remote operations.

31. Service access functions will be built using the model-view controller structure.

32. The result of the data-definition process shall be approved by all clients.

33. An efficient process for updating the results of the definition process shall be implemented.

34. All intermediate and final results of the definition process shall be stored in the dictionary/directory in a self-defining form.

35. End user verification for base data access will have a probability of circumvention of less than .01 percent.

36. Changes to the operational characteristics of the data integrity functions must be approved by the

CIO and verified by the internal auditing organization.

37. Client access functions will have different efficiency levels available to meet diverse capacity needs.

38. The client access function shall be designed as a separate system with well-defined interfaces to other data functions.

39. All data system functions will have access methods specifically designed for use by data management.

40. The number of servers defined for each level should decrease as the amount of detail in the level increases.

41. All intermediate and final results of the assignment process as it concerns data shall be stored in the dictionary/directory in a self-defining form.

42. The development of server-to-server assignment rules is the responsibility of the network engineering organization.

43. Server-to-server assignment rules must be approved by the network/system implementation organization and the network management organization.

44. The number of overlays defined for each level should be kept to a minimum while still meeting the anticipated design needs.

45. Active feedback transactions will consist of not more than .1 percent of maximum traffic or 5 percent of current traffic on any involved link.

C. Operational

1. Training programs for all system software operations personnel should be available as a network service.

2. All operations personnel should be trained on all operational software used in the enterprise.

3. No local alterations to the operating system should be made except in emergencies. Any changes made should be backed out as soon as possible.

4. System software updates should be spread out over time. Whenever possible, multiple updates should not be made simultaneously.

5. Changes to the network operating system must be made without bringing down the network.

6. All network system software functions should have 100-percent availability.

7. System software operator messages should be minimal. An expert system should be utilized to handle most interaction with the NOS.

8. All workstations will be connected to a physical or virtual LAN through direct coupling or via a remote access facility. Gateways will be utilized for access to other networks.

9. All network functions should have 100-percent availability.

10. Training programs for all system software operations personnel should be available as a network service.

11. All official data should have 100-percent availability.

12. All procedures that assign official status to transaction data must be approved by a designee of the CIO.

13. Only one copy of replicated data may be official.

14. Before any product server that has no deployed equivalent can be assigned permanently, an extensive test program must be completed successfully.

15. Before any physical overlay product that has no deployed equivalent can be assigned permanently, an extensive test program must be completed successfully.

352

16. Before any network management product that has no deployed equivalent can be assigned permanently, an extensive test program must be completed successfully.

17. The responsibility for network management will be placed in a network management organization that has no other operational function.

18. The network management system will be continuously available. No function will be designed such that it requires the network management system to be stopped for any reason.

19. The same organization will be responsible for the administration, planning, and operations aspects of network management.

20. Manual overrides to all automatic operation partition actions shall be provided. These overrides shall have appropriate levels of security provided.

21. The NOS should require only one operational point. That point should be able to be moved anywhere on the network.

22. Every OS should have the same core set of features and functions.

23. Access routines to service interface should allow complete portability of the service between network nodes.

24. If the same service exists on more than one network node, the service access routines must be able to spread the load among the instances of the service.

25. Network service access permission will be obtained automatically through the network administration function.

26. Service security is a function of the service access routine.

27. The interface of a service to network management is a function of the service access routine.

28. End users will be allowed to change their workstation characteristics to meet their individual needs
29. The definition of a data item shall be the same regardless of network location. Local definitions are not permitted.
30. All defined data items must be available subject to verification requirements.
31. Base data and transaction data should not be stored in the same physical DBMS.
32. No server shall be placed on the network unless it results from applying the concepts of the server architecture.

II. Standards
   A. Architectural
      1. Enterprise-defined interface standards should follow international or other industry standards when possible.
      2. Enterprise-defined system software standards should follow international or other industry standards when possible.
      3. Commercially available system software should be used when possible.
      4. Enterprise-standard interfaces to the NOS will be defined.
      5. Enterprise standards shall be defined for the design of each type of entry/presentation format.
      6. Enterprise access standards will be defined and utilized for all systems.
      7. Commercially available operating systems will be used.
      8. Enterprise access standards will be defined and utilized for all systems.
      9. All interfaces in the data system will be declared to be enterprise standards and defined as such

with appropriate documentation and enforcement means.

10. Data system standards should follow international or other industry standards when possible.

11. Commercially available products should be used in the data system when possible.

12. The standard data language will be SQL.

13. The data design methodology chosen should be used consistently. No deviations from the process should be allowed.

14. Enterprise standards will be developed for all data integrity functions.

15. Enterprise standards will be developed for all client access functions.

16. Enterprise standards will be developed for all data management functions.

17. The dictionary/directory will have a standard format for all contents. To the extent possible, this format will be self-defining.

18. The dictionary/directory will utilize relational technology for storage.

19. Standard data storage procedures will be developed and used by the enterprise.

20. All server selection candidates at any abstraction level will be declared to be enterprise standards.

21. Server standards should follow international or other industry standards when possible.

22. A standard set of attributes and associated values will be developed for each level.

23. A standard set of server selection candidates will be developed for each level.

24. The decomposition technique should follow an established industry standard.

25. If desirable, an enterprise-standard decomposition technique may be established that differs from other published procedures.

26. All generic overlays at any abstraction level will be declared to be enterprise standards.

27. Overlay standards should follow international or other industry standards when possible.

28. Recognized layered communication architecture standards shall be used.

29. The number of layered communications architectures used should be kept to a minimum.

30. Enterprise standards will be developed for all network management model interfaces and protocols used in the network.

31. No interface or protocol will be implemented and/or deployed unless it has been identified as an enterprise standard.

32. Industry standards or those developed by recognized standards bodies will be used whenever possible.

33. De facto standards set by a competing vendor will not be adapted unless it is required for competitive purposes. Such standards will be in addition to the one adapted by the enterprise.

34. A single reference model and architecture shall be defined and used in all networks used and/or deployed by the enterprise.

35. Approval of the reference model and architecture shall be required by the network management, software engineering, technology management, and implementation organizations.

36. Presentation layer functions that interface with humans shall be standardized by the enterprise.

37. Enterprise standards for network management applications shall be developed.

38. Each defined methodology will be designated an enterprise standard and treated as such.

39. No methodology will be used for application development unless it has been identified as an enterprise standard.

356

B. Design
   1. X-windows standard will be used for all screen devices.
   2. NTSC video format will be used for image input/output.
   3. Provision will be made for 6 RS-232C auxiliary ports.
   4. Enterprise-standard interfaces for all coupling devices will be defined and implemented.
   5. CCITT X.400 protocol will be used for electronic mail.
   6. All user-accessible databases will be relational.
   7. The DIF format will be used for spreadsheet and word processing data.
   8. ACM SIGGRAPH will be used as the graphics standard.
   9. Standards for all user functions will be defined.
   10. Any portions of the NOS developed by the enterprise will use object-oriented design.
C. Operational
   1. Enterprise-standard operational techniques will be developed and used.

III. Guidelines
   A. Architectural
      1. Enterprise-defined guidelines should follow accepted industry practices whenever possible.
      2. End user presentation and application protocols should have the same look and feel.
      3. Enterprise-defined guidelines should follow accepted industry practices whenever possible.
      4. System software should be selected in the following priority order:
         • From computer vendor
         • From software vendor
         • Internal development

5. System software messages and commands should be based on natural language processing.
6. System software should be able to recover automatically under fault conditions.
7. System software functions should be placed where they will have the widest scope.
8. Automatic interoperability between all users, functions, and services should be provided.
9. As few OS types as possible should be used in the network.
10. Every OS in the network should be widely used under similar circumstances in the industry.
11. As many data integrity functions as economically justifiable should be implemented.
12. Changes to the operational characteristics of the data integrity functions should be minimized.
13. Client access should be able to be transferred easily from one network location to another by the client.
14. Client access function requests for additional direction should be in natural language form.
15. Planning for data needs should be done on a five-year basis.
16. Relational technology should be used for storage whenever possible.
17. Once defined, the levels should not change from system to system.
18. Server selection candidates should be stable. Changes to the list should be minimized.
19. Once defined, level-to-level assignment rules should not change from system to system.
20. Server-to-server assignment rules should be stable. Changes to the rules should be minimized.
21. Decomposition should be a joint effort of the network engineering, implementation, and service definition organizations.
22. Decomposition should always be accomplished

using the same procedure. It should not vary from system to system if possible.

23. The number of layered communications architectures used should be kept to a minimum.

24. Assignment should be a joint effort of the network engineering, implementation, and service definition organizations.

25. The methodology should allow multiple module sizes depending on need.

26. The methodology should allow multiple languages to be used for final implementation.

27. The methodology should allow either conventional or object-oriented techniques to be used in both the design and implementation phases.

28. The methodology should provide a product structure optimized toward efficient change.

29. The methodology should be oriented toward the development of information systems.

30. The methodology should be able to utilize the architecture structure and principles effectively.

B. Design

1. Control should be based on finite state machine concepts and should utilize AI knowledge structures when possible.

2. Control should attempt to recover automatically from error conditions before alerting the end user.

3. Some amount of stand-alone functionality should be provided for all remotely accessed functions so that processing may continue for a time if the remote function becomes unavailable for a time.

4. All system software should be designed to detect and destroy any viruses that enter the system.

5. Data system design should follow good engineering practice.

6. The data system design methodology should be

similar in step structure to the network system design methodology.

7. The same client access system design should be used for all clients. Individual variations should be accomplished through the use of parameters.

8. As little client intervention as possible should be required in the view process.

9. Server selection candidates for all abstraction levels should follow good engineering practice.

10. Experts in the enterprise, as well as outside consultants when necessary, should be asked to contribute to the server-to-server assignment rules.

11. A procedure to verify and validate changes to the server-to-server assignment rules should be developed.

12. Assignment should follow good engineering practice.

13. Digital networks should be used whenever possible.

14. Artificial intelligence should be used as part of the network design process.

15. The network design should not be based totally on a tariff that is subject to unilateral change.

16. Geographically diverse facilities should be used for multiple access to any node.

17. Application development should follow good engineering practice.

18. Object-oriented techniques should be used whenever possible.

19. Functions should be located close to their intended user community. *Close* may be defined on either a network or a geographical basis.

20. Large developments should be partitioned into multiple smaller developments whenever this can be accomplished without affecting requirements or other architectural principles.

C. Operational

    1. Users should be allowed to select the specific coupling devices that are comfortable to them.

    2. Function processing should be performed as close to the end user as possible.

    3. Voice and text-oriented electronic mail shall be interconnected and accessed using the same procedures.

    4. NOS updates should not remove any functionality; only new functionality should be added.

    5. DBMS parameters should be examined continually and tuned as necessary.

    6. As few different types of DBMS products as possible should be used in the network.

    7. A help desk for data-related problems should be established.

IV. Rules

  A. Architectural

    1. The end user system will have the same interface regardless of the physical device or system software on which it is resident.

    2. Additions only can be made to the format set. No existing format may be eliminated or altered unless the network functions for which it was used are eliminated.

    3. The end user must not be required to know the network location of any function.

    4. Documentation for all system software will be in machine-readable form.

    5. An enterprise expert must be developed for all purchased system software before the software is deployed.

    6. Detailed criteria must be developed for selecting an OS.

    7. Documentation for the data system will be in

machine-readable form and will be available in the dictionary/directory.

8. A member of the data management organization will attend all application design inspections.

9. The data design process will use advanced computer aided design (CAD) techniques.

10. No local changes or additions to the data definition process will be allowed.

11. No application program from any source may be placed on the network unless the application system data verification procedure has been performed.

12. The data management function will be structured such that 95 percent of all problems will be resolved in two hours.

13. The dictionary/directory will support all data storage facilities on the network.

14. Every database management system on the network must have the following capabilities:
   • Dynamic transaction backout
   • Backward and forward recovery
   • Checkpoint/restart capability
   • Log generation
   • Kernel security at every data level

15. Documentation for the entire assignment procedure will be in machine-readable form.

16. No system will begin the deployment step of the development methodology until the assignment process is completed.

17. The number of candidate servers in the logical level will be between 10 and 20.

18. The number of servers in the physical level will be between 5 and 12.

19. Changes in the server-to-server assignment rules will be approved by the technology management organization.

20. Changes to the service attributes and associated

values must be approved as part of the strategic planning process.

21. No system will begin the deployment step of the development methodology until the assignment process is completed.

22. No more than six generic overlays will be defined for any abstraction level.

23. Enterprise-defined guidelines should follow accepted industry practices whenever possible.

24. Software transducers should be developed by the vendor of the software being affected whenever possible.

25. Software transducers should be proved correct using a theorem-proving technique.

26. All transmission lines, modems, multiplexers, switches, session control software, and application programs shall have transducers embedded in them.

27. The state of all transducers shall be made available on command.

28. Three or fewer separate transducers will exist in any one network entity.

29. All methodology documentation will be in machine-readable form.

30. The methodology will provide for all product development in a distributed/cooperative processing structure.

31. The LS methodology will provide for development in the large.

32. All network systems will use the deployment infrastructure systems that provide end user services, system software functions, data services, and network management services.

33. No network system will redefine or bypass any aspect of these services.

B. Design
1. The coupling devices, entry/presentation format,

and access procedures components shall be resident on the workstation.

2. A default format will exist for each system. Error notification to the end user must not disturb any other functions in process.

3. All workstations will have access to the following functions in addition to those specifically required to perform the user's job:
   - Spreadsheet
   - Relational database
   - Word processor
   - Desktop publishing package
   - Network function directory
   - Picture creation package
   - Electronic mail
   - Document storage and retrieval
   - Calendaring

4. Voice- and text-oriented electronic mail shall be interconnected and accessed using the same procedures.

5. The NOS will be optimized to support the enterprise standard network configuration.

6. Every OS must be able to be updated without taking down the node.

7. Every OS must be able to use the NOS directory structure.

8. Client verification will utilize "call-back" techniques when system network access is obtained through a public network.

9. Interface and protocol design should follow good engineering practice.

10. Object-oriented techniques should be used whenever possible.

11. Active feedback should be used sparingly.

12. The entities contained in a network group should have some synergy with one another.

13. Assignment should be a joint effort of the net-

work engineering, implementation, and service definition organizations.

14. Artificial intelligence should be used extensively in the network control center to keep human intervention to a minimum.
15. Artificial intelligence should be used extensively for network design.
16. Artificial intelligence should be used extensively in automating the administration functions.
17. Exceptions to any methodology architectural requirements must be approved formally by the architectural organization and senior enterprise management.

C. Operational
1. All workstations will support the following devices, and the end user system will be able to interface with them:
   - Keyboard
   - Color screen
   - Mouse
   - Speaker
   - Telephone handset
2. Every person in the enterprise will have a terminal attached to the network.
3. The NOS will support gateways to the following network types:
   - Public telephone network
   - Public packet network
   - Cable TV
   - Private service networks
4. A software maintenance contract must be maintained on every deployed OS.
5. The service access function will not add more than 3 percent overhead to any service.
6. All changes to official data will be transparent to the clients.

7. Client requests for new access privileges will be processed within one hour.
8. A software maintenance contract must be maintained on every deployed DBMS.
9. All changes to the server architecture must be approved by the network engineering, implementation, and technology management organizations.
10. All changes to the communications architecture must be approved by the network engineering, implementation, and technology management organizations.

BIBLIOGRAPHY

The references selected for inclusion in this section serve one of three purposes: they directly relate to specific material discussed in the book, they provide background information or additional detail for those areas, or they cover subjects mentioned but not presented in detail. The references have been selected to favor the most recently published information that adequately covers the subject. When there has been no suitable replacement, the original or classic publication in a subject area has also been included. Because a great deal of material in the book is new, in many cases, no previous publications are directly applicable. In this instance, references have been selected that provide a suitable background in the general subject area.

Because of the breadth of the material covered in the book, the references have been arranged by chapter to facilitate their use. When a given reference could be placed in more than one chapter, it has been assigned to the chapter that seems most appropriate. This process seems preferable to duplicating references. Because of the number of references, a comprehensive bibliography in all the subject areas is not feasible. However, the references provided should give you a good start in finding additional information about the subject of interest.

CHAPTER ONE

Brown, Marc H. *Algorithm Animation*. Cambridge, MA: MIT Press, 1987.
Green, P. E., Jr., ed. *Special Issue on Computer Network Architec-*

tures and Protocols. IEEE Transactions on Communications, vol. Com-28, no. 4 (April 1980).

Inmon, W. H. *Information Engineering for the Practitioner*. New York: Yourden Press, 1988.

Liskov, Barbara, and John Guttag. *Abstraction and Specification in Program Development*. Cambridge, MA: MIT Press, 1986.

McWilliams, Gary. "Integrated Computing Environments." *Datamation*. Vol. 35, no. 9 (May 1, 1989):18–21.

Perry, Tekla, S. and Glenn Zorpette. "Supercomputers: Entering the Mainstream." *IEEE Spectrum*. Vol. 26, no. 2 (February 1989):26–33.

Webster, Dallas E. "Mapping the Design Information Representation Terrain." *Computer*. Vol. 21, no. 12 (Dec.1988):8–24.

Zimmer, J. A. *Abstraction for Programmers*. New York: McGraw-Hill, 1985.

CHAPTER TWO

Ammeraal, L. *Programming Principles in Computer Graphics*. New York: Wiley, 1986.

Carroll, John M., ed. *Interfacing Thought: Cognitive Aspects of Human-Computer Interaction*. Cambridge, MA: MIT Press, 1987.

Ehrich, Roger W. and Robert C. Williges, eds. *Human-Computer Dialogue Design*. New York: Elsevier, 1986.

Gale, Anthony and Bruce Christie. *Psychophysiology and the Electronic Workplace*. New York: Wiley, 1987.

Garson, Barbara. *The Electronic Sweatshop: How Computers Are Transforming the Office of the Future into the Factory of the Past*. New York: Simon and Schuster, 1988.

Gasser, Morrie. *Building a Secure Computer System*. New York: Van Nostrand, Reinhold, 1988.

Guindon, Raymonde, ed. *Cognitive Science and Its Applications for Human-Computer Interaction*. Hillsdale, NJ: Lawrence Erlbaum Associates, 1988.

Kearsley, Greg and Robin Halley. *Designing Interactive Software*. La Jolla, CA: Park Row Press, 1987.

Linton, Mark A., John M. Vissides, and Paul R. Calder. "Composing User Interfaces with InterViews." *Computer Magazine*. Vol. 22, no. 2 (February 1989):8–22.

Lueder, Rani. *The Ergonomics Payoff: Designing the Electronic Office*. New York: Nichols Publishing Co., 1986.

Popov, E. V. *Talking with Computers in Natural Language.* New York: Springer-Verlag, 1986.

Potosnak, K. "Do Icons Make User Interfaces Easier to Use?" *IEEE Software.* Vol. 5, no. 3 (May 1988):97–99.

Sage, Andrew P. *System Design for Human Interaction.* New York: IEEE Press, 1987.

Schaffner, Stuart C. and Martha Borkan. "Segue: Support for Distributed Graphical Interfaces." *Computer.* Vol. 21, no. 12 (December 1988):42–55.

Shneiderman, Ben. *Designing the User Interface: Strategies for Effective Human-Computer Interaction.* Reading, MA: Addison-Wesley, 1987.

Thomas, John C. and Michael L. Schneider, eds. *Human Factors in Computer Systems.* Norwood, NJ: Ablex Publishing, 1984.

Tylutki, George. "Building a Self-Modifying User Interface." *Computer Language.* Vol. 6, no. 5 (May 1989):34–47.

CHAPTER THREE

Bhuyan, Laxmi N., Qing Yang, and Dharma P. Agrawal. "Performance of Multiprocessor Interconnection Networks." *Computer Magazine.* Vol. 22, no. 2 (February 1989):25–37.

Cheriton, D. R. "The V Kernel: A Software Base for Distributed Systems." *IEEE Software.* (April 1984).

Cheriton, David and Timothy P. Mann. "Decentralizing a Global Naming Service for Improved Performance and Fault Tolerance." *ACM Transactions on Computer Systems.* Vol. 7, no. 2 (May 1989):147–83.

Comer, Douglas. *Operating System Design: The XINU Approach.* Englewood Cliffs, NJ: Prentice-Hall, 1984.

Finkel, R. A., M. L. Scott, Y. Artsy, H.-Y. Chang. "Experience with Charlotte: Simplicity and Function in a Distributed Operating System." *IEEE Transactions on Software Engineering.* Vol. 15, no. 6 (June 1989):676–85.

Kurose, James F. and Rahul Simha. "A Microeconomic Approach to Optimal Resource Allocation in Distributed Computer Systems." *IEEE Transactions on Computers.* Vol. 38, no. 5 (May 1989):705–17.

Northcutt, J. Duane. *Mechanisms for Reliable Distributed Real-Time Operating System — The Alpha Kernel.* Orlando, FL: Academic Press, 1987.

Sun, Zhongxiu, Xing Xue, Jianqiang Zhou, Peigen Yang, and Xiho

Xu. "Developing a Heterogeneous Distributed Operating System." *ACM Operating Systems Review.* Vol. 22, no. 2 (April 1988).

Tanenbaum, Andrew S. *Operating Systems: Design and Implementation.* Englewood Cliffs, NJ: Prentice-Hall, 1987.

Tokuda, Hideyuki and Clifford W. Mercer. "ARTS: A Distributed Real Time Kernel." *ACM Operating Systems Review.* Vol. 23, no. 3 (July 1989):29–53.

Tripathi, A. R. "An Overview of the Nexus Distributed Operating System Design." *IEEE Transactions on Software Engineering.* Vol. 15, no. 6 (June 1989):686–95.

CHAPTER FOUR

Atre, S. *Database: Structured Techniques for Design, Performance, and Management.* New York: John Wiley & Sons, 1980.

Bancilhon, Franqois and Setrag Khoshafian. "A Calculus for Complex Objects." *Journal of Computer and System Sciences.* Vol. 38, no. 2 (April 1989):326–40.

Bhargava, B. and J. Riedl. "The Raid Distributed Database System." *IEEE Transactions on Software Engineering.* Vol. 15, no. 6 (June 1989):676–85.

Chen, P. P. "The Entity-Relationship Model: Toward a Unified View of Data." *ACM Transactions on Database Systems.* (March 1976).

Codd, E. F. "Extending the Database Relational Model to Capture More Meaning." *ACM Transactions on Database Systems.* (December 1979).

Cornell, D. W. and P. S. Yu. "On Optimal Site Assignment for Relations in the Distributed Database Environment." *IEEE Transactions on Software Engineering.* Vol. 15, no. 8 (August 1989): 1004–1009.

Date, Chris. *Introduction to Database Systems.* Reading, MA: Addison-Wesley, 1981.

———. *Introduction to Database Systems.* Vol. 2. Reading, MA: Addison-Wesley, 1982.

Demers, Greene, Irish Hauser, Shenker Larson, and Terry Swinhart. "Epidemic Algorithms for Replicated Database Maintenance." *ACM Operating Systems Review.* Vol. 22, no. 1 (January 1988):8–32.

Denning, Dorthy E. R. *Cryptography and Data Security.* Reading, MA: Addison-Wesley, 1982.

Dewan, R. M. and B. Gavish. "Models for the Combined Logical and Physical Design of Databases." *IEEE Transactions on Computers.* Vol. 38, no. 7 (July 1989):955–67.

Fong, Elizabeth, et al. *Guide on Logical Database Design.* Special

Publication # 500–122, Natural Bureau of Standards, Washington, DC, 1985.

Inmon, W. H. (Bill). "At the Heart of the Matter." *Database Programming and Design.* (July 1988):23–25.

Joseph, T. and A. F. Cardenas. "PICQUERY: A High Level Query Language for Pictoral Database Management." *IEEE Transactions on Software Engineering.* Vol. 14, no. 5 (May 1988):630–38.

Martin, James. *Strategic Data Planning Methodologies.* Englewood Cliffs, NJ: Prentice-Hall, 1982.

————. *Managing the Data Base Environment.* Englewood Cliffs, NJ: Prentice-Hall, 1983.

Ross, Ronald G. *Data Dictionaries and Data Administration.* New York: AMACOM, 1981.

Rapaport, Matthew. "Data Dictionaries: The CASE Connection." *Computer Language.* Vol. 6, no. 3 (March 1989):91–96.

Schkolnick, M. "A Survey of Physical Database Design Methodology and Techniques." *Proceedings of the International Conference on Very Large Databases.* (1979):474–87.

Shal, Rajkvmar R. and J. P. Lenoczky. "Concurrency Control for Distributed Real-Time Databases." Technical Report, Computer Science Department, Carnegie Mellon University, 1988.

Tsichritzis and Lochonsky. *Data Models.* Englewood Cliffs, NJ: Prentice-Hall, 1982.

Yao, S. Bing, ed. *Principles of Database Design.* Englewood Cliffs, NJ: Prentice-Hall, 1985.

CHAPTER FIVE

Aggarwal, S., D. Barbara, and K. Z. Meth. "A Software Environment for the Specification and Analysis of Problems of Coordination and Concurrency." *IEEE Transactions on Software Engineering.* Vol. 14, no. 3 (March 1988):280–90.

Giacolone, A. and S. A. Smocka. "Integrated Environment for Formally Well-Founded Design and Simulation of Concurrent Systems." *IEEE Transactions on Software Engineering.* Vol. 14, no. 6 (June 1988):787–802.

Killen, Michael. *The Making of the Common View.* New York: Harcourt Brace Jovanovich, 1988.

Layne, Richard, with Thomas Hoffman. "What Vendors Don't Tell You about Cooperative Processing." *Information Week.* (August 7, 1989):25–27.

Mariani, M. P., ed. *Distributed Data Processing: Technology and Critical Issues.* Amsterdam: North-Holland, 1984.

Martin, James. *Design Strategy for Distributed Data Processing.* Englewood Cliffs, NJ: Prentice-Hall, 1986.

Report. *Distributed Processing Services in the New Telecomputing Environment. INPUT.* Mountain View, CA, 1986.

Wang, Yu. "A Distributed Specification Model and Its Prototyping." *IEEE Transactions on Software Engineering.* Vol. 14, no. 8 (August 1988):1090–97.

CHAPTER SIX

Boesch, Francis T. *Large Scale Networks, Theory and Design.* New York: IEEE Press, 1976.

Bollobas, Bela. *Graph Theory: Introductory Course.* New York: Springer-Verlag, 1979.

Bracker, William E. and Ray Sarch, eds. *Cases in Network Design.* New York: McGraw-Hill, 1985.

Carre, Bernard. *Graphs and Networks.* New York: Clarendon Press, 1979.

Communications Architectures and Protocols. SIGCOMM '88 Symposium Proceedings. New York: ACM Press, 1988.

Conard, J. W. *Standards and Protocols for Communications Networks.* Madison, NJ: Carnegie Press, 1983.

Davidson, John. *An Introduction to TCP/IP.* New York: Springer-Verlag, 1988.

Doll, Dixon R. *Data Communications: Facilities, Networks, and System Design.* New York: John Wiley & Sons, 1978.

Dwyer, John and Adrian Ioannou. *MAP and TOP: Advanced Manufacturing Communications.* New York: Halstead Press, 1988.

Frederickson, Greg N. and Ravi Janardan. "Efficient Message Routing in Planar Networks." *SIAM Journal on Computing.* Vol. 11, no. 4 (August 1989):843–57.

Freeman, Roger L. *Telecommunication System Engineering: Analog and Digital Network Design.* New York: Wiley, 1980.

Green, Paul E., Jr. *Network Interconnection and Protocol Conversion.* New York: IEEE Press, 1988.

Greenspan, Sol J., Clement L. McGowan, and M. Chandra Shekaran. "Toward an Object-Oriented Framework for Defining Services in Future Intelligent Networks." *Proceedings of the International Conference on Communications.* June 12–15, 1988.

Halsall, Fred. *Data Communications, Computer Networks, and OSI.* Reading, MA: Addison-Wesley, 1988.

Joyce, Edward J. "Tales of EDI Trailblazers." *Computer Decisions.* Vol. 21, no. 2 (February 1989):62–65.

Klingman, D. and J. M. Mulvey, eds. *Network Models and Associated Applications.* New York: North-Holland, 1981.

Mandl, Christoph E. *Applied Network Optimization.* New York: Academic Press, 1979.

Martin, James. *Communication Satellite Systems.* Englewood Cliffs, NJ: Prentice-Hall, 1978.

Sarch, Ray. *Integrating Voice and Data.* New York: McGraw-Hill, 1987.

Seventh Annual ACM Symposium on Principles of Distributed Computing. Symposium Proceedings. New York: ACM Press, 1988.

Swamy, M. N. S. and K. Thulasiraman. *Graphs, Networks, and Algorithms.* New York: Wiley, 1981.

CHAPTER SEVEN

Bernstein, Lawrence, Robert W. Cronk, A. R. Johnson, and D. N. Zuckerman. "Expert Systems in Network Operations and Management." *IEEE Network.* Vol. 2, no. 5 (September 1988):5.

Bernstein, Lawrence and Christine M. Yuhas. "How Technology Shapes Network Management." *IEEE Network.* Vol. 3, no. 4 (July 1989):16–21.

Birkwood, P. N., S. E. Aidarous, and R. M. K. Tam. "Implementation of a Distributed Architecture for Intelligent Network Operations." *IEEE Journal on Selected Areas in Communications.* Vol. 6, no. 4 (May 1988):697–705.

Cronk, Robert N., Paul H. Callahan, and Lawrence Bernstein. "Rule-Based Expert Systems for Network Management and Operations." *IEEE Network.* Vol. 2, no. 5 (September 1988):7–21.

Day, John, and Ann Pettyjohn. "Update: OSI and Network Management." *Business Communications Review.* Vol. 19, no. 1 (January 1989):22–24.

Feridun, M., M. Leib, M. Nodine, and J. Ong. "ANM: Automated Network Management System." *IEEE Network.* Vol. 2, no. 2 (March 1988):13–19.

Filipiak, Janusz. "M-Architecture: A Structural Model of Traffic Management and Control in Broadband ISDNs." *IEEE Communications Magazine.* Vol. 27, no. 5 (May 1989):25–31.

Haenschke, D. C., D. A. Kettler, and E. Oberer. "Network Management and Congestion in the U.S. Telecommunications Network."

IEEE Transactions on Communication. Vol. 29, no. 4 (1981):376–85.

Klerer, S. Mary. "The OSI Management Architecture: An Overview." *IEEE Network.* Vol. 2, no. 2 (March 1988):20–29.

Leroy, Guy. *System Network Control Center (SNCC) Project Report.* IBM Technical Bulletin GG24–1643. Raleigh, NC: IBM Corporation, 1984.

Sahin, V., C. G. Omidyar, and T. M. Bauman. "Telecommunications Management Network (TMN) Architecture and Interworking Designs." *IEEE Transactions in Selected Areas in Communications.* Vol. 6, no. 4 (May 1988):685–96.

Sheehan, J. R. "Network Operations and Management of Data Networks: The Challenge of Complexity." Rec. IEEE 1988 Network Operations and Management Symposium, 1988.

Sluman, C. "Network and Systems Management in OSI." *Telecommunications.* Vol. 34 (1988):32–39.

Vetter, R. W., Jr. "Integrated Operations." *IEEE Journal on Selected Areas in Communications.* Vol. 6, no. 4 (May 1988):648–55.

CHAPTER EIGHT

Bailin, Sidney C. "An Object Oriented Requirements Specifications Method." *Communications of the ACM.* Vol. 32, no. 5 (May 1989):608–23.

Bhargava, B. "Constructing Distributed Systems in Conic." *IEEE Transactions on Software Engineering.* Vol. 15, no. 6 (June 1989):663–75.

Boar, Bernard H. *Application Prototyping: A Project Management Perspective.* New York: American Management Association, 1985.

Boehm, B. "Seven Principles for Software Engineering." *Journal of Software and Systems.* Vol. 3, no. 1 (1983):3–24.

Candullo, Carl, Jr. *System Development Standards.* New York: McGraw-Hill, 1985.

Jeffcoate, Judith, Keith Hales, and Valerie Downes. *Object Oriented Systems: The Commercial Benefits.* London: Ovum Ltd., 1989.

Kull, David. "Crisis in I/S — The Aging Systems Saga." *Computer Decisions.* Vol. 21, no. 1 (January 1989):42–47.

Neighbors, J. M. "The Draco Approach to Constructing Software from Reusable Components." *IEEE Transactions on Software Engineering.* Vol. 10, no. 5 (September 1984):564–74.

Nosek, J. T. and R. B. Schwartz. "User Validation of Information

System Requirements." *IEEE Transactions on Software Engineering*. Vol. 14, no. 9 (September 1988):1372–75.

Oile, T. W., H. G. Sol, and C. J. Tully, eds. *Information Systems Design Methodologies: A Feature Analysis. Proc. of the IFIP WG8.1 Working Conf.* York, UK. July 5–7, 1983. Amsterdam: North-Holland, 1983.

Scacchi, Walt. "The USC System Factory Project." *ACM Software Engineering Notes*. Vol. 14, no. 1 (January 1989):61–82.

Shriver, Bruce and Peter Wegner. *Research Directions in Object Oriented Programming*. Cambridge, MA: MIT Press, 1987.

INDEX

User personal needs, 68
User problem resolution, 291,
  292
User profile, 74
  See also Architecture, end user
User script, 96, 98
User skill level, 54
User types, 58, 59
User view
  of data. *See* Data view processing
  of network services. *See*
    Architecture, end user
    services

Validation/verification, 156, 318,
  320
Values of attributes, 137

WANGNET, 263
Wang Laboratories, 263
Wide area network (WAN), 260,
  262
Wisdom (as an item of
  intelligence), 127
Word (as an item of intelligence),
  126
Workstation, 87, 174